Sovereignty at Sea

New Perspectives on Maritime History and Nautical Archaeology

UNIVERSITY PRESS OF FLORIDA

Florida A&M University, Tallahassee
Florida Atlantic University, Boca Raton
Florida Gulf Coast University, Ft. Myers
Florida International University, Miami
Florida State University, Tallahassee
New College of Florida, Sarasota
University of Central Florida, Orlando
University of Florida, Gainesville
University of North Florida, Jacksonville
University of South Florida, Tampa
University of West Florida, Pensacola

Sovereignty at Sea

U.S. Merchant Ships and American Entry into World War I

Rodney Carlisle

Foreword by James C. Bradford and Gene Allen Smith

University Press of Florida
Gainesville/Tallahassee/Tampa/Boca Raton
Pensacola/Orlando/Miami/Jacksonville/Ft. Myers/Sarasota

Copyright 2009 by Rodney Carlisle
Printed in the United States of America.
All rights reserved

First cloth printing, 2009
First paperback printing, 2011

Library of Congress Cataloging-in-Publication Data
Carlisle, Rodney P.
Sovereignty at sea : U.S. merchant ships and American entry into World
War I / Rodney Carlisle ; foreword by James C. Bradford and Gene
Allen Smith.
p. cm. — (New perspectives on maritime history and nautical
archaeology)
Includes bibliographical references and index.
ISBN 978-0-8130-3420-1 (alk. paper); ISBN 978-0-8130-3762-2 (pbk.)
1. World War, 1914-1918—United States. 2. Merchant marine—United
States—History—20th century. 3. World War, 1914-1918—Naval
operations—Submarine. 4. World War, 1914-1918—Naval operations,
German. I. Title.
D619.C29 2009
940.4'514—dc22   2009022467

The University Press of Florida is the scholarly publishing agency
for the State University System of Florida, comprising Florida A&M
University, Florida Atlantic University, Florida Gulf Coast University,
Florida International University, Florida State University, New College of Florida, University of Central Florida, University of Florida,
University of North Florida, University of South Florida, and University
of West Florida.

University Press of Florida
15 Northwest 15th Street
Gainesville, FL 32611-2079
http://www.upf.com

Contents

List of Figures   vii

List of Tables   ix

Foreword   xi

Acknowledgments   xvii

Introduction   1

1. The Voyage of the *Vigilancia*   9
2. From *Falaba* to *Sussex*   16
3. The Flag under Fire: From *Frye* to *Pass of Balmaha*   31
4. The Flag under Fire: From *Leelanaw* to *Chemung*   48
5. Meetings at Pless Castle and on Pennsylvania Avenue   63
6. *Housatonic* and *Lyman M. Law*   75
7. A Telegram, *Algonquin*, and an Abdication   91
8. The Tipping-Point Ships: *Vigilancia, City of Memphis, Illinois*   106
9. The Agony of Woodrow Wilson   122
10. *Aztec, Missourian, Marguerite,* and *Congress*   141

Epilogue   161

Appendix A. Loss of the *Healdton*   167

Appendix B. Casualty Lists   173

Appendix C. Table of Ship Losses   175

Notes   177

Bibliography   205

Index   213

Figures

1. *Vigilancia* 10
2. Convening Congress 12
3. "Way of the Neutral Is Hard" 15
4. Uncle Sam after the *Lusitania* 25
5. *Gulflight* under repair 41
6. *Nebraskan* 42
7. *Leelanaw* 49
8. "Ruthless warfare" 64
9. Bernstorff as persona non grata 69
10. *Lyman M. Law* 82
11. Weary waiting 89
12. Riding to the inauguration 98
13. Cloture 99
14. *Algonquin* 101
15. *City of Memphis* 112
16. *Illinois* sinking 117
17. Colonel Edward House 125
18. *Healdton* 129
19. *Aztec* 142

Tables

1.1. The ten U.S. ships lost following the 1917 German declaration of unrestricted submarine warfare   13

3.1. Major encounters, U.S. ships with German warships, January 1915–November 1916   35

3.2. Minor encounters, U.S. ships with German warships or aircraft, December 1915–January 1917   35

4.1. Harriss-Irby-Voss ships lost, 1915–1916   58

10.1. Congressional mentions of U.S. ships sunk, debates over declaration of war, April 4–6, 1917   159

B.1. Names of Americans lost, by ship, February 5, 1917–April 1, 1917   173

B.2. Number of U.S. fatalities, by ship, February 5, 1917–April 1, 1917   174

C.1. U.S. flagship loss details, February 3, 1917–April 4, 1917   175

Foreword

Water is unquestionably the most important natural feature on earth. By volume, the world's oceans compose 99 percent of the planet's living space; in fact, the surface of the Pacific Ocean alone is larger than the combined surface area of all land bodies. So vital to life is water that NASA looks for signs of water as carefully as it does for air when testing for whether the moon or planets can sustain life. The story of human development is inextricably linked to the oceans, seas, lakes, and rivers that dominate the earth's surface. The University Press of Florida's New Perspectives on Maritime History and Nautical Archaeology series is devoted to exploring the significance of the earth's water while providing lively and important books that cover the spectrum of maritime history and nautical archaeology broadly defined. The series includes works that focus on the role of canals, rivers, lakes, and oceans in history; on the economic, military, and political use of those waters; and upon the people, communities, and industries that support maritime endeavors. Limited by neither geography nor time, volumes in the series contribute to the overall understanding of maritime history and can be read with profit by both general readers and specialists.

Since the dawn of the modern era, nation-states have contested for control of seas and oceans; empires have risen and fallen as a result of such struggles. This is particularly true for the nations of western Europe and North America. Since the founding of the United States, the right to freely navigate the North Atlantic Ocean has been a vital national interest. Defending that right was the primary cause of the Quasi War with France and the War of 1812 with Great Britain. The ability to use the oceans and deny their use to opponents played a crucial role in victories won in the Mexican War, the Civil War, and the Spanish-American War during the nineteenth century and the Second World War, Korean War, and Gulf War during the twentieth century.

Both of these factors played a critical role in the First World War, i.e., the right and ability of the United States to use the oceans—what President Woodrow Wilson called the principle of the freedom of the seas—caused both the American entry into the war on the side of the Allies and the defeat of the Central powers. President Woodrow Wilson made the institutionalization of "freedom of the seas" an American goal when he submitted a list of Fourteen Points to Congress on January 8, 1918, enumerating the principles upon which peace should be negotiated with the Central powers:

> Absolute freedom of navigation upon the seas, outside territorial waters, alike in peace and in war, except as the seas may be closed in whole or in part by international action for the enforcement of international covenants.

The importance Wilson placed on this principle was reflected by its standing second on the list behind his call for "Open covenants of peace, openly arrived at . . . in the public view."

At the outbreak of war in 1914, leaders of both the Central powers and the Allies believed that the conflict would be won quickly, like the Franco-Prussian War of 1870, rather than become a prolonged war of attrition like the Wars of the French Revolution and Empire, but such was not to be. Instead of a war of weeks, or months at most, World War I lasted more than four years. The conflict soon descended into a destructive bloodletting in which the ability to use the sea to transport the resources of the rest of the world to the battlefields of Europe brought victory to the Allies. Yet this advantage by itself did not bring victory to the Allies. Given the balance of resources between the two opposing sides, the Allies could not prevail on the battlefield until the United States entered the war in 1917.

The decision of the United States to join the fray became a, if not the key, determinant in the war. For nearly a century, historians have debated the reasons for American entry, almost all of them focusing on long-term causes. In the final analysis, the date of American entry was crucial and the key to understanding that timing lies with Woodrow Wilson and his request for Congress to declare war on Germany. When the war began in August 1914, Wilson hoped it would be brief, and even when that proved not to be the case, he, like many other American political leaders, wanted to keep the United States a neutral and from the outset sought a role in a negotiated peace settlement. Within months, the question of maritime rights began wearing away at American neutrality as both sides sought to prevent the United States from trading with the other, the British by erecting a blockade of both enemy and neutral entrepôts, and the Germans through the laying of mines and the execution of submarine warfare to isolate the Allies. Woodrow Wilson responded to these policies by announcing that the

United States would hold all belligerents strictly accountable to the tenets of international law, but those principles remained vague and unclear.

A year and a half into the war, a German submarine operating in the English Channel mistook a French passenger steamer for a minelaying ship and torpedoed it. That steamer, the *Sussex*, limped into port in France with several injured Americans on board. Responding to an American demand that it abandon attacks on passenger and freight-carrying vessels, Germany, on May 4, 1916, issued the *Sussex* Pledge, promising to end attacks on unarmed civilian ships that did not attempt to elude or resist capture. The Germans asked, in vain, that the United States in turn object to a number of British violations of American neutral rights.

A modus operandi appeared to have been reached, but by the end of the year Germany had grown desperate. At a meeting on January 9, 1917, German leaders concluded that the initiation of unrestricted submarine warfare was crucial to avoid defeat. They instructed the German ambassador to the United States, Count Johann von Bernstorff, to inform U.S. officials on January 31 that Germany would begin unrestricted submarine warfare against all ships, neutral or Allied, found in a war zone in the seas around the Allies, on the following day. Woodrow Wilson responded by announcing the severance of diplomatic relations with Germany based on that nation's violation of its *Sussex* Pledge, but he continued to hope that Germany would not resort to an "overt act" of war against the United States. For a month, most U.S. ships hesitated to depart for European waters.

Over the period from February 3 through April 4, 1917, the Germans sank a total of nine American ships. An additional ship, the *Healdton*, sank off the Netherlands. At the time, American officials and the press assumed that it, too, had been sunk by a German submarine. In fact, as demonstrated in this volume, that ship was probably lost to a British-laid mine.

Many in the United States, such as former president Theodore Roosevelt and many of Wilson's close advisors, believed the sinking of the first few of these ten ships represented overt acts of war. However, President Wilson continued to hope that that war could be avoided. A close look at the individual cases of ships lost and how they were interpreted reveals the lengths to which Wilson went in order to avoid war.

On February 24, British officials delivered to the U.S. State Department a copy of a message from Berlin to German ambassador von Bernstorff in Washington that its agents had intercepted and decrypted a month earlier. Known as the Zimmerman Telegram, it instructed von Bernstorff to order Germany's ambassador in Mexico to propose to officials there that, were the

United States to enter war against Germany, Mexico and Germany should form an alliance with a provision that Germany would assist Mexico in recovering territory it had "lost" to the United States during the nineteenth century. Even given this threat to American territorial integrity, Wilson, not considering it an "overt act," held back from declaring war.

Wilson and his cabinet refused to decide for war, even after three ships had been lost to German submarines: *Housatonic, Lyman M. Law*, and *Algonquin*. As this study shows, the sinking of *none* of these three ships could be considered a casus belli because of details of the ways in which they had been sunk and the legal conditions surrounding the registry of one of them. In fact, during the period of neutrality, in 1915 and 1916, eight other American-flagged ships had been sunk or confiscated by German submarines and surface ships. None of those little-remembered events had led to war. In various ways, the sinking of *Housatonic, Lyman M. Law*, and *Algonquin* fit into the pattern of the earlier losses. Wilson and his legal advisors had already accepted the eight losses over 1915 and 1916 as unfortunate events, but not as acts of war. Those earlier losses had led only to exchanges of relatively polite diplomatic notes. Because the first three 1917 losses conformed to precedents set in the earlier eight incidents, Wilson, the State Department, and the cabinet could not treat the new events as acts of war.

Wilson's cabinet finally decided, at a meeting on March 20, 1917, that an additional batch of losses did represent acts of war. Over the previous weekend, news arrived that three U.S. merchant ships, *Vigilancia, City of Memphis*, and *Illinois*, had been sunk by German submarines. Only by examining the details of these encounters and sinkings is it possible to understand why these three represented a casus belli, while all the previous incidents of German naval attacks on U.S. merchant ships did not.

This volume's examination of Wilson's decision process and "what the president knew and when he knew it," suggests the degree to which Wilson resisted war. After the weekend sinking of the three ships, he decided to convene Congress early, to meet on April 2, 1917. But he refused to disclose, even to most of his advisors, whether he would ask for a declaration of war. Before he made his decision known to anyone, the *Healdton* was lost off the Netherlands, apparently contributing to his final decision. Although Germany clearly stated that no German submarine was anywhere near that ship, the press, the State Department, and members of Congress were erroneously convinced that *Healdton* had been torpedoed by a U-boat.

On April 2, Wilson asked Congress for war. Two days later, the Senate passed a declaration of war on Germany by a vote of 82 to 6, and on April

6, the House of Representatives followed suit by a vote of 373 to 50. Wilson did not specifically mention the ten ships and their losses as a casus belli, but only referred to them in general terms. But several members of Congress, provided with information by pro-Ally Secretary of State Robert Lansing, discussed the details of ship losses, often confusing the facts, but nevertheless pointing to the loss of American-flagged ships as the final events that pushed the United States into war. Some congressmen included in their consideration numerous ships that the State Department and Wilson had already treated as matters for diplomatic exchange, not as acts of war.

In point of fact, when Wilson decided to convene Congress, only six American seamen had been killed by the action of German submarines under unrestricted submarine warfare. Nevertheless, the loss of *Vigilancia*, *City of Memphis*, and *Illinois*, and later, *Aztec*, *Missourian*, and *Marguerite* did constitute acts of war, because German military forces had intentionally targeted the American flag in those attacks, and had thus infringed on American sovereignty at sea.

Historians have long acknowledged the critical role of neutral rights in the coming of World War I, but the destruction of the *Housatonic*, *Lyman M. Law*, *Algonquin*, *Vigilancia*, *City of Memphis*, *Illinois*, *Healdton*, *Aztec*, *Missourian*, and *Marguerite* has never before been examined in detail. This volume traces the American and German views of neutral shipping rights from the start of the war through January 1917, then examines in depth events of the critical weeks from February 1 through early April 1917 as the United States moved from neutrality to war. Finally, this important topic receives its due!

James C. Bradford and Gene Allen Smith
Series editors

Acknowledgments

As in any work of this kind, the writer accumulates debts for the assistance provided by colleagues, archivists, and librarians. I want to especially thank colleagues James Muldoon and Andrew Lees at Rutgers University; Philip Cantelon, Brian Martin, Jamie Rife, and Keith Allen at History Associates Incorporated; Bill Thiesen at the Coast Guard Historical Office; and attendees at conference presentations at North American Society for Oceanic History, 2007 and 2008, who offered challenging questions and suggestions for finding the answers. The following librarians and archivists were of great assistance: Heidi Hackford (Woodrow Wilson Presidential Library); Gary Golden (Rutgers University Library); Jennifer Bryan (U.S. Nimitz Library, Naval Academy); and Jennie Cole (Seeley Mudd Collection, Princeton University Library).

In the new age of the Internet, it has become far easier to do international research and research in remote locations in the United States. The list of those reached by e-mail and by Internet sites, all of whom who were generous with their time and help, is quite extensive: Curatorial Officer Iain MacKenzie (of the Naval Historical Branch, Admiralty Library at Portsmouth, U.K); Laura M. Poll (Monmouth County Historical Society, N.J); Mark C. Jones (Morristown-Beard School, Morristown, N.J.); Claudia Jew (Mariner's Museum, Virginia); Oliver Loerscher (uboat.net); Michael Lowrey (uboat.net); Louisa Watrous (Mystic River Seaport); Roger Sarty (editor of *Northern Mariner/Le marin du nord*, which published my article reflecting the thesis of this book: "The Attacks on U.S. Shipping That Precipitated American Entry into World War I," July 2007); Emelie McAlevy (granddaughter of survivor of *Algonquin*); Chris Heather (British National Archives); Alma Topin (University of Glasgow, U.K.); Bruce Dennis (independent researcher, U.K.); Leigh Bishop (independent researcher, U.K.); Alan Dunster (independent researcher, U.K.); Leon Homburg (Dutch Marine Museum); Richard Webb (independent researcher, Germany); B. J. Meiboom (Dutch National Archives); and Johan Joor (independent researcher, the Netherlands). I must also thank John Boone for helping with the translation of several German works and passages, Professor Eladio Cortes for resolving some questions of Spanish surnames, and my wife, Loretta, who patiently heard the story of the *Healdton* so often that she knew it by heart.

Introduction

For the American merchant marine, the decade before World War I was an age of hardship and transition. Since the Civil War, American shipping had been in decline, and the low wages and harsh conditions aboard the privately owned schooners and coal-fired steamers of the era often made work aboard such ships a last resort for workers in seaport cities and towns. Despite the romance associated with the sea, in fact, work aboard oceangoing schooners, brigs, and other sailing vessels, as well as the newer steel-hulled steamers, driven by hot, noisy, but effective steam-piston engines, drew a class regarded and treated as the dregs of society. Increasingly, the crews aboard American-owned ships were made up of stranded and out-of-work men with few skills, often resident aliens who had never taken out any citizenship papers. Ships also employed recently naturalized immigrants and African Americans escaping the poverty and oppression of sharecropping in the South and low-paid industrial or mining jobs in the North.

The work was made even more difficult by the terms of employment. Workers signed up for the duration of the voyage, to collect their pay upon return to the home port, often after many months at sea. They were on call at all times of day, and often worked seventy or more hours a week with no extra compensation for overtime. The shipmaster's word was law, and although flogging had been outlawed, many captains enforced their rule by beating, confinement, or other corporal punishment.

Andrew Furuseth, union secretary of the Coast Seamen's Union based in San Francisco, devoted his life to improving conditions. In 1892, the Coast Seamen's Union and the Steamshipmen's Protective Union joined together to form the Sailors' Union of the Pacific. That union began endorsing specific political candidates and working for legislation to improve the lot of merchant mariners. However, only after Robert LaFollette, progressive senator from Wisconsin, backed a comprehensive seaman's reform bill, did it pass Congress. Even so, President Taft vetoed the bill late in his term. LaFollette persisted, however, and the Seaman's Act was signed into law by President Woodrow Wilson on March 4, 1915. Furuseth wrote to Wilson, thanking him for signing the bill, and pledging support of American merchant mariners in case the United States should enter World War I.

The Seaman's Act required that ships registered in the United States issue standard contracts to workers, and also required that any U.S. ship be staffed with officers who were American citizens and that 75 percent of crews understand English. Even so, ship rosters continued to include among officers some recently naturalized engineers, masters, and mates from European nations, particularly Britain and the Scandinavian countries. To conform to the law, the percentage of English speakers aboard was sometimes raised by employing a few more American cooks, stewards, and deckhands. The law also increased the size of living quarters aboard and outlawed the payment of advances, which had led to a form of debt servitude under seamen's boardinghouse owners over the prior decades. When times were good and jobs were readily available as in mid-1915, merchant ship owners, rather than raising the pay for shipboard labor, would continue to scour the waterfronts for men down on their luck and ready to accept the low wages and punishing conditions of the merchant marine.

In 1915, Andrew Furuseth, as head of the International Seamen's Union; Samuel Gompers, head of the American Federation of Labor; and T. V. O'Connor, leader of the International Longshoremen's Union, all decried efforts by German agents, some suspected of working through Irish American leaders, to provide strike relief funds in exchange for large-scale work stoppages. When U.S. involvement in the war seemed imminent in March 1917, Gompers rallied labor leaders and the rank and file to support the war effort, even though Furuseth thought such a call premature before a declaration of war by the United States. Nevertheless, in the period of neutrality as well as after the war began, sporadic efforts to tie up shipping in order to favor the Central powers were widely criticized by the conservative press and major labor leaders as unpatriotic. It seemed that both seamen and longshoremen viewed neutrality much as did American businessmen, as an opportunity to continue to ply their trades and to earn financial benefits.

On the whole, seamen and longshoremen sought to use their organizational power to ensure that they got a fair share of the money to be made from the trade as neutrals, not to throw their weight against the war itself. Consequently, there was no concerted effort by seamen or longshoremen to refuse to load or carry munitions to the Allies. As the danger of crossing the sea increased in 1917, however, seamen's unions and individual ship crews successfully organized short work stoppages in order to gain "bonuses" for travel through the war zone, generally settling for a 50 percent wage boost in some cases.

The middle-class American public had a very conflicted view of merchant mariners. On the one hand, some of the old-line Scandinavian, German, and British officers seemed to meet the stereotype of intrepid and hardy men of the sea. On the other hand, the ethnically and racially mixed crews drew ambivalent feelings from those in the middle classes. Some reform-minded middle- and upper-class activists, such as LaFollette, felt sympathy for the seamen's plight, but others, probably most of the comfortable and wealthy, felt simple disdain and unconcern for this and other underclasses. An exception to this pattern would be the fond regard held for officers and crews who manned the older class of sailing schooners, whose handling of wooden ships and sails evoked romantic images of an earlier era that was clearly in its waning days. Those sailors represented the ideal of masculinity, increasingly threatened by the industrial age, the organizational age, and other changes that were almost consciously seen as emasculating.

The shift from sail to steam helped account for the long-term decline in numbers of ships and American seamen at work over the decades following the Civil War, with the faster and larger steamships edging out the sailing vessels, particularly in long-distance transoceanic trade. One estimate put the decline in the number of American seamen employed as falling from 135,000 in 1870 to 105,000 in 1900.

The age of transition from sail to steam also had a profound impact on the popular imagination. While the salty tars who had shipped out aboard sailing vessels echoed the drama of the works of Richard Henry Dana, Herman Melville, and Joseph Conrad, it seemed that the steam-powered ships of the new era somehow reduced the heroic image of man versus sea evoked by those writers. Sweltering below decks, stoking the coal-fired boilers with shovels of fuel, and wiping the oily engine parts with bits of waste cloth hardly reflected the clean and beautiful image of man against elements aloft in the rigging of a clipper ship, whaler, or East Indies trading bark.

Another cultural icon of the era was the grand ocean liners—the floating palaces that competed to take passengers back and forth across the Atlantic in comfort and at high speed. A competition between the fast liners of the British, French, German, and American shipping firms had made good news copy as the voyage was reduced to five days from New York to Liverpool, or from ports in Ireland to the east coast of the United States. The ship with the fastest record was publicly heralded as holding the "blue riband," an imaginary symbol of the winner of the transatlantic race. From 1909 until 1929, no ship beat the speed record of the British Cunard liner *Mauretania*, which made the crossing, both eastbound and westbound, at an average of just over 25 knots (about 29 miles per hour) several times in the period.

With the rigid class structure aboard such ocean liners reflecting the social cleavages of the era, it was easy for the middle-class public to visualize the elegance of dining in first-class, or sweltering below decks in steerage class or the engine rooms. The elegant decor, the social prominence of some of the passengers, and a sense of the hazards of the sea that they faced made passenger liners a symbol for many of the concerns of the age. Not only did the ships reflect social class divisions, they also embodied the effort to use modern technology to harness and conquer the forces of nature. As symbols of both elegance and the triumph of science, engineering, and technology over nature and a harbinger of the marvels expected in the twentieth century, such ships and their voyages were the subject of newspaper features, magazine articles, travel books, and novels. Such media, conveying concerns and underlying meanings, help account for the sensational and long-lasting impact of the loss of *Titanic* after striking an iceberg on April 16, 1912, with the death of more than 1,500 passengers and crew.

Yet, whatever the symbolic import of shipping and seafarers, ships existed within a legal and diplomatic reality. When civilian merchant mariners shipped out from U.S. harbors, whether aboard the dwindling fleet of sailing vessels, or aboard the smelly and smoky freighters and tankers, if the ship was registered in the United States, the mariners and the ships themselves traveled under the protection of the American flag.

The flag was no simple piece of cloth or empty symbol. It represented an extension of American sovereignty at sea. Aboard ships that flew the American flag, American labor laws would apply. When survivors of a wrecked or sunken American vessel rowed into a foreign port in a lifeboat, they would be extended the protection and concern of American consuls there, who would report their condition immediately to their superior officers at the State Department in Washington, usually to the secretary of state himself. The State Department, in turn, would bring their conditions to the attention of the general public by immediately releasing consular dispatches to the press. The newspapers, in turn, would print the names and sometimes the addresses and next of kin of both survivors and casualties. Whatever their social standing, native-born Americans, naturalized citizens, and resident aliens who had shipped under the American flag were regarded and treated as under the protection of that flag.

Thus when war broke out in 1914 between the Great Powers in Europe, with Britain coming to the aid of Belgium, France, and Russia (the Entente, or the Allies) against the forces of Germany and Austria-Hungary (the Central powers), one of the most important ways that the war impacted neutral

America was through the policies of the belligerents toward merchant ships and their crews. Small numbers of American citizens worked among the crews of belligerent civilian ships, and larger numbers of Americans took passage aboard civilian liners operated by those warring states, particularly the British. The death of one or more Americans from the loss of a merchant ship or ocean liner registered to one of the countries at war would poignantly remind the public that the world war could make victims of innocent neutral citizens.

However, it was even more important that an American-registered ship, flying the American flag, could encounter a blockading warship or be torpedoed. If such an event were to occur, it would represent an attack on the sovereignty of the United States. That principle—that sovereignty at sea was defined by the registry and flag of a ship—could be traced back to the writings of Hugo Grotius in the seventeenth century. Affronts to the American flag on American ships on the high seas were events with the potential to draw the United States into the war.

In 1914, when the war began, President Woodrow Wilson urged Americans to be neutral in thought as well as deed. And his position was widely accepted, even among the ethnically and regionally diverse American public, who recognized that "we don't have a dog in that fight." Neutrality, however, did not mean that American businesses would cease trading with the belligerents. In fact, such trade was regarded as a "neutral right." Interference with, or any effort to limit, that trade by one or another of the belligerents was fraught with dangers for the United States.

As the conflict expanded from ground combat to economic warfare, with the Allies blockading the ports of Germany to prevent war materiel, and then food from supplying the Central powers, and as Germany applied their improved version of an American invention, the submarine, to interdict trade to the Allies with a form of submarine-enforced blockade, American ships and American seamen were sometimes caught in the crossfire. Yet despite more than two years of slaughter in Europe and across the world on the high seas as Allied warships and merchant ships of Allies and neutrals encountered German warships, the United States was able to remain neutral. That official neutral status lasted from August 1914 until April 1917.

As this work shows, the actual events that drew the United States into that war in early 1917 were entirely events on the oceans of the world. Those events had little to do with the high-minded concerns of idealism, democracy, the rights of peoples to self-determination, or some of the other values so loudly proclaimed at the time and so studiously examined by later generations. The actual cause of American entry into World War I, or the casus belli, entirely derived from maritime issues, most especially from events surrounding a little-remembered group of American-registered merchant ships. Understanding how the destruction of a few ships flying the American flag could cause committed neutralists, including some of Woodrow Wilson's most trusted advisors, members of Congress from states and districts with heavy German American populations, and finally, Wilson himself, to endorse war requires an explanation of some of the principles of what was increasingly called "international law" in the period.

Of course, no legislative body creating international law has ever existed; the term describes a convenient fiction, recognized by major powers when it suits their interests, but ignored when it does not. However, the idea that there was such a thing as international law, and that it could be developed to assist the human condition, caught on through the late nineteenth century and the first years of the twentieth century. Diplomats, legal theorists, and political thinkers believed that a body of international law could be developed that would reduce the likelihood of war through international understandings, treaties, and agreements. When wars threatened to break out between two nations, increasingly diplomats sought to bring the parties together to resolve their differences peacefully through arbitration or mediation. Further, diplomats sought to prevent a war between two nations from escalating to include other nations, with arrangements and principles that would limit the participation of others. Arbitration and negotiation had resolved many disputes between the Great Powers, including the United States and other nations, between 1890 and 1910.

Ironically, a part of the effort to prevent the spread of war involved the development of mutual defense treaties so that one nation, if feeling threatened by another nation, would enter into defensive alliances during peacetime. These defensive alliances represented a promise by one nation to come to the aid of a second nation if that second nation were attacked. Such alliances were developed on the principle that a promise of support would represent a deterrent to others. Thus, in this prenuclear age, the alliances marshaled tremendous weaponry and alignments of armed force to deter aggression. Leaders of a nation like Belgium could believe that treaties recognizing its neutrality signed by Britain, France, and Germany would prevent any of those nations from attacking it; similarly, the leaders of the small nation of Serbia might believe it was immune from attack from the neighboring empire of Austria-Hungary because Serbia had friendly relations and treaties with the Russian Empire.

Unfortunately, these very treaties not only failed to prevent war in August 1914, but the invoking of those alliances caused the war to escalate from an incident to a world war of immense proportions. The minor conflict arising when a group of Serbian nationalists assassinated the heir to the throne of the Austro-Hungarian Empire soon grew into a major war. In a tale of falling dominoes, that conflict soon engaged Russia and Germany, then France. And when German troops crossed Belgium to attack France, the British came in to honor their commitment to Belgium.

None of those events had any direct military or strategic effect on the United States since that nation, following a principle first enunciated by George Washington, had studiously avoided engaging in such mutual defense treaties. Thus it was quite natural, logical, and appropriate for the United States to remain neutral. Similar logic allowed all the independent nations of the Western Hemisphere, as well as Spain, Norway, Sweden, Holland, Denmark, Switzerland, and other countries, to make it clear that they would remain neutral. As events unfolded, however, some neutrals were drawn into the conflict, including Italy and Japan on the Allied side, and Bulgaria and the Ottoman Empire on the side of the Central powers.

Despite the failure of so-called "international law" to prevent the outbreak and spread of the war, some of the principles of international law continued to protect neutral nations from becoming drawn into the conflict. In 1908–9, a conference of the major maritime powers, including most of those later engaged on both sides in World War I, as well as the United States, sought to codify and capture the existing body of practices regarded as appropriate in the conduct of war at sea. Early in 1909, the group issued the Declaration of London, which included more than sixty rules or principles defining how navies should conduct war at sea, and how they should administer blockades against enemies and avoid risking the lives of civilian sailors aboard merchant ships. In particular, the Declaration of London was very specific regarding how a blockading navy should behave toward *neutral* ships and crews, in effect, defining the "neutral rights." Unfortunately, the Declaration of London was never ratified by the participating nations, and thus did not officially go into effect. Even so, all the major belligerents recognized that the declaration did embody appropriate practices, and all pledged to abide by its principles as far as possible, although retaining the right to violate those principles if necessity or conditions demanded.

The principles of the Declaration of London stated how a blockade should be conducted, how warships should deal with belligerent-owned and neutral-owned civilian ships attempting to run a blockade, and how the loss of life at sea from such encounters could be minimized. And, despite the horrors of war at sea, it is accurate to say that the principles of proper respect for the lives of civilians as enunciated in the unratified declaration meant that thousands of seamen of belligerent and neutral nations escaped death by gunfire or drowning because, to a very considerable extent, the British, German, and other navies respected the principles. In fact, during all of World War I from August 1914 to November 1918, by an official count, 132 American merchant ships were lost; on 88 of those ships, there were no casualties whatsoever, with all crew safely rescued or reaching shore alive.

Perhaps due to the ambivalent feelings of the American public and American leaders toward the American merchant ships and the crews who manned them, the episodes that drew America into the war have almost vanished from the American historical consciousness. The sailors who risked their lives in order to make a living, especially those on the dirty, small tankers and coal-powered freighters, drew little respect. Furthermore, the money-making businesses that funded American ships attempting to carry cargoes of arms, ammunition, transport equipment, or food for the armies of the belligerents hardly seemed to conform to the image of a high-minded and idealistic nation that was a defender of democratic principles.

How much more thrilling it was then, and still is, to believe that the United States engaged in the war to avenge the loss of innocent women and children, to oppose a brutally aggressive power, or to come to the aid of fellow democracies in a struggle against autocracy. The reality, as will be demonstrated, was far more mundane. The actual casus belli, or cause of war, for the United States came early in 1917, from the losses of a very small number of specific ships, and that is what this work sets out to make explicit.

1

The Voyage of the *Vigilancia*

The freighter *Vigilancia* steamed steadily eastward across the Atlantic on the clear and cold morning of Friday, March 16, 1917. Bound for Le Havre from New York, the 4,115-gross-ton steamship carried a general cargo including goods for France that Germany had declared contraband. In the hope that America's neutrality in the Great War would offer some protection, the American flag was painted directly on the hull on both starboard and port sides. Registered in the United States, the ship was owned by Gaston, Williams, & Wigmore, Inc., an American import-export firm that specialized in supplying motor vehicles and other goods to the Allies. The crew had a decidedly international makeup, recruited from seamen who were citizens of a half-dozen countries, all living in the ship's homeport of Wilmington, Delaware.

Vigilancia plowed steadily ahead as it approached the British Isles, some 150 miles west of Bishop's Light. At about ten in the morning, lookouts saw a greasy track they later decided was a torpedo, passing harmlessly aft the stern. A minute or so later, another torpedo struck near amidship. The ship lost headway and began taking on water.

Within five minutes, the crew lowered all four lifeboats, and the officers and men hurriedly piled in. The ship still wallowed forward, and the men evacuated under rough conditions. Two of the lifeboats capsized, one with the captain and the other with the third officer. The captain and most of the crew in his boat struggled into one of the upright lifeboats, but eleven of the twelve men from the third officer's boat and four from the captain's boat drowned. A lone survivor in the water, Assistant Engineer Walter Scott, worked out of his heavy clothes and swam about a mile to the lifeboats that drifted away. Scott, soaking wet and shivering in the March air, joined Captain Frank A. Middleton in one of the boats. Some thirty survivors in the two upright boats hoisted sails and headed toward land.

Fifteen men drowned, including six Americans: Neils North, the third officer; C. F. Aderholde, assistant engineer; Estphan Lopez, the mess boy; F. Brown, the carpenter; Joseph Siberia (possibly "Loeria"), quartermaster;

Figure 1. *Vigilancia*. The *Vigilancia* was the first American ship intentionally sunk without warning in World War I. Despite the clear U.S. flags marked on its sides, Otto Wünsche of *U-70* sent it to the bottom. There were fifteen fatalities, including six U.S. citizens. (Reprinted with permission from Mariners' Museum, Newport News, Va.)

and Alexander Rodriquez, oiler. The other nine who drowned included two each from South America and Greece, and five from Spain. They were Julio Montera from Peru and T. Rondon from Venezuela; A. Galitos and E. Dmitrios from Greece; and, from Spain, Joseph Livio, G. S. Sparrow, Juan Nesz, M. Vasquez, and R. Gonzales. The captain later reported that one of the engine room crew, possibly Walter Scott, suffered from partial paralysis due to his exposure in the frigid water.

The small sailing lifeboats arrived at the southwestern tip of Britain on Sunday, March 18, with all the crew exhausted from the ordeal and the cold. At Plymouth, the American consul, Joseph G. Stephens, interviewed the survivors and cabled a brief report to the State Department. U.S. newspapers received the news by wire too late for the Sunday editions, but published the details on Monday, March 19.

The event was front-page news because *Vigilancia* was the first American ship with casualties sunk by the Germans under their unrestricted submarine warfare policy announced on January 31, 1917. In the face of that January 31 announcement, President Woodrow Wilson, who had struggled to keep the United States neutral in World War I, decided he had to break diplomatic relations with Germany. In announcing the break before Congress on February 3, Wilson stated that he could not believe that German submarines would actually do what had been promised, that is, sink all ships in the war zone around Britain, whether neutral or Allied, without warning and without regard to the safety of seamen. Wilson said that if they did commit such "overt acts" against American ships, the United States would have to take stronger measures.

After Wilson's announcement and before *Vigilancia*, three U.S.-flagged ships had been sunk, all without any casualties: the *Housatonic* on February 3, the schooner *Lyman M. Law* on February 12; and the freighter *Algonquin* on March 12. In Wilson's eyes, for different reasons, the loss of none of these first three ships represented an overt act, or casus belli.

Vigilancia was different. The ship was U.S.-owned and U.S.-registered. It had not been warned. Fifteen seamen died, though not directly from the torpedo attack. But the submarine captain, Otto Wünsche, aboard *U-70*, had made no effort to come to their aid, and the casualties were clearly caused by the submarine. Although he was by no means the most successful or ruthless of the submarine captains, Wünsche's U-boat would eventually sink a total of fifty-three ships with a total just over 138,000 tons. Like other U-boat commanders at work in early 1917, he no doubt regarded the sinking of *Vigilancia* as a matter of routine.

When the news of *Vigilancia* was published in the United States on Monday, March 19, newspapers also announced that two other American ships, both in ballast, had been sunk over the previous few days. They were another freighter, *City of Memphis*, and a Texaco tanker, *Illinois*, both headed home to the United States. Each had been sunk by other submarines, the *City of Memphis* in the Irish Sea, and *Illinois* near Alderney, the northernmost of the British-ruled Channel Islands off France. The lifeboats from *City of Memphis* became separated, and for a few days, it was unclear whether all aboard that freighter had been rescued, until the missing survivors arrived in Scotland. By midweek, however, all from *City of Memphis* and *Illinois* had been accounted for.

Nevertheless, the fact that three American merchant ships had been sunk, and the three ship losses announced all at once, came as a shock to the American people, to newspaper editorial writers, to the cabinet, and to members of Congress. Many who had hoped to preserve neutrality were finally pushed to decide for war. Even Josephus Daniels, the avowedly pacifist secretary of the Navy, reluctantly came around to support the war, as did

Figure 2. Convening Congress. After the loss of *Vigilancia*, *City of Memphis*, and *Illinois*, Wilson changed the date of convening Congress to April 2. He refused to explain why, but the cartoonist Clifford Berryman noted that Congress was the "war-declaring body" of the government. American lives were lost in the ship losses, although the actual number was not emphasized. (Wilson Presidential Library, Staunton, Va.)

Postmaster General Albert Burleson, immediately after the loss of *Vigilancia*, *City of Memphis*, and *Illinois*.

When Wilson met with the cabinet on Tuesday, March 20, the *only* loss of life from attacks on U.S. ships since the German declaration on January 31 had been from the swamped *Vigilancia*'s lifeboats. In our modern age of concerted attacks by terrorists and weapons of mass destruction, the fact that the drowning of fifteen men, including six Americans, when openly attempting to steam through an announced submarine blockade, could be seen as a cause for war may seem astounding. At the urging of the cabinet, Wilson agreed to convene Congress early, on April 2. In the evening of that day, Wilson addressed Congress and asked for a declaration of war. The final vote in Congress was held four days later. By that time, the number of

Table 1.1. The ten U.S. ships lost following the 1917 German declaration of unrestricted submarine warfare

Ship	Gross tons	Date lost	U.S. lives lost	Total lives lost
Housatonic	3,143	3 February	0	0
Lyman M. Law	1,300	12 February	0	0
Algonquin	1,806	12 March	0	0
Vigilancia	4,115	16 March	6	15
City of Memphis	5,252	17 March	0	0
Illinois	5,225	18 March	0	0
Healdton	4,489	21 March	7	21
Aztec	3,727	1 April	11	28
Marguerite	1,553	4 April	0	0
Missourian	7,924	4 April	0	0
Total fatalities			24	64

American ships lost had climbed to ten. News of the last three ship losses of the ten arrived after Wilson began his speech.

The fact that six American men had been killed on March 16 was rarely mentioned in the heated debates over a declaration of war in the Senate and in the House of Representatives on April 4–6. One of the senators voting for the war measure, Claude Swanson (D., Virginia), specifically spoke of the fifteen deaths aboard the *Vigilancia* as among the acts of war by Germany against the United States. Several other members of Congress also listed some of the ships sunk, and included the loss of *Vigilancia* in their remarks. The House Foreign Relations Committee provided a report that mentioned the sinking of the *Vigilancia* along with a great many other offenses by Germany.

But like President Wilson, who couched his address to Congress asking for the Declaration of War in more idealistic terms, most of the congressmen and senators speaking to the issue did not focus on the specifics. Rather, they accused Germany of waging a ruthless war, without regard for rights of neutrals and civilians, and of trying to impose German rule across Europe. While such charges had some truth, they were not the specific legal acts that brought the United States into the war. The United States had no mutual defense treaty obliging the nation to go to war on the invasion of any other country; no territory of the United States had been invaded by Germany. The Zimmermann Telegram, decrypted and released to the public on March 1, had revealed that Germany was willing make an alliance with Mexico, *if war was declared*, but that offer itself was not an action that infringed American sovereignty. The only attack on U.S. sovereignty had been against the merchant flag aboard American-owned and American-registered cargo ships.

The vote in the House of Representatives was 373 in favor of war, 50 opposed; in the Senate, it was 82 in favor and 6 opposed. The United States would lose some 53,000 killed in action and another 63,000 deaths from other causes in the Great War. Although Wilson portrayed the war as one to make the world safe for democracy, and as a war to end wars, the actual tipping point for the American decision to enter World War I was the loss of *Vigilancia* and its forgotten seamen.

In the early twenty-first century, the American press and public asked U.S. presidents whether or not they entered wars for justifiable reasons. What did the president know, and when did he know it? Was the casus belli legitimate, or were the facts distorted to fit another agenda? In light of the Vietnam War, the Gulf War, the Iraq War, and many incidents such as the invasions of Grenada and Panama that have troubled the American conscience, these inquiries have become routine. But in 1917, such questions were not posed; in the years following World War I, historians, political scientists, and even psychoanalysts probed Woodrow Wilson's motivations on a higher plane. While many in organized labor, on the Left, or in regions far removed from either coast opposed the decision to go to war, the opponents never focused the debate on the key events that in fact moved Wilson from a position of neutrality to a decision for war.

Rather than investigating the specific events that constituted the reasons for the United States' entry into the war, many historians have sought out in the depths of Wilson's motivation factors that led him to take an unneutral policy favoring Britain and its Allies over Germany while officially remaining neutral in the Great War. A vast body of scholarship has grown up surrounding America's failed attempt to stay neutral in that war, with much of that writing examining the ideas of Wilson and the advisors and friends who influenced him. The nature of Woodrow Wilson's idealism has been thoroughly plumbed.[1]

In this work, the straightforward facts of the events are presented. The war began for the United States because the public, Congress, and the president concluded that the rights of Americans to use the seas of the world had been sorely infringed by Germany. German espionage, sabotage, the leaked Zimmermann Telegram offering a German-Mexican alliance, and the mistreatment of American diplomatic staff in Germany all contributed to the anger at Germany, but none of those developments had been acts

Figure 3. "Way of the Neutral Is Hard." The cartoonist Clifford Berryman captured the difficulty of Uncle Sam carrying the burden of neutrality along a perilous path marked with "contraband," "demand for embargo," "misuse of the flag," and other maritime problems. (Wilson Presidential Library, Staunton, Va.)

of war. After a series of affronts to Americans on the high seas, none of which quite rose to the level of an attack on the United States, the sinking of the *Vigilancia* and two other merchant ships on the same weekend stood out as a clear and undeniable casus belli. Despite the seemingly small scale of these incidents, events and circumstances that had developed over the previous two-and-a-half years made it clear that Germany had, with these attacks, initiated war against the United States. This book details the events and circumstances that made the loss of *Vigilancia* and the deaths of fifteen men who sailed aboard her, and the sinking of the *City of Memphis* and the *Illinois*, the overt acts of war that brought the United States into World War I.

2

From *Falaba* to *Sussex*

The sinking of U.S. merchant ships like the *Vigilancia* that carried the U.S. flag got the United States into World War I. However, the flag and sovereignty at sea issues that were the legal casus belli for American entry into the war have been obscured from view by contemporary and later concern over the loss of lives of American passengers aboard foreign ships during the period 1915–16. These events worsened U.S. relations with Germany and fed the popular image of German brutality at sea; the sinking of liners registered to Britain, France, Italy, and Russia helped create the mood, if not the legal grounds, for war.

American Neutrality

At the outbreak of World War I, because the United States had no alliances with any of the nations of Europe that would require that American troops come to the defense of any of the parties to the conflict, and because of his personal abhorrence of war, Wilson immediately declared American neutrality. Wilson's position was well-rooted in precedent. Traditionally, the United States had been able to follow George Washington's advice in his Farewell Address of 1796 to "steer clear of permanent alliances with any portion of the foreign world." Through the nineteenth century, Americans had easily stayed out of the Crimean War in 1853–56, the Austro-Prussian War in 1866, the Franco-Prussian War of 1870–71, and the Sino-Japanese War of 1894–95. Later, they stood on the sidelines of the Boer War of 1899–1902, and two Balkan Wars of 1912 and 1913.

From June 28, 1914, when Archduke Franz Ferdinand was assassinated in a touring car in Sarajevo, Bosnia, through August 4, 1914, the origins of the war seemed distant, horrible, and quite unlikely to engage the United States. In a speech to Congress on August 19, 1914, Wilson asked Americans to be neutral in "thought as well as in deed." He knew that Americans, with ancestry among both the Allies and the Central powers, could easily take sides in the conflict, and he hoped that the nation could put aside those sentiments, and also be very careful not to take any actions that would show a preference for, or provide aid to, one side over the other.[1]

American Passengers on Belligerent Ships

The German attacks on British passenger ships, carrying women and children, horrified Woodrow Wilson and the American public. Several incidents of German attacks on Allied passenger liners fitted in perfectly with the growing impression of German brutality created by their ruthless suppression of civilian resistance in Belgium and by British propaganda efforts exaggerating and even creating false stories of atrocities in Belgium, France, and Poland. The incidents involving British and French passenger ships resulted in heated exchanges of diplomatic notes and threats by Wilson to sever relations with the German Empire. Although the losses of liners registered to the Allies were not a cause for war for the United States, the facts of those events are quite pertinent to the unfolding story of sovereignty at sea in the period. Furthermore, the ways in which the British chose to interdict neutral shipping to Germany with a blockade also represented challenges to American sovereignty at sea.[2]

Wilson constantly argued that Americans voluntarily choosing to travel on the ships of belligerent nations should be immune from attack, and he believed that neutral rights included the right to travel unmolested during wartime. Wilson held this position despite the German government forcefully arguing that no such right existed. More than once, German diplomats pointed out that expecting submarines to refrain from sinking Allied ships carrying munitions or troops, or armed passenger ships because they also carried American tourists would be like asking Germany to refrain from targeting a British munitions wagon in the battlefield because Americans chose to ride on it. If Americans boarded a British ship, they assumed the risk, Germany claimed, arguing that such victims were guilty of irresponsible behavior.

The comparison of ships and ammo wagons was compelling, and many pro-German and neutralist Americans found it convincing. However, there was, in fact, a significant difference between riding a British ammo truck or wagon and traveling as a passenger on a British ship that carried war cargo. A whole body of international law and practice had grown up around the conduct of war at sea that made the situation very different.[3]

The major naval powers had convened in London from December 1908 to January 1909 in an attempt to codify the practices of proper naval warfare. Representatives from Britain, France, Germany, Austria-Hungary, the Netherlands, the United States, Italy, Japan, and Russia all diligently worked to capture correct practices regarding blockade, treatment of civilian ships, and other aspects of war at sea. The resulting Declaration of London of 1909, even though it had never been signed as an official multilateral treaty or convention, did in fact represent the commitment to paper of many existing "rules of war" as they applied to blockades and the treatment of neutral ships. The declaration had been approved by the Foreign Relations Committee of the United States Senate, and at the beginning of the war, the French government and others hoped it would form the basis of blockade operation. On the other hand, a few months after the war began, Lord Lansdowne, a member of the British cabinet, made clear that the Admiralty would selectively use parts of the Declaration of London, while ignoring other parts, as suited the exigencies of the war.[4]

Under accepted rules of blockade, as reflected in the Declaration of London, a belligerent or neutral civilian ship attempting to run through a blockade should be hailed by a blockading warship, and the ship should then be placed under a prize crew if it was found to carry contraband of war. If a prize crew could not safely be put aboard and the merchant ship had to be sunk, all civilian passengers and crew (belligerent and neutral alike) should be evacuated before the ship was destroyed.

The practices surrounding exactly how to stop and inspect merchant ships had been observed by the major nations with naval forces and were known as "cruiser rules" because they reflected the practices employed in earlier decades by naval cruisers enforcing blockades. Article 50 of the Declaration of London explicitly stated that passengers and crew aboard civilian (or "merchant") ships like liners and freighters carrying contraband should be "placed in safety" before a ship was destroyed. They should be able to travel without fear of being killed through an attack, unless the captain and crew of the ship engaged in flight, attempted to attack the warship, or worked in conjunction with enemy naval ships by communicating with them. Even during the American Civil War, Confederate raiders at sea scrupulously followed the cruiser rules, and although they destroyed more than 230 merchant ships, they carefully preserved the lives of *all* crews and passengers aboard them. Wilson was quite correct in viewing the sinking without warning of a peaceful civilian ship as a violation of the rules or practices of civilized warfare as they had evolved. The United States State Department through numerous notes, and U.S. ambassador James Gerard in person in Germany, made it clear that the United States expected Germany to follow cruiser rules in the use of U-boats. In fact, as will be seen in this work, German U-boat commanders during the period of American neutrality usually did adhere to cruiser rules when accosting American ships, allowing time for safe evacuation of crews.[5]

The United States government was rightfully concerned if American citizens traveling as passengers or crews aboard ships under the British flag and sovereignty were harmed. The United States should and did exercise its diplomatic influence to protect such American citizens. But sovereignty at sea followed the flag. When Wilson protested against German attacks on British liners, he was protecting individual American rights, not arguing for the defense of American sovereignty. The distinction may seem abstract, but it was crucial to the difference between the loss of American lives aboard a British ship and the sinking of a ship flying the American flag.

An attack on an American ship would be something entirely different. That would entail not only an attack on individual citizens' rights, but an attack on the nation's sovereign rights and would be a direct and much more serious affront to the United States under international law. The distinction was one that was very clear and very real to Wilson's legal advisor in the State Department, Robert Lansing.

Wilson consulted with Lansing over the issue of Americans traveling aboard neutral ships. Lansing had extensive experience in international law, and served as legal counsel to the State Department in 1914–15 while William Jennings Bryan was secretary of state. When Bryan resigned from his post in 1915, Wilson chose Lansing to replace him. Lansing understood that civilians would be at risk if they traveled on an armed ship of a belligerent nation, or on a ship whose captain decided to attack a warship or to escape from it. He understood that the "right" of Americans to travel on belligerent ships (especially those that were armed or carried arms) was not an absolute right and varied with the particular circumstances of the incident. The German government was quick to point out what they saw as the warlike behavior or equipment of the merchant ships that U-boats sank without warning. Even so, Wilson was extremely active in defending the rights of American passengers, even aboard ships known to be carrying weapons or war supplies such as the *Lusitania*. The State Department under William Jennings Bryan and, later, under Robert Lansing examined the particulars of every case very closely to vigorously protest any violations of American rights.

Lansing, who was extremely pro-Ally, supported Wilson's position regarding Americans traveling under Allied maritime flags. The vigor with which Wilson defended American individual rights was infectious. As the protest notes mounted and the press focused on them, those Americans who supported the Allied cause won converts from the more strictly neutral position. Wilson's protests, however, did not mean that he personally sought an excuse to go to war. He remained convinced that the United States should remain neutral and work for peace. His effort to provide some form of mediation between the warring parties has been well documented, and the effort, though a failure, was very genuine, lasting right up through the first weeks of 1917.

Saloon Class and Seamen

While the State Department lodged official protest notes with Germany and its ally Austria-Hungary regarding aspects of attacks on American merchant ships such as freighters, tankers, and cargo schooners, during the period of American neutrality, Wilson and Lansing gave such events far less attention than they gave to the fate of Allied passenger liners. Considering the significant difference between protecting the rights of individual American citizens on foreign ships and defending American sovereignty as represented by the merchant flag on American merchant ships, the disparity of concern is remarkable. A class-analysis view of the matter sheds some light on this disparity.

American passengers aboard British liners in "saloon class" included the elite of American society. It was also was possible to book transatlantic fares in second- or third-class accommodations at very low rates. But American travelers in first-class, especially during the war years, tended to be drawn from among the wealthiest and most socially prominent families, including literary figures, businessmen, and heirs to great fortunes, many of them well-known to the public. Newspapers carried lists of the arrival of first-class passengers and sometimes the cabin passengers as well aboard particular ships, suggesting the degree to which socially and financially prominent figures received attention, admiration, and respect from the public. In the era before electronic mass media, celebrity status tended to be reserved for the wealthy, and for playwrights, musicians, and other famous creative artists.[6]

By contrast, the crews of U.S.-registered merchant ships who were endangered in the same period were clearly members of an underpaid class at the bottom of the social ladder. The merchant ship crews were at this time often quite international in character, including members of ethnic groups usually held in low esteem by middle- and upper-class Americans of British or other northern European descent. Crew lists aboard American merchant ships during the war years included many Greeks, Spaniards, Latin Americans, Puerto Ricans, Filipinos, and African Americans, as well as European immigrants recently naturalized as U.S. citizens. Ethnic and class identity shaped the way that casualties were reported in the press, and how the events were viewed by government officials and politicians. Wilson and most mainstream journalists of the era clearly had more sympathy for white Anglo-Saxon passengers aboard luxury liners than they did for the polyglot crews aboard merchant ships.[7] Ultimately, when the United States went to war, it was such men who had been killed, but they had been killed aboard ships that flew the American flag, not the British flag. It was the attack on U.S. sovereignty, not on U.S. citizens, that represented the tipping point for war.

The fact that women and children were among the liner passengers, and were usually entirely absent aboard merchant ships, also helped account for the disparity in concern expressed by the press between that for liners and that for freighters. Gender values of the period tended to regard women as more fragile, more deserving of deferential consideration, and more entitled to sympathy than men. The accidental deaths of one or two middle- or upper-class women passengers during a lifeboat rescue or ship sinking received vastly more sensational attention in the press than did the death of a much greater number of the "black gang" who stoked the furnaces of steamships with coal or dozens of hardworking men who tended mules and horses being exported from the United States to the Allies.

One incident suffices to illustrate the class disparity in reporting. The British liner *Armenian* was sunk by *U-38* off Cornwall on June 28, 1915, on the way from Newport News, Virginia, to Liverpool, with the loss of twenty-nine lives. It carried no passengers, as it had been converted for carrying mules and horses to Britain. Among the dead were twelve African American men whose job it was to tend more than 1,400 mules aboard the ship. The *Armenian* incident and those twelve deaths received far less attention from the State Department and the press than the earlier death of a single American male passenger aboard the British *Falaba* or two American women passengers aboard the British *Laconia* in early 1917.[8]

Among the attacked passenger ships that stunned the American people, Wilson, and members of Congress, the most striking were, *Falaba*, *Lusitania*, *Arabic*, and *Sussex*. These four ships were the most notorious of the more than twenty passenger ships fired on by submarines through 1915 and

1916. While there were American passengers and crew aboard some of the other Allied ships attacked by German submarines, these four cases set the tone of diplomatic exchanges over the issues.[9]

Falaba

The steamship *Falaba*, operated by the Elder Line, had been built in 1906. The 4,086-ton passenger ship was capable of 14 knots, powered by triple expansion engines. It left Liverpool, bound for Sierra Leone on the west coast of Africa, on the evening of March 27, 1915. The next morning, some thirty-eight miles west of the Smalls Light, it encountered a submarine with a British flag. However, as the sub approached, it replaced the ensign with the German naval flag. The sub was *U-28*, under the command of Baron von Forstner. Von Forstner signaled with flags "stop and abandon ship," but Captain Davis of *Falaba* increased to full speed. The submarine then signaled, "stop or I will fire on you."[10]

Since the submarine was capable of a slightly faster surface speed than the *Falaba*, Davis stopped the liner and began to swing out the lifeboats. However, at a range estimated at 150 yards, *U-28* fired a single torpedo. *Falaba* immediately began to sink as the passengers and crew frantically tried to launch the boats. Although two nearby "steam drifters," a type of large fishing boat engaged in war duty, picked up survivors, 104 of the 247 passengers and crew aboard died, either in the water or shortly after being pulled out. One of the passengers who died was Leon Thrasher, thought to be the first American killed in World War I. It turned out that it was not clear whether he was an American citizen after all, as he was a longtime resident of Britain on his way to a job in West Africa; nevertheless, the event was a shock to the American public. By the strict letter of cruiser rules, the captain of *Falaba* had put the ship at risk by attempting to flee rather than immediately stopping when signaled to do so.[11]

The United States began protests of this event and was still engaged in exchanges with Germany over it when *Lusitania* was sunk.

Lusitania

The most disastrous of all the attacks on liners and the one that entered American popular memory as a great atrocity was the oft-retold sinking of the *Lusitania*, at 1415 (2:15 p.m.), on May 7, 1915. When Walther Schwieger of *U-20* fired a single obsolete torpedo against the four-stack Cunard British flag liner, the ship went down in about fifteen minutes. The death toll was 1,198 passengers and crew, including 217 women and 94 children.

The death toll included more than 100 American passengers and crew members. For many years, the total number of deaths and the number of Americans who died were variously recorded, but recent studies have tended to agree that the number of American citizens killed was 128, including a number of women and children who were unable to survive in the frigid conditions of the waters off the Irish coast. Among those who died was the well-known American millionaire Alfred Vanderbilt.

Schwieger was horrified when he saw the ship sink so rapidly after a secondary explosion. Later research has suggested the secondary explosion that spelled the rapid loss of the ship was probably due to coal dust in the fuel storage bunkers. Watching the tragedy unfold through the periscope, Schwieger noted: "there was a terrible panic on her decks. Desperate people ran helplessly up and down while men and women jumped into the water and tried to swim to empty overturned lifeboats. It was the most horrible sight I have ever seen. . . . The scene was too horrible to watch and I gave orders to dive to twenty metres and away."[12] Once the British learned the identity of the U-boat commander, he was vilified as a murderer. It only added to British and American distress that Schwieger was welcomed as a hero in Germany, and that medals and commemorative cards were manufactured and distributed honoring him and his attack. Wilson and the American public were stunned.

Official inquiries and historical treatments of the *Lusitania* episode pursued a great many questions. The German embassy had published in New York newspapers a warning against traveling on British ships before the *Lusitania* sailed. The ship carried a cargo that included small arms ammunition that German officials and commentators at first suggested had contributed to the secondary explosion.

Some of the facts brought out in the inquiries suggested that the captain of the ship and broader British policies were not entirely blameless in the *Lusitania* affair. Cunard Line officials had ordered the ship to operate on only two of its three engines to conserve coal. Although capable of speeds that would outrun any submarine, the *Lusitania* proceeded slowly as Captain W. J. Turner appeared to ignore certain orders to steam quickly past the danger zone and to avoid the headlands. Furthermore, British Admiralty wireless warnings to the *Lusitania* about the presence of submarines were not worded very clearly. British liners had been advised by the British Admiralty to take evasive action and to ram submarines, both of which practices, under cruiser rules, lost them immunity from attack. It was also a fact that *Lusitania* was listed as a naval auxiliary cruiser. None of these considerations lessened the horror of the event for Wilson, American editorialists, and many of the general public in the United States.[13]

Woodrow Wilson sent three protest notes to Germany regarding the sinking of the *Lusitania*, progressively raising the tone of anger and outrage in each. In the first note, sent on May 13 over objections from Secretary of State Bryan, Wilson insisted on the right of Americans to sail on any ship in international waters. Wilson said Germany should be held to "strict accountability" for any loss of civilian lives incurred by the actions of their ships at sea. Germany responded two weeks later, pointing out that the ship carried ammunition and war cargo. Wilson continued to believe that the central issue was the right to travel on the high seas, and that the Germans were evading the issue by discussing the ship's cargo and other points. Although no public announcement was made, the Kaiser issued a confidential order about a month after the loss of *Lusitania*, instructing U-boat officers not to sink *any* passenger liners without warning.

Wilson was a little shocked at the public outrage in the United States over the sinking of the *Lusitania*, and three days after the sinking, he gave a speech in Philadelphia trying to calm feelings, stating, "There is such a thing as a man being too proud to fight." Opponents and critics seized on the phrase as an indication of his lack of backbone, while supporters admired Wilson's high-mindedness.[14] As Wilson prepared his second and third notes to Germany insisting on the American right to sea travel, Secretary Bryan decided to resign from his post. Bryan left June 8, 1915, after making a heartfelt farewell to his colleagues in the cabinet.[15]

Wilson had been acting as his own secretary of state, with Bryan's role cut back to signing notes that had already been drafted by the president, and that factor as much as the content of the notes appeared to contribute to Bryan's departure. Even so, Bryan was a prominent pacifist, and his break with Wilson over the *Lusitania* notes was popularly viewed as one over issues as well as procedure. Wilson immediately replaced Bryan with Robert Lansing as acting secretary, to be confirmed later by the Senate. Lansing was willing to continue to act as Wilson's legal advisor rather than an independent secretary of state; even so, he privately took an even more anti-German position than did Wilson.

Wilson had other advisors through this period, who like Lansing, favored finding some reason for siding with the British. They included the informal advisor Colonel Edward House; Wilson's private secretary, Joseph Tumulty;

Figure 4. Uncle Sam after the *Lusitania*. The cartoonist Clifford Berryman depicted Uncle Sam struggling with the note to Germany, considering not only the loss of the *Lusitania*, but also the damage to the American merchant ship *Nebraskan*. (Wilson Presidential Library, Staunton, Va.)

the U.S. ambassador to Britain, Walter Hines Page; and Secretary of Agriculture David Houston, among others. Wilson tended to make his own decisions and had a reputation for ignoring advice with which he did not agree. For that reason, the influence of such pro-Ally advisors has remained very difficult to assess. Wilson certainly realized exactly where his advisors and associates stood, and could even predict ahead of time very accurately what particular positions they would take when an important issue came up. He persisted in working to keep the United States neutral while many of his closest advisors became increasingly bellicose.[16]

The *Arabic* and the *Arabic* Pledge

Despite the uproar from the American press and from other neutrals, German submarines continued to attack Allied merchant ships through the summer of 1915, usually warning the crews of smaller ships to evacuate. However, the policy of German submarine commanders toward the ships they attacked seemed to vary to some degree with the commander's personality, as well as with the specifics of the situation. When target ships appeared to be threatening or to be ignoring proper instructions to stop and be challenged, they definitely ran the risk of being sent to the bottom, having sacrificed immunity from attack. With so many variables, each incident was unique.

On August 19, 1915, Captain Rudolf Schneider of *U-24* sank the British steamer *Arabic*, carrying 433 passengers and crew on a voyage from Liverpool bound for New York. Evacuation proceeded fairly well, and only 44 aboard perished, including two American citizens. Schneider reported that the steamer had zigzagged, and he feared it had been attempting to ram the sub, a plausible story that the American press mostly found implausible.[17]

In response to protests, the Kaiser personally ordered that before any more liners were sunk, the ship had to be fully warned, and that both passengers and crew had to be safely aboard boats. German ambassador Johann von Bernstorff in Washington was ordered to assure the U.S. government of the policy, and on September 1, 1915, he gave a note to the State Department that said, "Liners will not be sunk by our submarines without warning and without safety of the lives of non-combatants, provided that the liners do not try to escape or offer resistance." The statement immediately became known as the "*Arabic* Pledge," although it was not clear to what extent it was a result of Bernstorff's own initiative, or whether it even represented a new policy. Even so, over the winter months of 1915–16, no more liners, large or small, were sunk without warning.[18]

In mid-1915, the British began using Q-ships. These were merchant ships rigged with concealed guns that would slowly steam through known U-boat cruising zones. When ordered to stop, a false "panic party" would scramble into lifeboats, apparently abandoning ship. As the submarine approached to dispatch the vessel with gunfire, panels on the deck of the supposedly innocent and apparently abandoned merchant ship would be thrown down, the British fighting ensign raised, and the guns aboard the Q-ship, manned by sailors of the Royal Navy, would open up on the submarine, sometimes with success. In one notorious case, on August 19, 1915, while the submarine waited for the crew of the British merchant ship *Nicosian* to get into lifeboats, the British Q-ship *Baralong*, which had at first flown a false U.S. flag, fired on the submarine and then shot the German crew in the water as they attempted to reach safety aboard the *Nicosian* lifeboats. British sailors also tracked down and murdered some of the German crew who had taken refuge aboard the *Nicosian*. American witnesses to the event filed affidavits that were forwarded to the State Department.[19]

In Germany, the debate over the best use of the submarine continued to simmer. Admiral Henning von Holtzendorff, who had risen to the post of chief of the German naval staff by late 1915, prepared a confidential memorandum spelling out calculations that if six hundred thousand tons of shipping could be sunk a month, Britain would face starvation within a few months. The policy was not initiated, and Holtzendorff "resolved to content himself" with treating all enemy armed merchant ships as warships: as a warship, an enemy armed merchant ship could be sunk without warning, the German navy reasoned. Some British merchant ships now mounted large, unconcealed guns for defense against submarines, and they were fair game under German policy.[20]

Q-ships and merchant ships with deck guns had become serious threats to the submarine. Consequently, on February 21, 1916, the German government announced that any Allied armed merchant ship, whether a liner or cargo ship, would be treated as a ship of war, and would be sunk without warning. German U-boats approached British merchant ships very warily to determine if they carried weapons; if they showed weapons, the submarines attacked the armed merchant ship without warning. By the German interpretation of cruiser rules, such attacks made sense, for if a U-boat warned an armed merchant ship with a gunshot, the submarine ran the risk of being immediately sunk. Submarine hulls were unarmored, and one or two holes from a deck gun could easily send a U-boat to the bottom.

Gore Bill and McLemore Resolution

By March 1916, some members of Congress feared that Wilson's policy of neutrality had, either consciously or unconsciously, evolved into a pro-Ally stand regarding the passenger ship question. Congressman Jeff McLemore of Texas introduced a resolution into Congress requesting the president to warn Americans against travel on any armed vessel. Since the British were arming liners, and the Germans had warned that they would sink without warning any armed merchant ship as if it were a warship, it seemed to Mc-

Lemore and his supporters that the United States could easily become embroiled if Americans persisted in traveling on such ships. A few days later, Senator Thomas P. Gore of Oklahoma introduced a Senate bill that would deny passports to any American who sought to travel on armed vessels. The Gore Bill further demanded that the Allies allow noncontraband trade with the Central powers. Gore, a nationally recognized figure, blind since childhood, and a strong defender of strict neutrality, was an advocate for the cotton trade, and no doubt he had that commodity in mind.

Wilson saw the McLemore Resolution and the Gore Bill as direct challenges to his presidential power to make and execute foreign policy. He asked Democratic Party leaders to have both actions stopped. Writing to Senator William J. Stone of the Senate Foreign Relations Committee, Wilson argued that if the United States would "once accept a single abatement of right [then] many other humiliations would follow." Stone, representing Missouri, had many German Americans in his constituency, and although a Democrat, opposed Wilson on many interpretations of neutrality. Wilson told Stone that he feared the "whole fine fabric of international law might crumble under our hand, piece by piece." If the United States were to yield on these principles and prohibit Americans from traveling on belligerent merchant ships, it would mean the "virtual surrender of her independent position among the nations of the world." Both measures were tabled, effectively killing them, by majority votes—the Gore Bill in the Senate on March 3 and the McLemore Resolution in the House on March 7, 1916. Although Wilson was able to get both these measures stopped, they were significant in that they showed ways that tensions with Germany could be reduced when passenger liners registered to one of the belligerent powers were targeted. Despite their failure, some convinced strict neutralists continued to hope that such measures, or variations on them, would require that contraband be sent only on belligerent, not American ships.[21]

The *Sussex* and the *Sussex* Pledge

On March 24, 1916, German submarine *UB-29* torpedoed *Sussex*, a French cross-channel passenger ship.[22] Originally owned by the British, the ship had been taken over by the French state railway service in January 1914. The torpedo knocked a large section of the bow entirely off. Surprisingly, the ship did not sink, and even though lifeboats were launched, most passengers and crew returned to the ship; it was later towed backward into Boulogne harbor, where it was declared unsalvageable. About fifty of the passengers aboard died, but none of them were American, although a few Americans had been injured in the incident. The U.S. State Department treated the attack as a clear violation of the *Arabic* Pledge.

After investigation, the German government claimed that the submarine commander thought that the *Sussex* was a minelayer of the *Arabic* class, a story widely disbelieved in the American press. The commander of *UB-29* that had attacked *Sussex* was Herbert Pustkuchen, who had apparently chosen to ignore recent orders about the safety of passengers. Although not a liner, the cross-channel ferry was certainly a passenger ship, and it has remained difficult to determine whether Pustkuchen made an honest mistake or displayed an excess of zeal. On his March 1916 cruise on his "UB" class coastal attack submarine, Pustkuchen sank several other ships without warning, and his methods may have been a matter of personal preference.[23]

Secretary of State Lansing urged Wilson to break diplomatic relations with Germany over the *Sussex* incident, but instead, Wilson had Lansing send a long, scolding, strongly worded note that ended with an ultimatum: "Unless the Imperial German Government should now immediately declare and effect an abandonment of its present methods of warfare against passenger and freight carrying vessels this Government can have no choice but to sever diplomatic relations with the Government of the German Empire altogether."[24]

The German response to Wilson's *Sussex* ultimatum came on May 4, 1916. The German government agreed that no more unarmed civilian ships, allied or neutral, would be sunk without warning, but agreed to do this only on condition that the United States insist that the Allies respect all the international rules of the sea with regard to shipping. In particular, Germany wanted the United States to get Britain to lift the blockade of food to Germany and to prohibit the use of the continuous voyage doctrine under which goods destined for European neutrals like Denmark and Holland were interdicted on the grounds they might be sent on to Germany by land. In explaining his position to Congress and in his reply to Germany, Wilson made it clear that he accepted the German promise to avoid sinking without warning, but that he would not take any notice of the counterconditions. In the tone of an instructor, he pointed out that it was not common international practice for one nation to ask another to abide by commonly accepted rules of behavior only on the condition that another nation do so.

Over the period from June 1916 through September 1916, German submarines more or less obeyed the so-called *Sussex* Pledge. Without officially abandoning the pledge, German submarines aggressively hailed ships and assaulted those that attempted to evade orders to stop and be evacuated, causing a few incidents.

Meanwhile, in a much less newsworthy fashion, and in a series of events much less treated by historians of the period, a series of United States merchant ships had their own encounters with German warships and submarines. Beginning with *William P. Frye* in 1915 and continuing through the loss or capture of another seven vessels through 1916, German ships and submarines established their own record against the less glamorous American-flagged merchant ships. Despite their humble character and lack of sensational casualties, those few ships were far more legally significant, for such attacks could represent violations of American sovereignty at sea. The reasons why none of these direct assaults on the American flag constituted a casus belli varied from case to case and are the subject of the next two chapters.

3

The Flag under Fire

From *Frye* to *Pass of Balmaha*

A few days before President Wilson announced his official neutrality policy, his first secretary of state, William Jennings Bryan, quietly told the banking community through J. P. Morgan that "in the judgment of this Government, loans by American bankers to any foreign nation which is at war are inconsistent with the true spirit of neutrality." Bryan's informal loan ban remained in place from August 1914 until September 1915, and meant that any belligerent had to draw on existing resources that they held in the United States in order to purchase any goods, including food, cotton, munitions, oil, or transport equipment.[1]

During that year, Britain and France were able to make purchases in the United States by drawing on some $2 billion in credit and bank deposits held by citizens and institutions of those countries in the United States. Germany purchased only an estimated $20 million worth of goods in the same period. The reason for the discrepancy in the dollar value of the trade was simply that Britain, with its vastly superior surface fleet, made it impossible for German ships to reach the United States. And by a combination of minefields and ship interdictions, Britain was able to prevent American and other neutral ships from carrying goods to Germany.

At first Britain did not prohibit trade in noncontraband goods with Germany, even allowing U.S. trade in cotton directly with German ports through the first months of the war. However, by late 1914, the British developed a form of blockade by beginning to mine off the North Sea and then offering pilots to help neutral ships find the channels through the minefields. During the process of getting a pilot in a British port, an American ship could be inspected. Port officials would even not release such a ship to go to neutral ports such as those in Holland or Denmark if the final cargo destination was German. Even after inspection in this period, only ships carrying noncontraband destined for Germany or for its bordering neutrals were permitted to proceed.

Technically, this practice of controlling trade to Germany through Holland or Denmark represented blockade under the "doctrine of continuous voyage." That is, the cargo was intended to pass on a continuous voyage by way of an intermediate port to an enemy destination. The 1909 Declaration of London had condemned as improper any sea blockade that used the doctrine of continuous voyage except in cases of weapons and other clear contraband items useful in war. With their mining and pilotage system, the British in 1915 began stopping trade even in items of "conditional contraband," that is, categories of goods declared by Britain to be useful to the war effort, but not directly identified as weapons or transport equipment. The cotton imports, they concluded, had been used in the manufacture of explosives, and they effectively cut off that trade.

By adopting the continuous voyage type of blockade with regard to conditional contraband, Britain was showing one of the several ways in which it selectively applied the rules listed in the Declaration of London. Because there were no formal treaties prohibiting the continuous voyage doctrine, and because the United States had actually employed it during the Civil War in the Union blockade of the Confederacy, the United States found it difficult to protest the policy.[2]

But the United States could protest delays and the related expenses for shipowners by the British policy of quarantining ships, and Bryan did so in a note on December 29, 1914. The weak protests against British practices angered members of the Senate Foreign Relations Committee, who expected a more vigorously neutral and balanced policy, and on January 20, 1915, Secretary of State Bryan tried to explain the U.S. position to the committee. No cargoes destined for Germany had yet been confiscated, but on the other hand, the British practices apparently discouraged American businesses from attempting to sell weapons and other strategic goods to Germany. Meanwhile, strategic materials, and even arms, ammunition, and transport equipment were regularly flowing from the United States to the Allies.

If there was an imbalance, Bryan pointed out, it was because Britain's control of the sea allowed it to exercise a more effective blockade. From the U.S. position, while American trade might be helping Britain and France more than the Central powers, it was not due to any violation of neutrality by the United States. Even faced with the loan ban, the British were simply buying what they needed, using funds already available in the United States and getting the cargoes to Britain by way of British ships or ships of neutrals like those of Norway, the Netherlands, and the United States.[3]

Fisher, Doyle, and Holtzendorff

Although Germany could not readily use surface ships to blockade Britain, Germany began to use its growing submarine fleet in retaliation for the British measures. The idea that submarines could be used as part of a warfare campaign against commerce (or *Handelskrieg*) had been developed and dreaded in Britain in the decade before the war. Admiral John "Jacky" Fisher had drawn attention to the possibility that submarines could be used to attack commerce in an article published in 1904 entitled "Submarines." Although ridiculed by others, the concept continued to haunt British commentators on warfare. Arthur Conan Doyle, the creator of Sherlock Holmes, published an article in *Strand Magazine* in July 1914, just before the war broke out, drawing the public's attention to the threat of a submarine blockade. German naval experts had first conceived of the submarine as a warship that could lay mines and provide coastal defense against enemy warships, but several German strategic planners advocated the concept advanced by Fisher and Doyle, including Admiral Henning Holtzendorff. Holtzendorff convinced Admiral von Tirpitz, secretary of state of the German Imperial Navy, to support the idea of using unrestricted naval warfare against all shipping to the Allies.[4]

Germany initiated the strategy by announcing the first unrestricted submarine warfare in a zone around Britain and Ireland in February 1915. Although the German navy had intended that the unrestricted attacks would include neutral as well as belligerent ships, the German chancellor, Theobold von Bethmann-Hollweg, overruled that policy and insisted that only belligerent ships should be sunk. Germany stated that any merchant or war ship under the flag of one of the Allies in the declared zone might be sunk without warning. Since Britain had urged British merchant captains to fly a false flag of a neutral country to avoid being sunk, Germany warned that sometimes a neutral ship might be accidentally sunk. Most of the submarine captains continued to warn merchant ships of whatever registry and evacuate crews before sinking, although some of the large fast liners belonging to the Allies, such as the *Lusitania*, capable of running away from a submarine or ramming it, were attacked without warning.[5]

German U-boats and American Merchant Ships

During the period of American neutrality, no German submarine ever accosted or attacked an American-registered passenger ship. Freighters and tankers, as discussed further below, were more difficult to identify, and two such ships were mistakenly attacked by German submarines and one slightly damaged by a bomb dropped from an aircraft.[6] In the two years between January 1915 and the end of January 1917, German submarines challenged or attacked American merchant ships about twenty times, but never accosted or attacked any U.S.-registered passenger liners.

One reason for the neglect shown by contemporaries and historians for the events aboard the American merchant ships assaulted during the period of American neutrality is quite straightforward. None of the attacks on American merchant ships in this period involved great tragic loss of life, and most before February 1, 1917, were resolved somewhat amicably through diplomatic notes and therefore subsided from the front pages. Putting aside questions of race, class, and gender, it was in fact true that the events involving attacks on American merchant ships in the two years from January 1915 through January 1917 were less newsworthy and far less dramatic than the loss of *Lusitania* or the attack on *Sussex*. Many of the events were hardly international incidents at all, and simply resulted from a submarine hailing a freighter with a gunshot.

Nevertheless, from the perspective of international law and the relations between belligerent nations and neutrals, the treatment by Germany of U.S. flag merchant ships was far more likely to create a true casus belli than was the sinking of a British flag liner. The encounters between U.S.-flagged merchant ships and German warships were scrutinized very carefully at the State Department and reported in some detail, especially in the pro-Ally New York press. There were eight major cases of such encounters.

Of these eight major cases of encounters between German warships and American-flagged merchant ships in the months between the outbreak of the war and February 1, 1917, two were admitted errors (*Gulflight* and *Nebraskan*), for which the German government offered compensation and apology. Only in the case of the accidentally damaged *Gulflight* were there *any* deaths, two seamen and the captain who later suffered a heart attack. The fact that no more than three lives were lost, all from that one accidental encounter, during incidents of gunfire and the challenge or sinking of ships that carried a total of more than five hundred officers and crew is striking. More than once, the German government pointed out correctly that the intentional sinking of neutral ships rarely, if ever, resulted in the loss of life in this period.

Some ten or twelve minor incidents involving U.S. merchant ships also briefly drew the attention of the State Department or the press during the

Table 3.1. Major encounters, U.S. ships with German warships, January 1915–November 1916

Ship	Date of Encounter
William P. Frye	January 27, 1915
Gulflight	May 1, 1915
Nebraskan	May 26, 1915
Pass of Balmaha	July 24, 1915
Leelanaw	July 25, 1915
Lanao	October 28, 1916
Columbia	November 8, 1916
Chemung	November 26, 1916

period of American neutrality.[7] But none of the minor cases involved casualties, in none was the ship seriously damaged or sunk, and none resulted in claims for financial damages. Those that can be substantiated and documented are shown in table 3.2.

Five other U.S. ships were lost to mines in the period of neutrality, and they were sometimes listed as German affronts to the U.S. flag, but such damage and losses did not represent willful acts of the German navy, and no matter how they happened, could not be construed as acts of war by

Table 3.2. Minor encounters, U.S. ships with German warships or aircraft, December 1915–January 1917

Ship	Date	Circumstances
Cushing	April 18, 1915	Aircraft attacked, on assumption was Allied ship; slight bomb damage
Muskogee	April 30, 1915	Submarine commander removed, and detained two seamen, thought to be enemy aliens
Petrolite	Dec. 5, 1915	Austrian sub asked for and obtained food; nature of exchange debated
Owego	Aug. 3, 1916	Sub fired warning shots; captain of *Owego* did not respond (ship incorrectly identified as "*Oswego*" in some documents)
Communipaw	Dec. 3, 1916	Sub possibly hailed tanker with warning shots
Rebecca Palmer	Dec. 14, 1916	Sub fired warning shots; slight damage; sub disappeared
Norlina	Jan. 4, 1917	Sub caused damage, no casualties
Sacramento	Jan. 6, 1917	Sub fired warning shots, but vanished before ship's boat could reach it
Nyanza	Jan. 13, 1917	Sub caused damage; no casualties
Westwego	Jan. 31, 1917	Sub asked for and received three barrels of oil

Germany. In fact, in some of the cases of ships sunk by mines, the State Department and the press assumed the mine had been one of those laid by the Allies, either British or Russian, and that it had drifted from its moorings. When an American ship sought to trade with Germany through a river or harbor the Germans had mined, German practice was to provide a pilot who knew the minefields to shepherd the ship through.[8]

Despite the fact that all of the major and minor incidents of encounters between German ships or submarines and American merchant ships were handled by relatively temperate exchanges of diplomatic notes, they were carefully recorded by some of those who advocated war with Germany. They saw the events, even the very minor encounters of submarines and U.S. ships and the handful of losses to mines, as part of a cumulative series of offenses. After February 1, 1917, when there were more serious intentional attacks that did constitute acts of war, some of these earlier events were recalled as part of the overall affront to the American flag. If one simply listed all the major incidents together with the minor incidents and cases of ships lost to mines, without offering any explanation of how the incidents were resolved, it would make a seemingly serious list of some two dozen or so attacks on the American flag at sea. However, at the time the ships were damaged, seized, or lost, none of these cases constituted a casus belli, each for very different reasons.[9]

Even though the details of the encounters over 1915 and 1916 rather quickly receded from public memory in the face of other more tragic events and dramatic headline news, some of the major encounters were treated as important legal precedents by the State Department. If the United States were willing to accept German explanations of the sinking of American ships under the American flag through 1915 and 1916 as more or less legitimate, those facts established and reflected some principles and ground rules. The specifics of the early incidents set and demonstrated the premises for evaluating later encounters, and show why none of them rose to the level of acts of war.

William P. Frye

The first encounter between an American merchant ship and a German warship during World War I took place on the afternoon of January 27, 1915, off the coast of Brazil, well out in international waters. The four-masted sailing bark *William P. Frye*, owned by the Arthur Sewall Company of Bath, Maine, carried a cargo of 5,200 tons of wheat from Seattle bound for Queenstown in Britain. The company owning the ship was a rather old-fashioned joint stock company of 128 shares, with most shareholders owning only a handful of shares.[10]

The bark was almost becalmed when the German auxiliary cruiser *Prinz Eitel Friedrich* approached and ordered it to lay to. When the German commander of the cruiser, Korvettenkapitän Max Thierichens, learned that the *William P. Frye* carried wheat destined for Britain, he ordered the cargo destroyed. When Captain Herman H. Kiene and his crew aboard the *William P. Frye* refused to obey, a German officer and a squad of men were sent aboard and forced the *Frye*'s crew to begin throwing the grain overboard by shovel. While they were at work, the squad was recalled, and the *Prinz Eitel Friedrich* sailed off in pursuit of another ship, the French bark *Pierre Loti*, also becalmed. The warship returned after sinking *Pierre Loti*, pulling alongside the *Frye* at about ten in the evening.[11]

Finding the disposal of the grain going very slowly, Thierichens sent about fifty men aboard the *William P. Frye* to assist in the job. After several hours, Thierichens decided that the bark would have to be sunk. The American captain Herman Kiene evacuated his wife and two sons, as well as all his crew to the German cruiser, where, in his words, they were "shown every courtesy throughout the remainder of the voyage." The next day, January 28, the bark was sunk with explosives placed aboard.[12]

The loss of the *William P. Frye* was not known in the United States until about six weeks after the event, on March 10, 1915, when the German auxiliary cruiser put into Hampton Roads, Virginia. There, Thierichens released some 342 members of crews and passengers from ships he had destroyed during his 30,000-mile cruise from the formerly German-held enclave of Tsingtao, China. The released civilians from *Prinz Eitel Friedrich* were quite cosmopolitan in composition, since the other ships destroyed by the auxiliary cruiser besides the *William P. Frye* were five British, four French, and one Russian. The *Prinz Eitel Friedrich* had been a German passenger liner with accommodation and cabins for hundreds of passengers. Kiene and his family were given the "bridal suite," and all the crews and passengers from the other ships had comfortable accommodations.

All the released passengers and crews complimented Thierichens on their treatment, and the American press reported the incident in March 1915 as a matter of maritime drama rather than as an international incident that might precipitate war. The U.S. quarantine officer at Old Point, Dr. H. W. McCafferty, "found all on board well and happy. The band was playing German national airs. The food supply was good and there was a feeling of good-fellowship among the people on the ship, many of whom were taken from destroyed merchant vessels.... Every one on board was satisfied that they had received the kindest treatment from the officers of the vessel.... I was impressed with the good appearance of the men and women on the cruiser." Another report, filed with the secretary of the Treasury by Norman Hamilton, inspector of customs at the port, also indicated the passengers and crews of the destroyed ships were in good spirits.[13]

After arrival in the United States, the detained passengers and crews from the merchant ships were repatriated, and the German commander gave his word of honor that his crew members would not leave the port in Norfolk, Virginia. The sailors busied themselves building a small replica German village out of scrap lumber at the harbor, complete with church, picket fences, and flower gardens, where they entertained tourists for a small charge over the next two years. However, at least three of the crew did break their parole, an action that was met with mild rebukes and protests from the U.S. State Department. The *Prinz Eitel Friedrich* was impounded, and later, after the United States entered the war, served as the USS *Dekalb*. The remaining German sailors of *Prinz Eitel Friedrich* were transferred to a prisoner-of-war camp at Fort McPherson, Georgia.[14]

On April 3, 1915, the United States presented to Germany a claim for $228,959.54 for the value of the *William P. Frye*, but stated that it was not filing a claim for the cargo. The German government replied immediately, pointing out that under treaties between Prussia and the United States of 1799 and 1828, still in force, Germany would be obliged to also pay for the cargo, and suggesting that the issue be brought before a prize court in Hamburg, since the German captain had obeyed the rules of the Declaration of London and Germany's own prize ordinance. The U.S. State Department replied that it did not regard the Declaration of London as in force, and since it did not seek compensation for the cargo, but only the ship, that a settlement should be worked out amicably by diplomacy rather than through a prize court.[15]

The diplomatic exchanges over the *William P. Frye* case dragged on for months, with the U.S. position continuing to be that it was happy to settle for the value of the ship, and the German position being that, while the U.S. might have a claim on both the value of the ship and the cargo, the matter should be resolved by the German prize court under the terms of the Prussian–United States treaties. Late in 1916, the two governments moved toward an agreement to submit the amounts in dispute to international arbitration at the Hague. There the case stood over the eventful weeks during which the United States finally decided for war in early 1917. Although the two countries did not work out the specific financial remuneration over the *William P. Frye* before the United States entered the war, it was significant that the United States did not regard the sinking of a merchant ship carrying contraband, as long as the crew were safely evacuated, as an act of war.

In several of the other later cases of German attacks by submarines rather than auxiliary cruisers, the issues seemed somewhat similar to those in the case of the *William P. Frye*, and the *Frye* case was explicitly mentioned as a "precedent" both in official statements and in news items and editorial opinion pieces. The United States would admit that an American ship sunk by Germany carried contraband, protest the action, and demand compensation; and the German government would investigate, offer compensation, or offer to adjudicate the differences along the lines of the *Frye* incident. Even though aspects of the *Frye* precedent might apply in some cases, the other incidents all had unique features.

Gulflight

Gulflight was a 5,189-ton oil tanker owned by Gulf Refining Company, built in Camden, New Jersey, and put in service in August 1914. The tanker was under way toward Rouen, France, escorted by two British patrol boats, carrying a cargo of oil. *Gulflight* was torpedoed about 1300 on May 1, 1915, some fifteen miles west of the Bishop Rock Lighthouse. The light itself lies about four miles to the west of the Isles of Scilly off the southwest tip of Cornwall in Britain. The crew rapidly abandoned ship into two lifeboats, with the exception of two men. The wireless operator Short, and one seaman, Chapaneta, jumped overboard at the first shock of the explosion, and drowned. As in many other newspaper accounts of the loss of lives of merchant seamen in the period, their first names were not reported. The captain, Alfred Gunter, died sixteen hours later, apparently from a heart attack. He had suffered no injuries during the torpedoing of the ship.[16]

Captain Gunter, who was fifty-two years old, had been with Gulf Refining for ten years and was in apparent good health before expiring aboard the rescue ship. A year earlier, in January 1914, he had been in command of the Gulf tanker *Oklahoma* that broke up off Cape May, New Jersey, in a storm. Among the ironies of the *Gulflight* case noted in the press, Gunter had been rescued in peacetime 1914 from the sinking *Oklahoma* by a German ship, *Bavaria*, of the Hamburg-American Line.[17]

The crippled *Gulflight* was towed to Crow Sound in the nearby Isles of

Scilly, and the damage was later repaired. The surviving thirty-three members of the crew were taken aboard one of the patrol boats, the *Iago*, to the Isles of Scilly, and then carried by the steamer *Lyonesse* into Plymouth.[18]

The incident caused an uproar in the American and British press, although some writers speculated whether the *Frye* precedent would apply, especially if the ship carried contraband cargo destined for France, and if it had been properly warned. Such speculation was soon eclipsed by the sinking of the British liner *Lusitania* on May 7, 1915, as well as by the realization that there had been no warning issued to the *Gulflight*. Since the *Gulflight* incident came almost in conjunction with the *Lusitania* tragedy, some American newspapers opined that the former was an unprovoked attack on the United States and constituted an act of war.

However, the German government investigated, and on June 1, 1915, Gottlieb von Jagow, the German foreign minister, sent an apology to U.S. ambassador James Gerard, who immediately forwarded it to Washington. Von Jagow explained that the German submarine commander had observed *Gulflight* as an unknown steamer, apparently being convoyed by two armed British trawlers, one of which had a radio antenna. German records showed that the submarine that attacked *Gulflight* was *U-30*, under the command of Erich Rosenberg.[19]

Rosenberg could not make out any distinguishing neutral markings or flags on the steamship, so, on the assumption that *Gulflight* was an important British ship, he launched a single torpedo. One of the patrol boats swerved toward the submarine with apparent intent to ram, so the submarine submerged. The apology from von Jagow ran in part as follows:

> The fact that the steamship was pursuing a course which led neither to nor from America was a further reason why it did not occur to the commander of the submarine that he had to deal with an American steamship.... According to the attendant circumstances there can be no doubt that the attack is not to be attributed to the fault of the commander, but to an unfortunate accident. The German Government expresses its regrets to the Government of the United States concerning this incident and declares itself ready to furnish full recompense for the damage thereby sustained by American citizens. It begs to leave it to the discretion of the American Government to present a statement of this damage.[20]

The State Department immediately released the German statement to the press, and in the midst of the heated controversy surrounding the *Lusitania*,

Figure 5. *Gulflight* under repair. The accidental damage to *Gulflight* was extensive. The three fatalities from this episode were the only ones incurred on an American-flagged ship by German action in the period of U.S. neutrality. (Reprinted with permission from Mariners' Museum, Newport News, Va.)

von Jagow's note regarding the *Gulflight* led some commentators to take a more restrained line. In any case, the dramatic loss of more than one hundred American passengers aboard *Lusitania* seemed far more significant than the mistaken assault on American sovereignty in the form of the damage to *Gulflight* and the loss of three merchant seamen.[21]

Nebraskan

The steamer *Nebraskan* was built in Camden, New Jersey, in 1902 for the American-Hawaiian Line to carry sugar. The ship was commanded by Captain J. S. Greene of San Francisco. In the early evening of May 26, 1916, about forty-eight miles west of Fastnet off the south coast of Ireland, headed from Liverpool, the ship suffered an explosion. Greene was unsure whether he had struck a mine or had been torpedoed.[22]

Figure 6. *Nebraskan*. Commander Claus Hansen of *U-41* said he did not see any neutral markings on this ship and fired one torpedo at it on May 26, 1915. As in the case of *Gulflight*, Germany offered compensation for the damage. (Reprinted with permission from Mariners' Museum, Newport News, Va.)

The crew immediately took to lifeboats, but when the ship did not appear to be sinking, and no further detonations took place, the crew returned to the ship in the calm seas. The ship had suffered no serious damage, but the foreholds were full of water. Greene headed the ship at about 8 knots back for Liverpool, flying signal flags that read, "I am not under control." As *Nebraska* passed the British naval base at Queenstown, an armed trawler came out to accompany the ship. Meanwhile, the British press clamored that the attack was an act of war.[23]

Although some American headlines also hinted at war, cooler heads prevailed. In a small *New York Times* story run over from page 1 to page 2, the Washington correspondent pointed out "government officials today gave no sign of excitement or worry over the affair. The general disposition in Government circles is to suspend judgment until all the facts connected with the incident have been ascertained." Even so, the location of the incident, remote from any known minefields, suggested that the explosion came from a torpedo, not a mine. Officials speculated that if the ship had been torpedoed, the German government would repudiate the attack, especially since the vessel was in ballast, carrying no cargo, and was headed home, and since it showed no hostile behavior. The German government had only recently notified the United States that it had instructed its submarine commanders not to attack any neutral ships.[24]

A *New York Times* editorial commented that if it should turn out that the ship had been intentionally attacked by a submarine without warning, "It would amount to an act of war, either to be so regarded or to be repudiated by Germany immediately." The State Department lined up naval technical experts in Britain to examine the ship to see whether a mine or a torpedo had caused the damage.[25]

Within two days, the American consul at Liverpool received detailed reports from Lt. John Towers, U.S. naval attaché at the U.S. embassy, and assistant naval attaché and naval constructor L. B. McBride, who examined the ship, as well as further testimony from Captain Greene and members of the *Nebraskan* crew. The consul forwarded his report to U.S. ambassador Walter Hines Page in London, who sent a summary on to Washington. Secretary of State Bryan immediately released some of Page's memorandum to the press, in which the chief engineer reported that he had seen a white streak in the water perpendicular to the starboard side of the ship immediately before the explosion in hold number one. By May 30, it was certain to officials and to the press that the ship had been torpedoed.[26]

After two weeks and an investigation in Germany, the German government provided Ambassador Gerard in Berlin with another apology and explanation. The report did not identify the sub or its commander, but later disclosed records show it was *U-41* under Claus Hansen.[27] He reported that he had met a steamer bound westward off Fastnet without a flag and no neutral markings on its freeboard. No lights were on to illuminate either a flag or such markings, and in the twilight, the name of the ship could not be made out. The report went on:

> Since the commander of the submarine was obliged to assume from his wide experience in the area of maritime war that only English steamers and no neutral steamers traversed the war area without flag and markings, he attacked the vessel with a torpedo, in the conviction that he had an enemy vessel before him. Some time after the shot the commander saw that the vessel had in the meantime hoisted the American flag. As a consequence, he of course, refrained from any further attack. Since the vessel remained afloat, he had no occasion to concern himself further with the boats which had been launched.[28]

The attack was not meant for the American flag, the apology stated. Although it was "not traceable to any fault on the part of the commander of the German submarine [the attack] is to be considered an unfortunate accident." The German government expressed its regret and offered to make compensation for the damage, continuing with language almost identical to that used in the *Gulflight* admission note. Further, the German note suggested that, as in the case of the *Gulflight*, the amount should be set, or, if there was doubt as to the figures, an expert should be appointed to fix the compensation.[29]

Although the incident blew over, the case of the *Nebraskan* demonstrated a couple of important points. If the attack had been intentional, not only the British press, but some American newspapers were ready and almost eager to declare the action as a clear act of war, which indeed it would have been. However, the attitude of the State Department was that all the facts had to be ascertained before jumping to conclusions. The exchange of notes and published commentary also showed that if American captains wished to announce the neutrality of their ships, they should not only fly the American flag, but should keep it well illuminated at night, and should paint the ship's name and nationality along the side of the ship in the freeboard area between the waterline and the deckline. Those practices did in fact become common over the next months. The *Gulflight* and *Nebraskan* cases, and the very minor damage done to a railing aboard the Standard Oil tanker *Cushing* by a bomb from a German aircraft in the North Sea on April 18, all showed that the German government, after investigating the events, would avoid a crisis in the case of errors of identification by admitting an "unfortunate accident," by assuring the United States that it intended no affront to or attack on the American flag, and by offering to pay for damages.[30]

Pass of Balmaha

Undoubtedly the most dramatic and adventurous of the tales of American ships that encountered German ships or submarines in the two-year neutrality period was that of the *Pass of Balmaha*.[31] Built in 1888 in Glasgow by the firm of Robert Duncan, the steel-hulled sailing bark was given the rather cryptic name of a pass in the hills behind the town of Balmaha on Loch Lomond in Scotland. The region was famous in literature, due to Sir Walter Scott's Arthurian-style epic poem *Lady of the Lake*. The 245-foot-long sailing bark had been registered in Canada through 1914 and was transferred to

U.S. registry early in 1915, and at the time of the incident was owned by the Harriss-Irby-Vose Company of Boston.[32]

On an earlier run to Germany in February 1915, with cotton shipped by the Harriss-Irby-Vose Company, *Pass of Balmaha* had been boarded, held, and released by the British. With the issuance of British Orders in Council establishing the blockade of cotton goods to Germany, the vessel again sailed with a cargo of five thousand bales of cotton that were originally intended for Germany, but changed over to be consigned to Archangel, in Russia. The ship departed New York on June 24, 1915.[33]

North of Scotland, *Pass of Balmaha* was stopped by the British auxiliary cruiser *Victorian* on July 23, 1915, and a small prize crew of one officer and four crew members put aboard to take the ship into the port of Lerwick in the Shetland Islands for examination. However, on July 24 the bark was stopped by the German submarine *U-36*, under the command of Ernst Graeff. Graeff put aboard a petty officer, a coxswain's mate named Lamm. Under the control of Lamm, with the British prize crew locked below, the bark sailed for Cuxhaven, Germany, arriving August 3, 1915.

The first the American press or State Department heard of the capture of the ship was on August 4, 1915. The German press reported that the British prize crew had been "hiding below" rather than "secured below," giving the story a slant that disparaged the courage of the British seamen. The *U-36* went on to encounter the Q-ship *Prince Charles* later on the same day it had captured the *Pass of Balmaha*, July 24, 1915. *Prince Charles* sank the *U-36* with gunfire during the engagement off the small island of Rona to the southwest of the Shetlands, and rescued fourteen of the submarine's crew of thirty-three, in the first of several Q-ship ruses that worked against German U-boats.[34]

After *Pass of Balmaha* arrived in Cuxhaven, the five members of the British prize crew were interned as prisoners of war and the American crew released. The cargo was unloaded and the ship transferred to Hamburg for prize court proceedings. The court eventually awarded Harriss-Irby-Vose $625,000 for the cargo, but retained the ship; Robert M. Harriss, representing the firm, personally appeared in Hamburg to collect the funds. The grounds for the seizure of the ship were that the German government did not regard as legal any transfers of registry from an enemy belligerent to a neutral flag, if the transfer had taken place after the war began. Since the ship had been Canadian through 1914, the rule applied.[35]

Ambassador James W. Gerard protested that the ship had been effectively

American in ownership before transfer and that it was now fully American as owned and registered in the United States. The protest was ineffective, as the German position remained that transfers of registry after the war began, from belligerent to neutral flags would represent a type of evasion, an argument that the United States opposed. The provision regarding transfers of registry from a belligerent to a neutral flag in time of war had been thoroughly covered in the Declaration of London; the United States had taken an exception to that provision, arguing that the burden of proof of the guilt of the transfer should fall on the nation challenging the transfer. However, since Germany, Britain, and France had all ruled that such changes of registry from belligerent to neutral status in search of a safer flag would be disregarded by them, it was a difficult position to sustain, and the U.S. protest seemed rather pro forma in nature.[36]

Count Felix von Luckner, a German officer and commander of the German training sailing ship, had suggested that Germany outfit a sailing vessel as a disguised commerce raider, and the Imperial Navy accepted his proposal. Accordingly, the steel-hulled, four-masted sailing ship *Pass of Balmaha* was converted into the *Seeadler*, armed with ordnance and machine guns, and given an elaborate cover as a Norwegian ship.

Beginning its cruise December 21, 1916, the *Seeadler* with von Luckner as commander sank fifteen Allied ships in its nine-month career. The fact that *Pass of Balmaha* had been converted to *Seeadler* was not known to the Allies until April 1, 1917, when some of the captured seamen from the *Seeadler*'s victims were released. During the cruise of this notorious sea-raider, only one seaman was reputed to die from wounds during an encounter; all the others were treated with courtesy and released unharmed. *Seeadler* was finally wrecked while careened on a remote Pacific island, August 2, 1917, from a wave tossed up by a storm or tsunami.[37]

Although the capture and conversion of the *Pass of Balmaha* was unique among the treatments of U.S. ships by the German navy during the period of U.S. neutrality, the event did reveal certain aspects of German practice regarding shipping that would serve as precedents. Germany demonstrated that it was quite willing to pay for cargo under the 1828 treaty between Prussia and the United States. In this case Germany did so, to the firm of Harriss-Irby-Vose. Secondly, the transfer of registry from an Allied flag to the U.S. flag was no protection. In other words, by shipping aboard a vessel that had transferred from Canada, the company was taking on the same risk, from the German point of view, as they would have if they had shipped the cargo aboard an enemy British or Canadian vessel. A transferred ship would be regarded as still under the original flag, and subject to destruction.[38]

After the capture of *Pass of Balmaha* and its conversion to *Seeadler*, the German command decided that the practice of putting a prize officer from a submarine aboard a captured ship was too risky. Admiral Reinhard Scheer, justifiably proud of coxswain mate Lamm's performance, decided not to risk submarine personnel in such ventures in the future. The *Pass of Balmaha* was apparently the only ship captured at sea by a submarine and brought into a German port under a prize crew.[39]

Harriss-Irby-Vose lost another ship to a German submarine within days of the capture of the *Pass of Balmaha*, also in the waters off Scotland. That event and the remaining major cases of assaults on the American flag at sea during the period of neutrality are recounted in the next chapter.

4

The Flag under Fire

From *Leelanaw* to *Chemung*

Leelanaw

Another of the ships owned by the Harriss-Irby-Voss Company, the oil-burning steamer *Leelanaw*, ran into trouble off the Orkney Islands, north of Scotland, immediately after the capture of the *Pass of Balmaha*. The *Leelanaw*, under the command of Captain Eugene Delk, had left New York on May 17, 1915, carrying a cargo of cotton consigned to Russia via Gothenburg, Sweden. After being detained for four weeks by the British at Kirkwall, the ship was released June 26 to proceed via Sweden to Russia. After delivering the cotton cargo, the steamer left July 8 from Archangel in Russia, bound for Belfast, with a cargo of flax. The submarine accosting *Leelanaw* was *U-41*, the same that had torpedoed but not sunk the *Nebraskan*. *U-41* hailed the *Leelanaw* on July 25, 1915, and on examining the ship's papers, Claus Hansen of *U-41* determined that the flax was contraband. He ordered the steamer crew to take to their boats, bringing their personal belongings with them, and come aboard the submarine. When they were all aboard, the sub fired about five shots from the deck gun, a torpedo, and two more gunshots, finally sinking the steamer.[1]

With the crew of *Leelanaw* on deck of *U-41*, the submarine motored on the surface until in sight of land in the Orkneys. Hansen ordered the crew into their boats, and then towed the boats shoreward. The crew all made it safely to Kirkwall. American consul E. H. Dennison ordered the crew sent on to Dundee, where he was stationed, so that he could obtain further details.[2]

Recognizing the significance of the fact that the crew of the ship was largely made up of Americans, the *New York Times* carried a list of names and hometowns. Even resident aliens in the United States were identified, with hometowns ranging across the United States from Maine through New

Figure 7. *Leelanaw*. This stubby 1,924-ton U.S. flag freighter was sunk by the Germans in 1915. Woodrow Wilson did not treat the episode as a casus belli, because the crew was warned and safely evacuated and because the ship was indeed carrying a contraband cargo. (Reprinted with permission from Mariners' Museum, Newport News, Va.)

York, New Jersey, and Delaware, to Texas and California. With this notice, the *Times* began the practice of identifying crew members by name, town, and later, even by street address. In addition to making identification of survivors easier for friends and relatives, the hometown listing had the effect of stressing the "Americanness" of some of the ships destroyed.[3]

George Hoyer, a representative of the Harriss-Irby-Vose cotton exporting company, pointed out that the sinking differed from the case of the *William P. Frye* in that the cargo of flax belonged to a citizen of a country that was an enemy of Germany. Even though the ship was American, the ship had been chartered to carry flax to Belfast, Ireland. The company had anticipated that the ship would unload in Belfast and refuel with oil for the return trip to the United States. Hoyer explained that on the outward-bound trip from the United States, the ship had been detained in Kirkwall by the British on suspicion that the original cotton cargo was destined for Germany, via Sweden, rather than for Russia. The British had only released *Leelanaw* on condition that the cotton would not be offloaded in Gothenburg, but would be carried all the way to Archangel.[4]

First reactions from the State Department indicated a degree of bristling at the fact that the *Leelanaw* crew had not been given a chance to surrender the cargo to the German submarine, and that they had been forced to take to their lifeboats. The parallels and differences between the *Leelanaw* case and the *Frye* case were explored with the press, and "high officials," probably State Department spokesmen acting on Secretary of State Robert Lansing's authority, "were inclined" to look on the *Leelanaw* incident as a "serious aggravation of the situation." By contrast with the somewhat milder protests over the *Frye* case, the *Leelanaw* episode was seen as exhibiting "contemptuous" disregard for the treaties of 1785, 1799, and 1828 between Prussia and the United States. The *Times* speculated that, depending on the outcome of notes, the destruction of the *Leelanaw* might be regarded as a "serious and important incident, especially if it appears as a deliberate repetition of violation of treaty obligations."[5]

In a lengthy exposition of the international law and treaty issues, the *New York Times* pointed out that the United States took the position in the *Frye* case and would take the position in the *Leelanaw* case, that even if the ship carried contraband, the contraband should have been removed and the ship released if the ship was that of a neutral. Sinking the ship should occur only if it was impossible to take the ship for prize court proceedings.

At this point, the State Department continued to argue that it was quite possible for the German submarines to either remove a cargo and release a ship, or to put aboard a prize crew and take the ship in for adjudication in Germany. Taking a captured steamer back to Germany in the face of British patrols and minefields would be risky, and a contraband cargo could not be dumped at sea with British patrols in the region. Nevertheless, the American position was that the situation was governed by the eighteenth- and nineteenth-century treaties and practices, and if submarines engendered their own special risks, those were Germany's problem, not those of neutrals.[6]

Some of the considerations concerning the submarine's tactics were brought to the public's attention with the report of Captain Delk of the *Leelanaw* and his crew on their arrival in Aberdeen. One member of the crew noted that the German submarine commander commented that they were not in the habit of throwing contraband cargo overboard, and had "no alternative but to sink the ship."[7]

Some press quotations of statements by the crew derived from reports from the consular offices in Dundee and London, and from reports from Ambassador Page, all released immediately to the press. A fuller report from Consul Dennison in Dundee announced that the crew would be sent home on the U.S. liner *St. Paul*. Dennison explained in further detail what had happened on July 25. The *Leelanaw* was about sixty miles northwest of the Orkneys when the submarine was spotted, firing warning shots from a distance of about two miles. After sending the ship's papers, the crew was given "ample time" to leave the ship. Towing the lifeboats, the submarine approached the Orkneys, and after spotting another steamer, the crew was ordered into the boats. Captain Delk refused the submarine commander's demand for the ship's papers, retaining the register, customs manifest, and bills of lading. He had no complaint about the treatment of himself or crew aboard the sub.[8]

After the German investigation of the incident, Gerard in Berlin forwarded the German reply to the State Department's protests and inquiries. In a "Note Verbale," dated October 16, 1915, the German Foreign Office confirmed the details, with a bit more precision as to time and position. After determining the ship's cargo to be flax and therefore contraband, the commander decided to sink the ship. The note explained the problem imposed by the use of a submarine: "Since the German commander was unable to take the steamer into a German port without exposing the submarine to danger or impairing the success of the operations in which it was engaged, he was justified in destroying the vessel." The justification was based on Article 113 of the German Prize Ordinance and Article 49 of the Declaration of London, both of which the United States refused to recognize. Some of the language of the German note was an almost verbatim version of the language used in Article 49 of the Declaration of London. The note further explained that the commander fulfilled his obligation as to the safety of the ship personnel and the ship's papers, as required by Article 116 of the German Prize Ordinance and Article 50 of the Declaration of London. Naval authorities forwarded the report to the Hamburg prize court, and the German government noted that the owners of the ship had already retained an attorney in Hamburg to represent them. The German note also referred to the *Frye* precedent and pointed out that under the Prussian treaties, Germany would have the right to confiscate the property of neutral Americans only when it was brought into port.[9]

Lansing replied to Gerard several weeks later. Lansing told Gerard to inform the German government that there would be no representation for either the *Frye* or the *Leelanaw* at the prize court in Hamburg, and that the United States desired that the amount of compensation "be adjusted by diplomatic negotiations."[10]

Despite the first angry reactions, after several months, the *Leelanaw* case came down, as had the *Frye* case, to whether the compensation for damages would be adjusted by the prize court in Hamburg, as the Germans preferred, or by diplomatic negotiations, as the United States preferred. *Leelanaw*, even more than *Frye*, receded from the public eye. But the pattern had been set, with German recognition, under the Prussian treaties, that it should compensate American neutrals for ship or cargo under certain conditions.

As made clear in the *Pass of Balmaha* case, the compensation for the ship would only be if the ship was clearly of U.S. registry and had not been transferred to the United States from a belligerent after the beginning of the war, and if it was owned by Americans. The cargo would only be compensated if it was owned by American citizens. Furthermore, if an American ship were discovered on the high seas with a contraband cargo destined for an enemy of Germany, the ship would have to be sunk, as long as the crew and its papers could be secured. Whether or not the United States approved of the Declaration of London or the German Prize Ordinances, the German Foreign Office was going to cite those provisions and offer compensation based on the principles spelled out in them when they superseded the Prussian treaties. While the U.S. State Department would continue to contest the details, it seemed the United States was willing to treat incidents conducted by these principles as unfortunate, but well short of acts of war.

Lanao

The *Lanao* was built in Bowling, Scotland, in 1912 and, at 692 tons, was a very small steamship even by the standards of the era. Early in 1916, this vessel had been owned by an American company based in Manila, in the Philippines, but had been sold before leaving to a Norwegian firm, to bring rice from French Indo-China to France. *Lanao* sailed from Saigon, and passed through the Suez Canal on August 30, 1916, with a cargo of rice, bound for Havre. The *Lanao* was sunk off Portugal on October 28, 1916, with no casualties. The loss of this ship was sometimes included in later published lists of U.S. ship losses since the Philippines were a U.S. territory, and since the American captain of the ship, Henry Mainland, was flying the American flag at the time of the capture and sinking.

Even so, as the news broke in the United States on November 7, 1916, the State Department noted a complication. On July 26, the American consul in London had reported that negotiations were under way by the owners, Findlay, Miller & Company, in Manila to sell the ship to Hans Hannevig of

Christiana and to transfer the ship to the Norwegian flag. Awaiting information about the registry of the ship and details of the sinking, the State Department deferred comment until more detailed reports came in.[11]

Delay in the news was partly due to the fact that, after the *Lanao* was sunk, the crew transferred to a Norwegian ship, the *Tromp*, which carried the survivors to the port of Barry in Wales. There, Captain Henry Mainland gave his story to the *London Daily Chronicle*. He explained that the *Lanao* had been passing St. Vincent, on the coast of Portugal, when the ship encountered a submarine that was in the process of sinking a Norwegian ship and attempting to sink a British ship. Mainland slowed to see if he could pick up survivors from the Norwegian ship. The submarine, which German records show to have been the *U-63*, under the command of Otto Schultze, fired three warning shots.[12]

Chief Officer Godinez from the *Lanao* rowed over to the submarine in one of the lifeboats, and there he was greeted by Schultze, who spoke excellent English. Schultze ordered the *Lanao*'s crew to all gather on the submarine, removed navigation instruments, and then had an explosive planted on *Lanao*, sinking the small steamer. After cruising on the surface, the submarine placed the *Lanao*'s crew aboard the *Tromp* and vanished from the scene.[13] The chief engineer confirmed the particulars of the captain's account, adding that the submarine also sank an Italian ship while the *Lanao*'s crew were aboard.[14] The German records show that ship to have been the Italian steamer *Selene*. Captain Mainland claimed that the *Lanao* was under Philippine registry and flying the American flag when destroyed.[15]

The report of U.S. Consul Lorin A. Lathrop, from Cardiff, Wales, backed up the report that the ship was flying the American flag. In discussing precedents and the law surrounding the case, the *New York Times* and the State Department again referred to the *Frye* case. There was "no disposition to raise the question" of the right of Germany to destroy the cargo of rice, since it was contraband destined for France, but the State Department still held that the ship should have been allowed to proceed after removal of the cargo.[16]

After receiving preliminary reports from the U.S. consul in Wales, Secretary of State Lansing asked Joseph Grew, *chargé d'affaires* in Berlin, to make inquiry of the German government regarding the *Lanao*.[17] After receiving the report from Otto Schultze, the commander of *U-63*, the new German foreign minister, Arthur Zimmermann, sent a note to Washington via Grew. He again pointed out that the ship was sunk because to escort it to a port in Germany or to a German-allied port would have exposed the crew to the danger of sinking. Regarding the registry of the ship, Zimmermann pointed out that the ship had been sold by Findlay and Miller to the Hannevig Brothers of London in July, and since then had sailed "under the English flag." The Hannevig firm was owned by Norwegian subjects, the sons of Christian Hannevig of Borre, Norway.[18]

Captain Mainland apparently knew of the sale and may have flown the American flag in the hope that he and the crew would receive better treatment than if they flew the British flag, which certainly would be true. On the other hand, it was a remote possibility that he was unsure if the change of registry had been completed, although that seems unlikely as he had sailed from Saigon at about the time of the sale of the ship and the whole operation of the rice trade from Saigon to Havre had been under the new ownership. He certainly had the opportunity to learn of the July transfer when he passed through the Suez Canal at the end of August.

Since all the crew, including the Americans aboard, had been safely provided for, and since the ship was Norwegian-owned and British-registered, it was clear the United States could not protest the action further, and the matter was dropped. As in other cases, the *Frye* precedent had been repeatedly cited by the press, but the registry matter closed the incident.

Columbian

The 8,579-gross-ton *Columbian*, built in San Francisco in 1907 and owned by the American-Hawaiian Steamship Company, had sailed from New York City on October 18, 1916, and from Boston on October 21, bound for Genoa, Italy. Under charter by the France and Canada Steamship Company, based in New York, the *Columbian* touched at St. Nazaire, France, on November 2, and departed the next day for Italy. On November 8, off the northwest coast of Spain in the Atlantic, the radio operator aboard sent a wireless report that *Columbian* was being shelled by a submarine. Officials speculated whether that meant that the ship was attempting to run away from the submarine, "thereby sacrificing her immunity from attack."[19]

By this time, the press was well aware that by Declaration of London rules and generally accepted practice, if a merchant ship did not heed warning shots and attempted to escape, German submariners might sink the ship without first evacuating the crew. Reports were slow in reaching the State Department, but the American consul in Bilbao on the north coast of Spain wired a report that the ship had been sunk thirty miles off Cape Ortega and the crew all saved.[20]

The crew arrived at La Coruña, Spain, on November 11.[21] Further reports came in, indicating that the German submarine commander had stood by the *Columbian*, waiting for the seas to calm from November 6 to November 8. Only then did the submarine order the crew to abandon ship, and then sink it. Captain Frederick Curtis of the *Columbian* was taken on board the submarine and held with others in a small cabin. He was aboard the sub when it fired two torpedoes to sink the *Columbian*, and then was taken below. He found his confinement in the small quartermaster's cabin with three other merchant ship captains "disagreeable," as the room was kept dark, and had only three bunks for the four men. The ship smelled of "benzene," and the food provided was meager, although it seemed likely that it was exactly what the submarine crew had to eat.[22]

The submarine stopped and signaled a Swedish steamer, the *Varing*, off the Spanish port of Camarinas on November 9, and the *Varing* picked up the crews from both the *Columbian* and a Norwegian ship, *Balto*, that was also sunk. Although Curtis claimed to have been held aboard for six days, that seemed impossible as his account was filed from shore on November 13; if he was taken aboard *Varing* on November 9 or 10, he was probably transferred to that ship less than three days after the reported sinking.[23]

The facts in the case were clarified by details brought out in a later report by Richard Hartman, the commander of *U-49*. The U.S. chargé d'affaires in Berlin, Joseph Grew, relayed an account of the incident from Hartman's viewpoint to the State Department on December 17, 1916. Hartman reported that he had at first stopped the *Columbian* at 1430 on November 7, in clear weather, but heavy seas. After firing a warning shot, the steamer stopped. When the submarine approached at periscope depth, Hartman discovered that the steamer flew the U.S. flag and was the *Columbian* from New York. Judging from the wooden structures on deck, Hartman assumed the ship had carried horses to England or France, and was on a return journey. He signaled, "you are released," and both the sub and the steamer proceeded on course.

However, soon afterward, Hartman's radioman reported that he had picked up the wireless broadcast from the *Columbian*, in plain English, giving the ship's location and stating that he had spotted a German submarine. Hartman regarded this reporting of his whereabouts as constituting collaboration with the enemy, and under the rules of war, he would be justified in regarding the *Columbian* as having taken on the nature of an enemy combatant ship. He altered course and warned the *Columbian* to reduce wireless range, then ordered the ship to accompany him, along with the Norwegian ship *Balto*, on which Hartman had placed a prize crew. The next morning, when the weather cleared, he examined the papers of *Columbian*, and then decided to sink the steamer "for un-neutral service."[24]

The Declaration of London had made it clear that a merchant ship in communication with warships had taken on an un-neutral character. After the seas had calmed sufficiently to allow the lifeboats to be launched, Hartman transferred the crew of *Columbian* to the *Balto*; later all the crews were put aboard the Swedish ship *Varing*, and both the *Balto* and the *Columbian* were sunk. According to Hartman's report, he kept Curtis aboard until November 10 (two days, not six), and sent him ashore at Camarinas.[25]

Although the U.S. State Department had received a report that the *Columbian* was empty and in ballast when sunk, the ship's documents and testimony by Curtis revealed that there was a mixed cargo of steel, copper, motorcycle parts, and other conditional contraband aboard, all of which would have justified the sinking of the ship by German rules. The freighter had been bound for Genoa, "well known to be an Italian naval and military fortress and a base of operations and supplies for the Italian land and naval forces." German foreign minister Zimmermann suggested that the State Department inform the "American parties interested in the ship and cargo" to advance the rights to which they laid claim before the German prize court. There is no published record that the U.S. State Department pursued further protests over the *Columbian* after receiving this report. Newspaper reports had already mentioned the wireless remarks regarding a submarine, and since U-boat commander Hartman's report explained the inconsistencies in the published accounts, there was no reason to doubt that he had given a quite accurate account of the event.[26]

The behavior of Curtis reflected the fact that American merchant officers seemed unaware of the protocols that the Germans expected. Several other cases showed the same pattern. In at least one minor incident, that of the *Owego*, in August 1916, the captain of an American merchant ship had simply ignored the German submarine commander's signals, running the risk, as the German Foreign Office pointed out, of more tragic consequences.[27] Alfred Gunter, the experienced tanker captain of the *Gulflight*, may not have been aware that steaming in apparent convoy with two armed British ships made his ship a more suspicious target than proceeding on course separately. In the case of the *Nebraskan*, Captain Greene apparently was unaware that taking down his flag at twilight in an announced war zone was a risky procedure. When Captain Mainland flew the American flag despite the fact that *Lanao* was transferred to British registry, he was either ignorant of the consequences or attempting his own personal *ruse de guerre*, at some risk to his ship and his men.

In light of these considerations, it is quite possible that Curtis, aboard the *Columbian*, had no idea that reporting the location of a submarine by wireless constituted "un-neutral service." He may not even have been aware that his cargo of steel, copper, and motorcycle parts destined for one of the Allies would justify the sinking of his ship from the German point of view. From reports in the press, he certainly seemed peevish about his brief incarceration aboard the U-boat, even though from the German perspective, he had committed the serious criminal offense of a civilian supporting a military action. More than once, Germany had executed civilians for such behavior.

Chemung

The *Chemung* was the fifth American ship lost during the neutrality period owned by the same firm, Harriss-Irby-Vose Company. The company was a cotton brokerage and exporting firm with connections in Oklahoma, Texas, and New York. Early in the war, Harriss-Irby-Vose was urged by the Foreign Trade Office of the State Department to undertake the export of cotton to Germany. As noted, until February 1915, the British permitted this trade, and consequently, the price of cotton in the United States, which had collapsed, began to rise. Harriss-Irby-Vose or its ship-operating firm, Harby Company, made several successful runs to Germany in the period before February 1915, although ships carrying the cargoes, including the *Evelyn* and the *El Monte*, encountered mines and had other harrowing experiences.[28]

Britain imposed a partial blockade on Germany in February 1915 through Orders in Council, extended a year later to formally include food and other products. Harriss-Irby-Vose was quite active in the trade to Germany early in the war. But to conduct the export business to Germany, the firm ran into trouble, with their ships quarantined and examined by the British, with the ships exposed to minefields and to boarding by both British and German naval forces. Later, the company and its related firms were blacklisted by the British for trading with Germany. Before the United States entered the war, the company lost five ships.

The firm was persistent in attempting to run the British blockade to trade with Germany, and later, in attempting to carry cotton and other goods to the British allies, the Italians. The fact that three of the four genuinely American flagships intentionally seized or sunk by the German naval forces

Table 4.1. Harriss-Irby-Voss ships lost, 1915–1916

Ship	Circumstance	Date
Evelyn	Sunk by either a British or German mine	Feb. 19, 1915
Vincent	Sunk by a mine thought to be Russian	Sept. 30, 1915
Pass of Balmaha	Boarded by *Victorian*, confiscated by *U-36*	July 24, 1916
Leelanaw	Sunk by *U-49*	July 25, 1916
Chemung	Sunk by *U-38*	Nov. 26, 1916

in the period 1915–16 belonged to this one firm is probably due to the fact that the company aggressively sought to export cotton and other goods to Europe during the conflict. William Harriss, the president of the firm, made his aggressive trading practices perfectly clear when he protested the British listing his company among twenty-two other American firms blacklisted from doing business with Britain.[29]

In a rare public statement, Harriss complained that his company had gone into the cotton exporting business at the behest of Robert F. Rose, the foreign trade advisor to the State Department under Secretary Bryan. Perhaps with some justification, Harriss took credit for the rise of the price of cotton from the "disastrous price" of six cents a pound to twelve cents a pound, once his company undertook the exporting plan. Even before the United States would offer war risk insurance, and with no access to bank financing, the company had successfully taken a few cargoes of cotton into Germany. "By so doing we opened a large market for the great product of the South and blazed the way for other American exporters," Harriss claimed. However, after following the urging of the State Department, he found his company placed on the British blacklist for doing business with Germany. When his complaints to Washington went unheeded, Harriss felt the State Department had abandoned him. No doubt the administration's change from the extremely neutralist Secretary Bryan to the more anti-German Lansing lay behind Harriss's frustration and the resignation of Robert Rose from government service.[30]

Although blacklisted from Britain and finding the routes into Germany effectively blocked by minefields, Harriss formed two other companies—Harriss, Magill & Company, and the Harby Steamship Company—that attempted to carry some cargoes to Italy.[31] *Chemung* was owned by Harby Steamship Company and operated by Harriss, Magill & Company, both located at the same address in downtown New York City as Harriss-Irby-Vose.[32]

By the end of November 1916, when *Chemung* was sunk in the Mediterranean, off the coast of Spain, the reaction of the United States to such events had been well established under the precedents. Quoting the released notes over the *Frye* incident, the *New York Times* expected that, since no one on the crew had lost their lives, and since the ship carried contraband destined for an Allied port, there would be no major protest from the State Department.[33] However, the State Department did file a formal protest in Vienna with the Austro-Hungarian government.[34]

Max Valentiner, the German commander of the *U-38*, was flying an Austrian flag, rather than a German flag. The ruse had been adopted by the German submarines operating out of bases in the Adriatic, because until August 27, 1916, Germany was not formally at war with Italy, although Austria was. Seeking to interdict cargoes bound for Italy as well as France in the Mediterranean, German submarines operating in the Mediterranean had adopted the false flag practice. This fact led to press reports that the submarine was Austrian, although a report cabled from Paris correctly identified the submarine as German.[35]

John L. Duffy, a "stocky, square-jawed, weather-tanned" mariner, captain of the *Chemung*, refused to lower the U.S. flag from the mainmast of his ship when he was signaled to do so, and was later quite proud that it went down with the ship. The crew of thirty-four safely evacuated into two lifeboats, and watched as the submarine shelled the *Chemung*. One shell hit a cargo of blasting caps that detonated, flinging debris a thousand feet in the air and all around the lifeboats and the nearby U-boat.[36] Then the submarine circled around, passed lines to the lifeboats, and towed them for two hours until spotting the Spanish steam-powered fishing vessel *Salvatore Giner*. The Spanish fishing boat took the crew aboard, and towed the lifeboats to Valencia, where the crew boarded the liner *Alicante* on November 28. The *Alicante* sailed for New York by way of Cadiz, on December 11. At Cadiz they were joined by the crew of the *Columbian*, and the *Alicante* brought both groups of survivors to the United States, arriving in New York January 1, 1917.[37]

In reporting the *Chemung* incident in response to the American diplomatic protest, the Austrian foreign ministry relayed information from Valentiner. He noted that Jacobsen, first officer of the *Chemung*, when he finally came aboard the submarine with the ship's papers, had mentioned that the cargo contained blasting caps. Not recognizing the term, Valentiner was unaware that the ship carried explosives, and hence was surprised at the major detonation when one of his shells detonated the cargo. Although only

100 meters away, the submarine was not damaged by flying debris, and the crew in the lifeboats were safe.

Valentiner suspected that Jacobson intentionally deceived him in hopes that the explosion would damage the sub, but Jacobsen explained that he had explicitly mentioned "blasting caps" and assumed the term was understood, and Valentiner let the matter drop. The naval section of the Austro-Hungarian foreign ministry, however, continued to argue that the *Chemung*'s crew had intended to damage the submarine.[38] The Austrian report came through in late January 1917. Further pursuit of the matter became impossible, as the *Chemung* incident was overtaken by events.

Sovereignty Assailed But Peace Preserved

Up through the end of January 1917, no American ship had been intentionally sunk by a submarine without warning and evacuation of the crew, and the three accidental deaths from the *Gulflight* remained the only American fatalities that could be attributed to U-boat action in all of the events. The various cases of German attacks on, or encounters with, U.S. ships in the two-year period of 1915 and 1916, did in fact show that the German government and the German naval officers made a fairly serious effort to avoid potential clashes with the United States. The loss of four American ships carrying goods declared contraband, with no casualties whatsoever, demonstrated that the German submarine commanders exercised considerable restraint. The few American merchant ships lost to mines in the period could not be attributed to willful acts by Germany, Britain, or Russia. The other, very minor incidents of encounters with German submarines, during which the submarine did not attempt destruction, also showed restraint by Germany toward American shipping and a respect for American neutrality through January 1917.

American reactions to the events had been mixed. Responsible voices in government and the press constantly referred to the *Frye* precedent, showing that American neutrality could be preserved, albeit somewhat awkwardly in the face of the German submarine blockade of Britain and France, and the "Austrian" blockade of Italy. American merchant captains and other merchant marine officers seemed to be very ill-informed about German practices, and the tone of German (and Austrian) notes regarding the various incidents tended to come across as somewhat arrogant. Several of the German notes placed the blame for the risks run by Americans on the ignorance or technical misbehavior of the American merchant mariners themselves. The same attitude—that the errors lay with the victims—had characterized the German position regarding passengers aboard ships like *Lusitania*. While such a position infuriated many in the United States, it was difficult to argue against such claims in the merchant ship cases.

In notes to the United States, an even more critical tone was taken by the German Foreign Office regarding the evasive maneuvers, weaponry, and actual attacks on submarines by British merchant ships. The United States refused to recognize procedures the Germans insisted were the binding legal framework, including the unratified Declaration of London and the German Prize Ordinance, insisting instead that diplomacy and treaties were the operative legal structure for adjudicating differences.

Other disagreements between the United States and Germany over submarines having to do with whether or not Americans traveling aboard armed belligerent passenger liners should be immune from attack continued to simmer. Those issues picked up with the loss of several smaller armed Allied ships in the last months of 1916. Six Americans had died when the British ship *Marina* was sunk October 16, 1916, and, as in the earlier incidents involving Americans aboard British ships, the loss of the *Marina* warranted a State Department inquiry. The *Marina* had mounted a 4.75-inch gun on its stern, and the American position remained that defensive armament was no reason for a submarine not to issue a proper warning before sinking such a ship.[39]

Out of the total eighteen major and minor encounters between U.S. flagships and German or Austrian ships or submarines between January 1, 1915, and January 31, 1917, there had been only three fatalities, all aboard the accidentally damaged *Gulflight*. In all of the incidents, including the sinking or seizure of ships, or cases of very minor damage, confiscation of supplies, or warning shots only, the level of diplomatic exchanges and notes had been far less heated than the exchanges over the British *Falaba*, *Lusitania*, and *Arabic*, and the French *Sussex*.

Although the exchanges over the Allied passenger ships were heated, the United States had not come close to going to war over those episodes. Furthermore, America and the Central powers would certainly not have gone to war over the eighteen events involving U.S. merchant ships in the period up through January 1917. War would not have come because of differences of legal interpretation, disagreements over the venue for compensation awards, understanding of protocols and procedures between submarines and neutral ships, or an arrogant tone of diplomatic exchanges. And war did not come to the United States even after German rulers openly announced a new phase of unrestricted submarine warfare that would target ships flying the American flag, in ways that violated the established conventions and rules of war at sea. It would only come after that new policy was implemented.

5

Meetings at Pless Castle and on Pennsylvania Avenue

On January 31, 1917, the German government delivered a note to the United States stating that the next day, February 1, German submarines would sink ships of all nations, without warning, within a designated war zone around Britain and France in the Atlantic and around France and Italy in the Mediterranean. The note detailed other arrangements, such as a safety lane to the Netherlands and another to Greece, and provisions for one clearly marked U.S. passenger ship per week to make the crossing. According to Wilson's private secretary, Joseph Tumulty, when the president received the note, his face turned ashen, and in shock, he said, "The break that we have tried so hard to prevent now seems inevitable."[1]

When Wilson met the next day with Colonel House, his personal advisor, he was "sad and depressed." House noted that Wilson said he "felt as if the world had suddenly reversed itself; that after going from east to west, it had begun to go from west to east." House, Wilson, and Lansing discussed how to react.[2]

The announcement of unrestricted submarine warfare that would now include attacks without warning on neutral ships represented a complete break with the prior German practices, and indicated that the carefully structured justifications for sinking neutral ships under the Declaration of London would not even be offered. Suddenly, every American ship, from liners, through freighters, tankers, and sailing schooners, was to be targeted if found in the war zones, and sunk without any warning. The new method was to be "ruthless," and was so regarded in Germany, Britain, and the United States. The German word for "ruthless"—*rücksichtslos*—was regularly employed in the German press to describe the new policy. In the original German, the term seemed to imply "without regard for consequences," without quite the overtone of unfeeling cruelty suggested by the English translation as "ruthless."[3]

Figure 8. "Ruthless warfare." Americans and the British translated the German word for "unrestricted" as "ruthless." The German announcement that all ships would be sunk in the war zone without being individually warned brought the United States closer to war. (Wilson Presidential Library, Staunton, Va.)

Although Wilson, his cabinet, and the American press reacted to the announcement with stunned surprise, there had been many indications that Germany was about to change its policy. James Gerard, U.S. ambassador in Berlin, and Joseph Grew, *chargé d'affaires* at the U.S. embassy in Berlin in Gerard's absence, had reported open discussion in the German press of proposals to renew unrestricted submarine warfare. In conversations with other diplomats, Grew had gone over the developments of internal politics in Germany, as conservatives pressured the chancellor to agree to the policy, long advocated by von Tirpitz and advanced by his followers even after he left office. Elements of the German press and political establishment urged the Kaiser to unleash submarine warfare in retaliation for the British blockade that was bringing food shortages to Germany. It seemed that parts of Holtzendorff's calculations about the shortages that could be brought to Britain through unrestricted submarine warfare had been leaked to the press and to supporters of the concept.[4]

David Houston, Wilson's secretary of agriculture and one of the most pronounced advocates of war in the cabinet, remarked when he learned of the announcement, "there had been rumors for some time that [Germany] might pursue this course, but I could not believe that she would be so stupid."[5] The decision seemed "stupid" to Houston because he thought it very probable that such an action would move the United States from its confirmed neutrality to war.

That neutrality was not simply a position held by Wilson, but it was one that had been endorsed, albeit narrowly, in the American presidential election of 1916. In November 1916, Wilson had won a second term over Republican candidate Charles Evan Hughes in one of the closest elections in American history. Wilson supporters had developed the slogan, "He kept us out of war," and that position and sentiment was widely and probably correctly assumed to have accounted for his narrow victory in states in the American West. Wilson's son-in-law, William Gibbs McAdoo, was quite convinced that women, voting in several states, such as Illinois, would swing the vote in Wilson's favor because they tended to come out to vote because of the peace issue.[6] In California, the vote was only a few thousand apart, and the crucial determination of that state's electoral votes was not known for several days after the election. Even so, with the vote, the American electorate had endorsed Wilson's diplomatic strategies that had steered a somewhat neutral course between the European belligerents, and the fact that, after all, Wilson *had indeed* kept the United States out of the war.

Through December 1916 and January 1917, Wilson put out peace feelers, attempting to get both the Central powers and the Allies to announce their war goals in preparation for a meeting to discuss a negotiated peace. On January 22, he had delivered a speech including the memorable phrase, "peace without victory." Although the phrase and the speech irritated pro-Ally advisors like U.S. ambassador Walter Hines Page in Britain, who urged Wilson to delete the phrase when he saw a draft of the speech, the effort was widely seen as another Wilsonian gesture of conciliation toward Germany. British indignation erupted at Wilson having regarded Britain and Germany as on the same moral plane in that speech. The German announcement of unrestricted submarine warfare clearly had been in preparation while Wilson still tried to open peaceful negotiations, and the timing of the announcement certainly seemed to many editorialists to represent another example of German perfidy. Not only did the announcement represent a complete reversal of the *Sussex* Pledge made in March 1916, it demonstrated that during the period of the pledge, through the remainder of 1916 and January 1917, while Wilson had tried his best to bring about a peace that Germany could accept, the German navy had been building a massive submarine fleet and preparing the new phase of the war.[7]

Ambassador Gerard was appalled that the plans had been in preparation while the Germans discussed the American peace proposals. In the United States, the press speculated about the months of work that must have gone into building up the submarine fleet, and the fact that the decision must have been reached well before it was announced.[8]

Pless Castle, Silesia

Gerard's speculation and that of the press about preparation were correct. The final German decision had been taken on January 9, 1917, at a closed meeting at Pless Castle in Silesia (Germany's wartime capital in this period), well before Wilson's "peace without victory" speech. The chancellor, Bethmann-Hollweg, who had opposed the resumption of submarine warfare against unarmed liners and merchant ships, was somewhat set up at the meeting, when he was confronted by Chief of the General Staff von Hindenberg and First Quartermaster General Ludendorff and the careful calculations of Admiral Henning von Holtzendorff. The military officers had met earlier and reluctantly agreed to get Bethmann-Hollweg aboard their decision, rather than have him resign and give a public appearance of disunity. At the meeting, Bethmann-Hollweg noted that he had heard and understood the memorandum by Holtzendorff indicating that Britain would collapse before "the next harvest" if the submarines were allowed to sink all shipping bound for Britain, including both Allied and neutral ships.[9]

The German decision went further toward the *"rücksichtslos"* policy than many German advocates of unrestricted submarine warfare anticipated, but did reflect Holtzendorff's concept that *all* shipping, belligerent and neutral, had to be interdicted. Instead of simply unleashing the submarines to attack without warning all British ships, the submarines would be instructed to attack without warning *all neutral* ships as well. This would entail acts of war against Norway, the Netherlands, Spain, Brazil, Argentina, and the United States, as well as other countries. Unleashing the submarines against British liners would violate the *Sussex* Pledge and in itself would probably mean that the United States would make good its threat to break diplomatic relations. But to sink unarmed merchant vessels of all the neutrals could vastly widen the war by bringing some of them in on the side of the Allies. On the surface, it seemed a reckless, as well as ruthless, concept.

The generals assured the chancellor that the European neutrals—the Netherlands, Switzerland and Denmark—could be handled, even if they went to war over the issue. As for the United States, all agreed that Britain's collapse would come about long before American participation in the war could be effective. Bethmann-Hollweg's reluctance to adopt the ruthless policy was reflected in the official transcript of the meeting, when he hinted correctly that if he continued to refuse the policy, he could be dismissed by the Kaiser. "If the military authorities consider the U-boat war essential, I am not in a position to contradict them," he said for the record, carefully noted by his secretary. Georg von Muller, chief of the naval cabinet, who had come around to the idea of unrestricted submarine warfare with not much enthusiasm himself, noted that the chancellor said that "he could not oppose" the policy. "It was not so much approval," he remembered, "as acceptance of the facts." The chancellor agreed to initiate the policy at the end of the month, giving the German navy time to issue the secret orders and prepare the submarines.[10]

At the White House

Wilson received the German announcement on January 31, 1917, and for several days, he hesitated to react officially. On January 31, after meeting with Wilson, Lansing came away shocked and nervous, fearful that the president would fall back on delivering another note. Wilson's "tone of indecision," noted Lansing, "had depressed me." The next day, after meeting again with Wilson, this time with Colonel House in attendance, he felt convinced "that the President had almost reached a decision to send Bernstorff home." Lansing, although familiar with Wilson's very deliberate thought process, was clearly frustrated.[11] In Britain, U.S. ambassador Walter Hines Page fumed at the presidential inaction, while in Berlin, Ambassador Gerard scanned the newspapers as well as his incoming cables for some indication of how Wilson would react.[12]

Wilson convened the cabinet on February 2, and opened the meeting with a question: "Shall I break off diplomatic relations with Germany?" he asked. In the hubbub of responses, several, including William Gibbs McAdoo, were for "prompt action," implying war.[13] The discussion went on for two hours, but Wilson would not reveal his plans. He "appeared to be resisting the idea of a break with Germany," Lansing noted. Although he considered this resistance one of Wilson's methods of drawing out opinion on both sides, Lansing was "morally certain" Wilson had his mind made up when he came to the meeting.[14] When the press questioned Tumulty and Lansing, both appeared "strangely reticent" to discuss Wilson's position. Later that day, Wilson informally visited the Capitol Building, and, in a hastily convened impromptu meeting that lasted over an hour and a half with fifteen or sixteen Democratic senators who remained in the building, he sought their opinions. Although the meeting was private, the senators later told the press that most had advocated breaking relations with Germany, and all had pledged to support Wilson in whatever he decided to do.[15]

Even though the cabinet and the group of senators all urged severance of relations with Germany, as Wilson had indicated he would do in the American ultimatum delivered after the *Sussex* incident, it was still unclear exactly *how* that would be done. On Thursday and Friday, February 1 and 2, there appeared to be three possible courses of action, discussed in news stories coming out of Washington. One choice was an immediate break of relations. A second choice was not to respond at all but to await some overt act on Germany's part and only *then* break relations. The third alternative was to send a note reiterating the declarations of the *Sussex* ultimatum and give a final warning that if the German intention was put into effect, then diplomatic relations would cease.[16] Wilson refused to discuss which alternative he would take, and on Friday after his meeting with the senators, he told newsmen he would reflect on the question overnight.

At the Capitol

The next morning, Saturday, February 3, Wilson made arrangements to appear before a joint session of Congress at the other end of Pennsylvania Avenue from the White House. He appeared precisely at 2:00 p.m. that afternoon, and he had Lansing prepare a document to be delivered at the same moment to German ambassador Bernstorff. As he began his address to Congress, Lester Woolsey, one of Lansing's close legal staff, delivered a paraphrase of Wilson's planned speech to Bernstorff, explaining that U.S. ambassador James Gerard would be recalled from Berlin, and that Bernstorff and his delegation were no longer welcome. In the phrase adopted at the time, Bernstorff was "handed his passports."[17] By beginning the speech at the same time as the notification to the ambassador, Wilson made sure

Figure 9. Bernstorff as persona non grata. After receiving the notice of unrestricted submarine warfare, Wilson told a joint session of Congress that he was breaking relations with Germany, and he had a State Department official "hand his passports" to German ambassador Johann von Bernstorff. (Wilson Presidential Library, Staunton, Va.)

that neither Congress nor the ambassador heard of the decision through the press, but rather, directly through official channels. It was characteristic of Wilson that he kept such crucial decisions to himself and that he preferred to release them through proper channels, not through press leaks.

Members of Congress, like the press and the public, were not sure in advance of the speech exactly which alternative Wilson had chosen, and the assembled crowd hung nervously on his every word. It was clear that the German announcement represented a complete abandonment of the *Sussex* Pledge. To the more pro-Ally members of Congress, the German announcement seemed a direct slap in the face, demanding stern action, while others, like Missouri senator William J. Stone, head of the Senate Foreign Relations Committee, favored a wait-and-see attitude. Perhaps the variety of opinions accounted for Wilson's curious language that was at once stern and pacific.

The precise words he chose would become crucial over the next weeks, and those words help account for the strange way in which the sinking of some ships did not lead to war, but the sinking of others did.

Wilson explained the German note received on Wednesday and how he had "no alternative consistent with the dignity and honor of the United States" but to break diplomatic relations. Therefore he directed the secretary of state to notify Bernstorff and "to hand to his Excellency his passports." This element of the speech got a furious round of applause. The members of Congress fell silent again as they listened carefully to Wilson's key predictions of what might happen next.

Wilson characterized the German decision as a "sudden and deplorable renunciation of its assurances" that had come in response to the *Sussex* crisis. But even in the face of this "unexpected action," he said, "I refuse to believe that it is the intention of the German authorities to do in fact" what they had warned. Wilson said he could not bring himself to believe that they would "destroy American ships and take the lives of American citizens in the willful prosecution of the ruthless naval program they have announced their intention to adopt." In a key phrase, he added, "Only factual overt acts on their part can make me believe it even now." However, he went on, if his "inveterate confidence" should "prove unfounded, if American ships and American lives should in fact be sacrificed," he said he would come again before Congress to ask for authority to use "any means necessary" for protection of "our seamen and our people."[18]

The more prowar members of Congress again leapt to their feet in applause, taking these phrases to mean that "any means necessary" would constitute a request for a declaration of war. However, the key paragraphs of his address contained several essential elements revealing his continued search for peace:

1. Wilson twice stated that destruction of American ships and the lives of American citizens would have to occur before he made a more serious move. There was no mention of the possible loss of American lives aboard the ships of belligerents such as Britain or France.
2. Only "factual overt acts" would convince him that Germany had adopted a new policy. In other words, the German *threat* to take action was not itself the action that would require another American step, but only the actual sinking of American ships would constitute the overt acts. Read closely, it was also notable that Wilson

did not say that a single "overt act" would convince him that other steps were needed, but only *plural* "overt acts."
3. Wilson did not actually threaten to ask for a declaration of war in the event of overt acts, but only to ask for authority to use any means necessary. Conceivably such an action could be armed neutrality, convoying of American ships, or other measures short of war.

Even though couched in a conciliatory tone in that he asserted that he refused to believe that Germany would do what they said they would do, the statement came much closer to a threat to go to war than any public statement Wilson had made up to that date. Although Wilson had sternly admonished the Germans that they would be held "strictly accountable" for loss of American lives aboard belligerent ships after the *Lusitania*, the worst he had previously threatened had been to break relations with Germany, making the threat explicit after *Sussex*. Although still not quite a threat to go to war, after relations had been broken, "any means necessary" certainly sounded bellicose, coming from Wilson.

Across the United States, the press response varied, depending on the leanings of the different editorial positions of the newspapers. Generally speaking, the responses had a tone of "rallying around the flag." However, the more neutralist newspapers praised Wilson for his forbearance and his conciliatory position, while the more hawkish press, including several papers in New York City, suggested that he had already shown more forbearance than he should have, but that at least he had finally acted consistently with American honor and dignity.[19]

Wilson had chosen his words carefully, apparently preparing his speech on his own typewriter in "the still watches of the night," on February 2-3. Wilson had once again been eloquent, and had heightened the drama of the moment by not revealing his intentions ahead of time. And his carefully worded position did not offend the committed neutralists of his own party, while still showing a commitment to stand by his earlier threat to break relations if the *Sussex* Pledge were violated.

Wilson mentioned that his alternatives were constricted in a very explicit fashion when he noted in the February 3 address that there was "no alternative consistent with the honor and dignity of the United States" but to break relations. *There was no alternative because Wilson himself had stated in the Sussex ultimatum a year earlier that if Germany should not renounce unrestricted warfare against liners, the United States would have to break dip-*

lomatic relations. The German announcement of January 31 explicitly stated that *all* ships, belligerent or neutral, would be sunk in the war zone. "All" would include not only tankers, freighters, and schooners, but large and small liners as well. Lansing, the rest of the cabinet, the senators at the February 2 impromptu meeting, and newspaper editorialists all had reminded Wilson that he had made such a threat, reducing his alternatives, *consistent with honor*, to the limited set of choices about exactly how he would break relations. To Lansing, the delay from Wednesday, January 31, until Saturday, February 3, had already stretched beyond the point of honor. There had been press speculation that during this delay, back-channel negotiations had been at work to get the Germans to modify their threats. Indeed, correspondence later released showed such efforts at work by Swiss diplomats and some unauthorized individuals.[20]

Bluster in Berlin and Oyster Bay

In Berlin, Gerard was certain that Wilson had no other choice but to break relations and anxiously awaited word. Foreign Minister Zimmermann told Ambassador Gerard on January 31 of the resumption of unrestricted submarine warfare. On Saturday, February 3, at a social dinner, Zimmerman confidently and somewhat arrogantly chatted with Gerard, telling him: "as you will see, everything will be all right. America will do nothing, for President Wilson is for peace and nothing else. Everything will go on as before." The next day, the news of Wilson's speech and final decision about breaking relations reached Berlin, and on Monday, Gerard went to Zimmermann to demand his passports. Although Zimmermann was composed, Gerard knew that he was surprised at Wilson's decision. "I cannot imagine," Gerard mused, "why intelligent men should think that the United States of America had fallen so low as to bear without murmur this sudden kick in the face."[21]

Wilson's high-minded approach of trusting Germany not to do what it said it would do left Germany an option: it could decide *not* to implement its threats, and could avoid sinking American ships and taking American lives, thus avoiding the "overt acts" that would require Wilson to take some as yet undefined, more drastic steps. His position had the advantage of putting the moral onus on Germany. The strategy, employed not only in this crisis, but in the *Sussex* affair, and more generally through all the inquiries and exchanges of notes, was seen by Wilson's supporters as leaving American hands clean and placing all the fault for any difficulties with Germany.

A drawback of the method was that it left Germany free to decide for war or peace. Wilson had always left the next move in the dangerous game of diplomatic relations with the major belligerents to the other side, and his February 3 speech very explicitly did it again.

To pro-Ally advisors like Lansing, Page in London, and Colonel House, and pro-Ally Republicans like Theodore Roosevelt and Henry Cabot Lodge, it seemed that Wilson, by adopting this approach, had avoided his responsibilities, scolding like a schoolmaster instead of taking action like a president. Theodore Roosevelt, writing from his home in Oyster Bay, New York, dreamed of getting command of a division of American troops and getting them personally into the trenches at the front. He was particularly incensed at what he saw as Wilson's inaction in the face of provocation. He regarded Wilson as a "cold & selfish man; a very timid man when it comes to dealing with physical danger." Roosevelt thought Wilson was not "capable of understanding the emotion of patriotism." He believed that Wilson, "by his side-stepping trickery, timidity, & shuffling," had created the "pacifist party." Then, when those people opposed a stronger action on his part, "he whines for sympathy" and used them as the excuse "for not taking fearless and honorable action in international matters." In private letters and public speeches, Roosevelt continued to fume at Wilson's efforts to preserve American neutrality.[22]

To men like Roosevelt and Page, the moral imperative was that the United States should simply decide, on the basis of a long list of German affronts to American sovereignty, to go to war. Lansing, who worked closely with Wilson through all of these crises, understood that Wilson did not like to be forced by events to take an action, accounting for his tendency to delay and search for pathways through crises.[23] Even though events closed in on him, Wilson still tried to leave some options by stating that in the case of German overt acts, he would approach Congress to ask for authority to take further steps, not stating in advance exactly what those steps might be.

Wilson had left the door open to Germany "even now" to avoid the "overt acts" that would precipitate the United States' entry into war. Over the next weeks, crisis after crisis inundated the White House, the State Department, and the American public. In the hectic weeks following Wilson's address on February 3, several American ships would indeed be sunk as German U-boats began to implement the policy that Holtzendorff had long advocated. The circumstances surrounding each ship loss would be scrutinized very closely to see whether Germany had committed the overt act. Wilson's phrase "overt act" entered popular discourse, and during the sixty days following his speech, the press and other observers debated whether one or another action by Germany constituted the particular type of overt acts that Wilson would regard as war.[24]

After February 1, 1917, when Germany announced unrestricted submarine warfare, if the German commanders acted with as much discretion and care for the safety of the crews as displayed in the earlier cases over 1915 and 1916, it would be very difficult for the United States to officially claim that the later actions were acts of war. As will be seen in the next chapters, German submarine commanders after February 1 did at first conform to the precedents of *Frye, Leelanaw, Columbian,* and *Chemung,* and that behavior helps explain why the United States and Germany remained at peace for fully two months after the policy was announced. Word of the sinking of the first American ship under the new policy, the steamer *Housatonic,* on February 3, arrived on Sunday, February 4, just as the American public attempted to fully digest the implications of Wilson's speech.

6

Housatonic and *Lyman M. Law*

By one of the mysterious coincidences so often encountered in tales of the sea, the first American ship sunk by the Germans under their unrestricted submarine warfare policy had the same name as the first ship ever sunk by a submarine in warfare. Almost exactly fifty-three years before the sinking of the merchant ship *Housatonic* on February 3, 1917, the Confederate submarine *Hunley* sank the USS *Housatonic* off Charleston, South Carolina (February 17, 1864). However, "Housatonic" was a common ship name, derived from the Housatonic River and Housatonic Valley in Connecticut. The name was truly coincidence, not the mysterious working of Fate.[1]

Unlike the Union navy's *Housatonic* sunk by *Hunley*, the World War I *Housatonic* was a commercial merchant ship, not a warship. it had originally been built in 1890 by Barclay, Curle & Company of Glasgow for the German Hansa Line, based in Hamburg. First named the *Pickhuben*, it was a 3,143-gross-ton ship, 331 feet long with a 41-foot, 1-inch beam. It was straight-stemmed, with one funnel and two masts. The ship could achieve a speed of 11 knots, and boasted accommodation for ten first-class passengers and over two hundred in steerage. It sailed on its maiden voyage to Quebec and Montreal on April 15, 1891, and then began Hamburg–New York runs and Hamburg-Montreal runs in 1892. It was renamed *Georgia* and began service in 1895 from Stettin via Helsingborg and Gothenburg to New York. It was switched to the Odessa–New York route in 1904.[2]

In 1914 as the Great War began in Europe, the German ship took refuge in the United States, and in 1915, it was granted American registry as *Housatonic* under the provisions of the U.S. maritime code enacted August 28, 1914, that allowed ships of foreign registry to be transferred to the American flag. It was then employed as a freighter, operated in early 1917 by a specially formed Housatonic Company carrying grain and flour to Britain. Among those who had incorporated the firm was Edward Sandford, who had served as an attorney representing the Hamburg-American Line and who had defended Karl Buenz, head of that line. Buenz had been accused of sending ships out from American harbors to resupply German warships at sea, in defiance of American neutrality law. Two other ships of the Hamburg Line that had been sold to American firms had been treated as belligerent ships by the Allies. The *Dacia* had carried a shipment of cotton to Germany before Britain declared cotton as contraband, and then was captured by a French cruiser and interned in a French port as a lawful prize of war. The Hamburg Line *Alexandria* was renamed the *Sacramento*, and its cargo of coal was taken over by German warships in the Pacific, some thought through collusion of the officers of the merchant ship. There was no evidence, however, that the manager of the Housatonic Steamship Company, Edward F. Geer, planned any trips to Germany.[3]

Under the command of Captain Thomas A. Ensor, *Housatonic* sailed from Galveston for Britain on January 6, 1917, more than three weeks before the announced submarine policy.[4] The ship put in at Newport News, Virginia, and began its crossing of the Atlantic on January 16, still more than two weeks before the German unrestricted submarine warfare policy was announced.[5] About sixty miles off the Isles of Scilly at the southwest tip of Britain, it was hailed by the commander of U-boat *U-53*, under the command of Hans Rose.[6]

The *U-53* and Lieutenant Rose were well known to the American public because he had made a dramatic entry with the same U-boat into the Newport harbor on October 7, 1916, and had visited for a few hours before slipping out again. Rose, as a handsome and intelligent German naval officer, had impressed reporters and shipboard visitors with his command of English and his altogether proper manners. Described by journalists as about thirty-three years old, with dark hair, a clipped mustache, and blue eyes, and "of more than medium height," Rose had exchanged "felicitations" with American naval officers in the port, and asked that a letter be posted to Ambassador von Bernstorff in Washington. A newspaperman took the mail to the Newport post office for Rose. Despite the newsworthy sensation Rose caused, he was careful not to disclose any hint of his plans to journalists or others.[7]

The aide to the commandant of the U.S. naval station in Newport and the commander of the destroyer forces' staff visited the *U-53* while it was in the American port, getting a tour of the submarine and meeting the officers and crew, some of whom refused to disclose their names. The youthful crew stayed on deck, playing a phonograph, while the officers conducted a below-deck tour of the vessel for the American visitors.[8]

Lieutenant Rose was well aware that neutrality rules would limit his stay in port to twenty-four hours, and that only necessary stores and repairs could be made. He stated that he was not in need of any stores, and that his ship was in fine repair. Apparently he made the visit simply to show that it could be done. He left at 5:30 on the same day. After leaving Newport, Rose then sank five ships off Nantucket Lightship, while sixteen American destroyers looked on and rescued the passengers and crews of the stricken ships. Those destroyed were the three British ships, SS *Stephano*, SS *Strathdene*, and SS *Westpoint*, the Dutch SS *Blommersdyk*, and the Norwegian SS *Christian Knudsen*. Each of these steamships was an average size for the day, capable of carrying freight and a few passengers, running in tonnage between 3,300 and 4,850 gross tons.[9]

Rose's 1916 visit had stimulated an extensive debate in the press over submarine policy, revealing the ability of submarines to cross the Atlantic and, at the same time, showing the American public that submarines could conduct warfare by "cruiser rules" just outside the three-mile limit.[10] Admiral Bradley Fiske, the U.S. Navy's most articulate exponent of technological advancement and preparedness, saw Rose's visit and subsequent operations off the U.S. coast as an excellent warning to the American people about the future of naval warfare. Fiske pointed out that if *U-53* "could go into Newport harbor she could go into New York harbor" in time of war.[11] Apparently shocked that the U.S. Navy had to stand by helplessly, Woodrow Wilson sent a note to Bernstorff insisting that such attacks just off American shores should not be repeated.[12] However, in February 1917, Hans Rose initiated the series of events that constituted acts of war, not in New York Harbor or off Nantucket, but in the sea lanes approaching the British Isles.

The American merchant captain Thomas A. Ensor recorded the details of the February 3, 1917, encounter between Rose's *U-53* and the *Housatonic*. Ensor recounted how, at 10:30 a.m., his ship was hailed by a submarine that fired two warning shots. Following signaled instructions, he took his papers aboard the submarine, where Rose first spoke in German, and then in "perfect English." After reading over the ship's documents, Rose said: "I find that the vessel is laden with grain for London. It is my duty to sink her." He explained, "You are carrying foodstuffs to an enemy of my country, and though I am sorry, it is my duty to sink you." Ensor asked to be towed landward, but the commander refused because of the danger of British warships. The third officer of the U-boat boarded the *Housatonic* and smashed off several seacocks. Finally, after more pleading, Rose agreed to tow the crew in lifeboats toward land.[13]

The submarine crew engaged in scuttling the ship took the opportunity to remove a quantity of soap from the *Housatonic*, explaining it was in short supply in Germany due to the demands of the munitions industry for glycerin. As the thirty-seven members of the *Housatonic* crew watched from the lifeboats, the submarine fired a torpedo, and Ensor observed Rose taking photographs of the sinking. Then sailors on *U-53* threw a tow line, *Housatonic*'s crew tied it to the two lifeboats, and the submarine began towing the boats northward. Operating on its diesel engines, the sub churned away from the site of the attack, and Ensor and his crew could watch the *Housatonic* slowly sink beneath the waves, taking twenty minutes to disappear.[14]

After about two hours' towing, a British patrol boat was sighted on the horizon, and the U-boat stopped. Rose shouted out to Ensor, "I am going to leave you now, as that fellow will pick you up soon." Rose then realized the patrol boat had not spotted them, and called, "That fellow is asleep, but I will wake him up for you."

Rose ordered his 88mm deck gun to be fired, and then submerged when the patrol boat approached at "full speed with the thick black smoke belching out of her tall funnel." The boat was the trawler *Salvator*, which then picked up the *Housatonic* crew and took them to the coast of Cornwall.[15]

Hans Rose noted the encounter in his log, and his account fairly closely agreed with the reports from Captain Ensor, although he did not mention his own initial reluctance to tow the lifeboats.[16]

The *New York Times* and other American newspapers reacted cautiously to the sinking of the *Housatonic*, generally reflecting the State Department position held by unnamed "high officials" that the action did not represent the "overt act of war" to which Wilson had referred in his speech on February 3. Because the ship had left port before the announced policy, it was unclear whether the gentlemanly rescue by Rose represented a special case, or whether the Germans would continue to be as respectful and careful of human life aboard American ships that they sank. The striking fact that Rose had not only towed the lifeboats to safety, but that he had gone to the trouble to alert a British naval patrol boat by firing a shot, seemed to represent an extraordinarily courteous procedure. Whether or not Ensor had to ask to be towed or whether Rose had voluntarily made the offer, the submarine commander's behavior struck most observers as very humane. The *New York Times* noted that "the *Housatonic* was warned before being sunk and efforts were made by the commander of the submarine to put the crew in a place of safety. The *Housatonic*'s cargo of wheat for the British Government would be contraband under any interpretation of international law."[17]

The *New York Times* went on to take note of a hint in the German announcement of January 31 that "immunity from the new measures of warfare would be extended to all ships which had left their home ports before the effective date." Papers also reflected speculation "that this regard for the vessels already on their way to the war zone might prevent serious developments, affecting American interests, for two weeks or more. In some messages from Berlin, moreover, it has been intimated that the blockade policy would be conducted with a certain moderation at the outset, but would become more ruthless as the days went by."[18] As it turned out, these predictions were rather accurate.

Some publications speculated whether the lenient, cruiser rule–based treatment of the *Housatonic* was a matter of official German policy or the result of an individual decision of a particularly humane submarine commander. For example, the *Independent*, a journal of comment on political, social, and economic news, noted "that the Germans had been more scrupulous than usual in providing for the safety of the crew." Perhaps, the *Independent* implied, the more ruthless measures announced by the Germans were not in place at all.[19]

Lieutenant Hans Rose was indeed among the most humane of the U-boat commanders in his treatment of crews and passengers. In an account of the U-boat activities, the historian Edwyn Gray noted that Rose had allowed a French steamer, *Anna Maria*, to escape unharmed when he discovered its lifeboats were not seaworthy. Gray regarded the handling of the *Housatonic* situation as a "remarkable demonstration of both ruthlessness and humanity." Later in the war, after torpedoing a British Royal Navy destroyer, Rose radioed the exact position of the lifeboats with survivors to British forces in the Irish port of Queenstown so that they could be rescued.[20] However, it was quite natural in February 1917 for the American press to read into the *Housatonic* incident some indication of the trend of broader German submarine policy, not the behavior of an individual U-boat officer. The treatment, in fact, might have been due to both Rose's own inclinations and his close reading of his orders.

Much of the pro-Ally press, the more neutralist and pacifist press, and the State Department all agreed that Hans Rose's action was not an act of war. Indeed, the incident was not very different from the sinking of the *Leelanaw* or the *Chemung*. As in those cases, the submarine commander carefully saw to the safety of the crew, shepherding the lifeboats to rescue. If those acts had not been acts of war, clearly the *Housatonic* could not be treated as such. As Wilson had explicitly suggested in his February 3 address to Congress, when the news of the *Housatonic* arrived, his "inveterate confidence" in the German humanity had not been shaken, and the uneasy peace could be maintained.[21]

Although some observers who were more inclined to a hawkish position thought that the *Housatonic* incident represented more than a sufficient cause for war, they reluctantly, if critically, noted Wilson's evaluation of the incident. The *Outlook*, widely and correctly regarded as representative of the position of Theodore Roosevelt, expressed the frustration of the hawks, in a long opinion piece entitled "War with Germany," published March 7, 1917. The article detailed events that caused losses of American lives aboard *Lusitania* and other British ships in the period from early 1915 up to March 1917. It further noted some of the minor incidents in which American ships had been attacked or damaged with no casualties. Summing up the sequence, the article noted, "Steadily and unmistakably the United States has been and is moving toward war." In a somewhat scornful tone, typical of Theodore Roosevelt's attitude toward Wilson, the editorial piece noted that the sinking of the *Housatonic* was "condoned" as it did not represent the overt act: "So used have we become to these murderous attacks that we regard continued ruthlessness as its own palliative."[22] Throughout this period, Roosevelt continued to fume, venting his frustration over Wilson's policies in private correspondence as well as in public statements.

By listing the *Housatonic* along with many other prior incidents, Roosevelt's *Outlook* included this and other acts that Wilson chose not to regard as a casus belli, in the mounting case for war. Roosevelt and fellow hawks had no hesitancy in conflating the losses of American passengers and crew members on British ships with the losses of American ships and those of other neutrals, as part of making the case against Germany. Wilson, however, would not be pushed in February 1917 by incidents so ambiguous and so well within established precedents as the sinking of the *Housatonic*. That practice of conflating attacks on American ships with attacks on the ships of other neutrals and with attacks on British-registered ships that were known to be under orders to attack German submarines on sight was characteristic of those who urged Wilson to see Germany as the enemy. After the war, such conflation of events and statistics, and a careless treatment of distinctions and details became quite pronounced in the literature surrounding the lead-up to the war, and there was no hesitancy in including *Housatonic* along with other ship sinkings as part of the lead-up to war.[23]

In retrospect, it would become clear that *Housatonic* would be the first of the ships sunk under the new policy, and would indeed become part of the broader casus belli. Yet if it had been the only American-registered ship destroyed by Germany after February 1, there would have been no legal grounds for war, by the standards already established by Wilson and Lansing, and official State Department reaction to similar cases in the past. Furthermore if later ships were sunk with the same scrupulous attention for proprieties shown by Rose, there would have been no justification for an American declaration of war. Only when that sinking was viewed along with those of several that came later, in which there was a more flagrant disregard for American sovereignty at sea, did it appear that the torpedo that sunk *Housatonic* was the first of a series of shots and ships destroyed that led the United States into the war. At the time, Wilson was correct in his view; in retrospect, Roosevelt and the hawks were right.

Lyman M. Law

The schooner *Lyman M. Law* was the second United States–registered ship sunk by Germany after the February 1, 1917, initiation of unrestricted submarine warfare. The vessel was a four-masted wooden schooner, 1,300 gross tons, built in West Haven, Connecticut, by Gessner & Marr Company in 1890 for the Benedict-Manson Marine Company. In 1916 Benedict-Manson, based in New Haven, sold *Lyman M. Law* to a private syndicate based in Stockton Springs, Maine, headed by George A. Cardine.[24]

The *Lyman M. Law* sailed from Stockton Springs, Maine, on January 6, 1917, the same day the *Housatonic* departed Galveston, more than three weeks before the German policy was announced. The *Lyman M. Law* set sail for Palermo, Italy. It carried a cargo of 60,000 bundles of box shooks, thin wooden strips used in the construction of lemon crates, shipped through New York agents of Maritime Transportation Company of 25 Beaver Street. The shippers of the cargo were T. J. Stewart Company of Bangor, Maine, and the cargo, valued at $31,200, was consigned to an Italian firm, G. Cavallero, with an office in New York City.[25]

The schooner's captain was Stephen W. McDonough of Winterport, Maine. McDonough had been a sailing vessel captain for fifteen years, since he was twenty-four years old. Brusque, outspoken, and opinionated, he appeared fairly typical of sailing vessel masters of the period. He came from an old seafaring family, as did many in the schooner business, and his father, Walter McDonough, was still in the coasting trade. McDonough's first mate was William Lowe, also from a seagoing family, also resident in Winterport. Nine of the members of the original ten-member crew were Penobscot Bay

Figure 10. *Lyman M. Law*. The *Lyman M. Law*, shown here in dry dock for repairs, would become the second U.S. ship intentionally sunk after the announcement of unrestricted submarine warfare. It was carrying wooden shooks for making lemon crates, contraband of war under the German interpretation. There were no casualties. (Reprinted with permission from Mariners' Museum, Newport News, Va.)

sailors, who had been on many trips along the coast to the Grand Banks, Newport News, and other points on the U.S. Atlantic seaboard. For most of them, the offer of high wages on this trip had enticed them away from the coastal trade to an ocean crossing to the Mediterranean.[26]

The schooner was sunk on February 12 off Sardinia, and the crew safely landed at Cagliari, a port on the island. From Cagliari, initial reports from the American consul in Rome and reports in the press incorrectly assumed the ship was sunk by bombs placed aboard from an Austrian submarine. American consul Roger Culver Tredwell at Rome sent a dispatch to the State Department on February 13, sparking the report of the Austrian flag on the submarine, which seemed to be based on the testimony of one of the schooner's crew other than the captain. Tredwell's hasty first report not only erred in describing the submarine as Austrian, but misspelled Cape Spartivento on Sardinia as "Spartimento."[27]

In fact, the schooner had been sunk, not by an Austrian sub, but by another of Germany's most talented submarine crews, captained by Lothar von

Arnauld de la Perière. Von Arnauld established a record as the most accomplished U-boat "ace" during the war, sinking some 539,000 tons of shipping, by contrast to the 210,000-ton record set by Hans Rose. With reddish hair, a sophisticated appearance and a strong intellect, von Arnauld was descended from a line of military men, originally from France, who had entered the service of the German Empire. Working out of Cattaro, an Adriatic port used as a U-boat base, von Arnauld operated one of twenty-five submarines that successfully slipped through nets and barriers established by the British across the Straits of Otranto, where the Adriatic joins the Mediterranean.[28] Similar to Max Valentiner of *U-38*, who had sunk *Chemung* in November 1916, von Arnauld may have been flying the Austrian flag in continuation of the 1916 policy.

Von Arnauld's submarine, the *U-35*, strictly followed protocol. Von Arnauld would sink an armed enemy naval vessel without warning, once sending the French cruiser *Gallia* to the bottom with more than two thousand troops and sailors aboard. However, he would carefully warn crews of merchant vessels, examine their papers, and set the crews adrift in lifeboats with directions to shore before sinking the ship by planted explosives, gunfire, or torpedoes. Sometimes he would take the merchant ship captains as prisoners, keeping them aboard until he could return to port with them. On his voyage in February and March 1917, he brought aboard a movie cameraman, who filmed the sinking of several merchant ships. The surviving film from that cruise contains a clip of a four-masted schooner, very possibly the *Lyman M. Law*, being consumed in flames, and quickly sinking into the sea. Von Arnauld was fluent in several languages, and his ability to listen in on wireless messages and determine the location of target ships from the information he gleaned no doubt contributed to his outstanding record.[29]

Von Arnauld lowered his own flag when he saw the American flag, and sent an officer aboard the schooner to determine the nature of the cargo. At first he was inclined to release the schooner, but after discussions with the officer who visited the schooner, decided that the crew should be put off in boats, provisions should be removed, and the schooner destroyed. Using the motor launch, McDonough divided the crew between the two boats, and towed the other lifeboat some twenty-five miles to land. He coasted along the shore to Cagliari, arriving after about twenty-five hours at sea. Since the weather and sea state were mild, the crew was in no danger and all arrived safely.[30]

Mistakes and confusion in reports abounded. The exact location of the schooner when attacked was not clear. The fact that Germans considered lumber as contraband, and that the lemon-crate shooks technically constituted a form of lumber, made the determination that the cargo was contraband a rather debatable point. Cagliari, where the schooner crew first took refuge, is a remote port on the southern tip of the island of Sardinia. News from there was filtered by delay, confused reports, and apparently some interpretation and speculation by newsmen along the pathway of news from the island to Italy to the American newspapers and readers. As a consequence, the American public got a somewhat mixed impression of what had happened to the *Lyman M. Law*.

Since the German government had announced that there would be a safety zone in the western Mediterranean Sea between Sardinia and the coast of Tripoli, and the spot of the loss of the *Lyman M. Law* was very close to that zone, the press speculated whether the sinking had conformed to the German announcement or not. The Italian minister of marine had reported that an Italian ship, putting in to the island port of Malta, had spotted the schooner in flames at latitude 38 degrees 32 minutes north, and 7 degrees 58 minutes east, a point that was just outside the safety zone. However, reporters speculated whether the ship had been stopped and then set afire inside the safety zone and had drifted into the position where it was seen aflame, because the consul's report had stated that the ship was set on fire seventy miles southwest of Cape Spartivento. If accurate, that location would have been inside the safety lane.[31]

Again as in the case of the *Housatonic*, the *New York Times* immediately interpreted the attack as not likely to be seen as an "overt act," or a casus belli, even before all the facts had been established, and following comments from State Department personnel, explicitly raised the precedent of the *Frye*. Noting that the *Lyman M. Law* carried lemon shooks and that as lumber, the shooks might be regarded as contraband, the newspaper noted, "In this respect the destruction of this schooner, provided warning was given, would resemble the case of the American sailing vessel *William P. Frye*." The story reminded readers that the *Frye* "was sunk in the Pacific by the former German auxiliary *Prinz Eitel Friedrich* for carrying wheat bound for a British port."[32]

After the safe landing of the captain and crew ashore, further reports continued to muddle exactly what had happened. A full crew list of the *Lyman Law* was published, noting that all the crew were Americans "except the negro cook . . . who hails from Jamaica, and is a British subject." Although correct on the score of national identity, the cook's name was spelled in more than one way, as were several others in the list.[33] The minor confusion in reporting the names only indicated the haste with which the list was compiled, and reflected the prompt effort of newswriters to establish the American identity of the ship by giving the hometowns of the crew.[34]

George W. F. Green, president of the Maritime Transportation Company in New York City, reflected the same theme: that the State Department and the president should step up and defend this "very American ship." Green was indignant, and said that he intended to file a protest with the State Department. Green suggested that the American flag should protect hardy New England sailing vessel sailors, especially since they had deep American ancestral roots. Green pointed out that "Captain McDonough is a 'down Easter,' an American of three generations, a sailor out of New England ports for more than twenty years." Reflecting a bit more of the current ethnic values, Green went on to say that the "men, with one exception, are stanch [sic] New England stock. Their ancestors fought in the Revolution. Now, if they are not entitled to protection, who the devil is?"[35]

By February 18, six days after the sinking, further details of the event began to reach the American press. In particular, a report from Cagliari, based on an interview with Captain McDonough, conveyed a sense of outrage. Considering other statements made by McDonough, it appeared that the tone of the interview reflected a little creative writing by reporters. The story quoted McDonough as saying, "It was a nasty piece of privateering." McDonough went on to claim, "A big, fat man, who seemed to be the boss, ordered us arrogantly, as though we were his slaves, to leave the boat immediately.... It seemed to me that my attempts to argue irritated the boss, and he began to threaten us. My understanding of what he said was that he would send us all to the bottom of the sea, from where we might appeal to President Wilson." McDonough concluded, "overcome with rage, I was obliged, together with my crew to leave the vessel, which was destroyed in a few moments by bombs set off by the submarine crew."[36]

A somewhat more balanced report was printed along with the one above, providing a paraphrase of comments made by Captain McDonough to the American consul and to several reporters. According to that report, the submarine commander made sure the crew had a supply of food, water, and gasoline to power their launch.[37]

After noting that Tredwell and the embassy were investigating whether the cargo could be considered contraband, the report further detailed McDonough's opinion that the schooner had been sunk because the sub crew wanted to confiscate the food aboard.[38] In a report with further information, the *New York Times* noted that McDonough was confident the commander was German, and that the submarine had taken $1,700 worth of stores from the schooner before ordering the ship destroyed because it carried contraband.[39] The details in these reports were in accord with the official note sent to Washington by Nelson Page, U.S. ambassador to Italy. By telegram, Page reported on the affidavits signed by both McDonough and his crew. Page confirmed that McDonough believed the "need for the stores caused the sinking" of the schooner.[40]

When interviewed in Rome, McDonough continued to stress the apparent piracy-like theft of supplies in the incident, noting "that the vessel had a large supply of canned goods, especially meat, chickens and vegetables, which doubtless attracted the officers and crew of the submarine in their search for food." He described the submarine crew as "about forty men—all big, blond, husky fellows." McDonough said: "If my ship had been armed with a five-pounder I could have destroyed the submarine as easily as buttering a piece of bread. Neither myself nor my men lowered our dignity by showing any resentment. I didn't ask them to spare the ship and left her smilingly, while the Germans also smiled." Despite the note of polite and diplomatic behavior suggested in this last comment by McDonough, the bellicose phrase regarding the five-pounder gun made it into the story's headline.[41]

McDonough reiterated his notion that the reason the ship had been sunk was to get its provisions, fleshing out the larceny story a bit: "I may be mistaken, but my impression is that we are the victims of robbery." After the submarine commander first said he would release the schooner, something changed his mind. McDonough thought it was the "large and rather select supply of food we possessed," spotted by the officer who inspected the ship. When that officer returned to the submarine, McDonough saw an "animated discussion" and then the submarine commander "finally decided to blow up the *Law* after having ransacked her."[42]

The fact that the news reached the United States in several ways, through consular reports released to the press in Washington, in news stories reproduced from the Italian press, and in reports wired to the United States from Cagliari, Civita Vecchia, and Rome, helps account for the somewhat varied tone of the reports. Headline writers naturally emphasized the most sensational aspects of the accounts. Not only was there some confusion about whether the submarine was Austrian or German, when in fact it was German, but discrepancies about other details such as the schooner's exact location when accosted and destroyed, and whether or not the cargo could be regarded as contraband, all surfaced in these preliminary reports. The stories about the requisition of food supplies may have been partially or totally fabricated, and tended to get more play as time wore on. The claim that a small cannon would have provided protection came during increasing agitation in mid- and late February for a policy of arming merchant ships to protect them from submarine attacks.

Even ten days later, when the *Independent* offered a comment on the incident, the facts remained unclear. The *Independent* offered the opinion that "The Law case is of more importance than would appear from the comparatively slight [financial] loss, for it may be the 'overt act' on which President Wilson threatened strong measures." While admitting that the loss of Americans embarked on belligerent ships would leave debatable how much responsibility the United States should take, the fact that the schooner and its crew were Americans was understood to be highly significant to this opinion journal. The *Independent* doubted whether the lemon shooks could be regarded as contraband, and dismissed the question of the ship's exact location. Whether or not the schooner was in the permitted safety zone or in the barred zone "would not matter much since the United States does not recognize the legality of the danger zones designated."[43]

The hurried and confused reporting of the *Lyman M. Law* incident was fairly typical of many stories of ships lost at sea, as fragmentary and conflicting accounts filtered back from different sources. However, through the disparate tales, the outlines emerged, indicating to an objective observer and any careful reader of the reports at the time that cruiser rules had been obeyed, that the crew had not been harmed in any way, and that the sinking of the schooner was in accord with the precedents in the cases of the *Frye*, *Leelanaw*, and *Chemung*. Viewed as an event at a moment in time, it could not constitute a casus belli by itself or even in conjunction with the sinking of the *Housatonic*, but when viewed in the context of later attacks on American ships, it would become one of the string of several events that would lead the United States into war.

However, as the end of February approached, the United States appeared to be no closer to war with Germany than it had been on February 1. Theodore Roosevelt believed Wilson was a coward, and wrote to that effect to Henry Cabot Lodge. "I have begun to doubt whether he will go to war under any circumstances," said Roosevelt. Wilson, Roosevelt thought, "is trying to sneak out of going to war under any conditions." The conditions, however, were putting severe pressure on Wilson.[44]

The Cabinet and the Shipping Crisis

Through February, President Wilson and his cabinet began to take note that a voluntary embargo of shipping to Germany had set in. Shipping companies and merchant ship crews were reluctant to commit themselves to crossing the Atlantic in the face of German attacks. In response to inquiries from shipping companies, the United States Hydrographic Office in Washington published a detailed description of the boundaries of the war zone as defined by Germany, giving the nautical bearings for the safe lane to Holland and the safe lane through the Mediterranean to Greece.[45]

At the February 6 regular Tuesday meeting of the cabinet, the first after the German announcement and the sinking of the *Housatonic*, "the situation of our American merchantmen occupied attention," recalled David Houston, secretary of agriculture, and strong advocate of war with Germany. None of the cabinet members knew what to expect. They recognized that the owners of merchant ships had a right to go to sea, but did not know whether they would exercise the right, or simply "tie up in our ports." Should the postmaster general insist that ships meet their contracts to carry the mail? Houston suggested that the shipowners be told to use their own discretion, and if they chose to sail, the government should tell them they had a right to arm in self-defense. Other members of the cabinet objected that no such advice should be given. Still others said that the responsibility should not be left to ship owners. A decision of sorts was reached, to tell shipowners that their rights were "just the same as if Germany had said nothing, and that they could arm for defense."[46]

Wilson convened extra meetings of the cabinet, and on Friday, February 9, a few days before the loss of *Lyman M. Law*, David Houston remarked that "the shipping situation had not been cleared up"; ships were not sailing, and they were "showing every sign of interning." The members of the cabinet varied considerably in suggesting courses of action. Some suggested selling, lending, or giving guns to the merchant ship owners, and furnishing gun crews. Secretary of War Newton Baker, known as one of the leading pacifists in the cabinet, suggested a convoy technique, so that "inoffensive merchantmen should not be exposed to danger." The February 9 meeting adjourned without reaching a consensus on what to do. It was against the background of these discussions, leaked to the press, that the "five-pounder" comment attributed to Captain McDonough was published, by implication supporting the armed merchant ship concept.[47]

Figure 11. Weary waiting. After the sinking of the schooner *Lyman M. Law*, no American ships were sunk for four weeks, as most had voluntarily "interned" or stayed in port. Americans anxiously scanned the news, awaiting the next crisis. (Wilson Presidential Library, Staunton, Va.)

The shipping crisis continued. According to a summary published later in the *New York Times Current History*, Standard Oil had recalled its steamers by wireless and the International Mercantile Marine Company had postponed all sailings indefinitely. During the first nineteen days after the announced German policy, only five American freighters had sailed.[48]

On February 21, Wilson began preparing an address to Congress to ask for authority to provide arms for merchant ships. As Wilson worked on the speech, he asked Lansing for the file on both the *Housatonic* and the *Lyman Law*.[49] When he presented the address on February 26, he explicitly repeated his observation that the sinking of the *Housatonic* and *Lyman Law* did not give a cause for war. Although the submarine policy was "fraught with danger," he observed, "We can only say . . . that the overt act which I have ventured to hope the German commanders would in fact avoid has not occurred."[50]

On February 23, after the detailed reports from the *Lyman Law* had come in, and after Roosevelt had vented some of his mounting anger to Lodge, Secretary of the Navy Josephus Daniels found the cabinet meeting even more "stormy" than usual. Lansing noted in his desk diary that the two-hour meeting included a "very hot debate on action." The war hawks in the cabinet, David Houston, Franklin Lane, and William Gibbs McAdoo, "insisted on immediate action" in arming merchant ships. Wilson replied, "You are trying to push us into war," and grew irritated when Lane inquired into a rumor that wives of American diplomats had been strip-searched before being deported. However, Daniels observed, it was not the suggestions of the cabinet members but the German attitude that brought Wilson around to the concept that he might choose to arm merchant ships in self-defense.

"Daniels," he said, "has the Navy the gunners and the guns for the job?"

"We can arm them as fast as the ships are ready," replied Daniels. To many observers the concept of arming ships seemed the only way to get the ships to sail and to resume trade with the Allies.[51] The only question in the minds of the cabinet members was whether or not Wilson needed congressional authority to take the action of putting guns and gun crews on private merchant ships.

Wilson thought he had the authority, but also wanted to get congressional "power behind him" so that he could take the action when he wanted to do so, "at the proper time." Franklin Lane, McAdoo, and Lansing grew increasingly frustrated at what they saw as Wilson's delaying tactics. Lane said he was "slower than a glacier—and things are mighty disagreeable, whenever anything has to be done."[52]

The Sixty-fourth Congress was about to end its second and last session in another week, on Sunday, March 4, and the Sixty-fifth Congress would not regularly convene until the first Monday in December 1917. If the Sixty-fourth Congress were to approve an Armed Ship Bill, it would only have the last week of its current session, from Monday, February 26, to noon on Sunday, March 4, to act. Lansing left town for a long and well-earned three-day weekend at White Sulphur Springs, West Virginia, over February 24–26. He was confident nothing of importance would happen over the weekend. It turned out that he was quite mistaken. On Saturday evening, February 24, Acting Secretary of State Frank Polk (during Lansing's absence) brought to the White House an urgent long telegram from London.[53]

7

A Telegram, *Algonquin*, and an Abdication

On January 17, 1917, William Reginald "Blinker" Hall, director of the Intelligence Division (DID) had worked his way through a docket of papers with an associate in Room 40 of the British Admiralty building. At about half past ten, Lt. Commander Nigel de Grey, one of the cryptanalysts, ran in, excited.

"DID," he asked, using Hall's title, "d'you want to bring America into the war?"

"Yes, my boy," answered Hall. "Why?"

"I've got something here which—well, it's a rather astonishing message which might do the trick *if* we could use it. It isn't very clear, I'm afraid, but I'm sure I've got most of the important points right. It's from the German Foreign Office to Bernstorff."[1]

De Grey had just partially deciphered a note from German foreign minister Arthur Zimmermann to the German ambassador in the United States, Johann von Bernstorff. The note contained an astonishing proposal. Zimmermann requested that Bernstorff contact the German minister in Mexico City and offer that, if the United States went to war with Germany, Germany would enter an alliance with Mexico, with a promise to help that country regain territory lost to the United States in the Mexican-American War in 1846–48, including Texas, Arizona, and New Mexico.

Admiral Hall searched for a way to release the note to the Americans while concealing from them that the British had been tapping their own private diplomatic line, as well as concealing that source from the Germans. Finally, by late February, he had developed a version that appeared to have been intercepted in Mexico, and provided it to Ambassador Page in London. Page wrote a cover note and wired the whole long telegram to the State Department, where it was received on Saturday, February 24. Lansing was already at White Sulphur Springs, and the work of handling the telegram went to Frank Polk, Lansing's right-hand man. Finally, on Saturday evening, Polk took the decrypted telegram to Wilson. The telegram read as follows:

On the first of February we intend to begin submarine warfare unrestricted. In spite of this, it is our intention to endeavor to keep neutral the United States of America. If this attempt is not successful, we propose an alliance on the following basis with Mexico: That we shall make war together and together make peace. We shall give general financial support, and it is understood that Mexico is to reconquer the lost territory in New Mexico, Texas, and Arizona. The details are left to you for settlement. You are instructed to inform the President of Mexico of the above in the greatest confidence as soon as it is certain that there will be an outbreak of war with the United States and suggest that the President of Mexico, on his own initiative, should communicate with Japan suggesting adherence at once to this plan; at the same time, offer to mediate between Germany and Japan. Please call to the attention of the President of Mexico that the employment of ruthless submarine warfare now promises to compel England to make peace in a few months.[2]

Treatment of this grand episode of decryption is presented in Patrick Beesly, *Room 40*; in Herman Kahn, *The Codebreakers*; in Barbara Tuchman, *The Zimmermann Telegram*, and in other volumes. In her well-crafted history of the episode, Tuchman refers to the decoded Zimmermann Telegram as "Zimmermann's overt act, lying like an unthrown hand grenade" in the safe of Admiral Hall in Britain.[3]

The eventual revelation of the note did indeed stun Wilson, the cabinet, the press, and many Americans, like an explosion. However, to see it as the "overt act" that forced the United States into World War I is something of an exaggeration. Wilson learned of the note on Saturday evening, February 24, 1917. He released the note to the public on Wednesday, February 28, and it was published on March 1. Wilson did not decide to call Congress to meet on April 2 to consider a declaration of war until Wednesday, March 21, some twenty-five days after he received the decrypted Zimmermann Telegram. Unless the sinking of specific American ships is considered closely, it is impossible to explain the more than three-week delay between receipt of the decrypted telegram and Wilson's decision. If the Zimmermann Telegram was the overt act that Wilson required to go to war, he could either have gone to Congress immediately with a request for a declaration of war or asked them to reconvene immediately after his inauguration on March 5. He did neither, and continued to await some evidence that Germany would in fact do what it had promised.

Wilson had said in his address on February 3 that it would take the loss of American ships and American lives, as overt acts, to make him believe that Germany was willing to attack the United States. The shocking Zimmermann Telegram specifically noted that Germany hoped to keep the United States neutral, and only if that effort failed, Germany would like an alliance with Mexico. The note was a statement of a possible policy outcome, not an action, any more than the announced unrestricted submarine warfare policy was an action. Although many inside and outside of his administration strongly disagreed, Wilson did not see statements of plans or policies as "overt acts."[4]

Wilson found it extremely distasteful that the Germans had taken advantage of the permission he had granted them to use Western Union cables to communicate peace proposals in cipher between Berlin and Washington, to transmit this surprising proposal for an anti-American alliance. The route that Zimmermann used to send his telegram, in the words of Herman Kahn, the leading historian of codes and codebreakers, "was of such simplicity, perfidy, and barefaced gall that it probably remains unequaled in the annals of diplomacy."[5] When Lansing later explained how the message had been transmitted, through the undersea cable that Wilson had insisted be available to Bernstorff for diplomatic exchanges, Wilson was so appalled that he said "Good Lord" several times. Lansing thought it remarkable, for Wilson very rarely used such an expression.[6]

The unfolding of events through these crucial days showed that the casus belli, in Wilson's mind, had to be specific hostile actions that met his own requirements as overt acts. Clinging to his faith that the United States would be more effective as a peacemaker and a neutral, and not wanting to be forced to take an action he had fought for more than twenty-eight months to avoid, he would not recommend war until and unless Germany actually used force in an *act*, not in *words*, against the United States.

Wilson had finally agreed with cabinet members on Friday, February 23, that he should establish a system to arm merchant ships.[7] On Saturday, February 24, Polk brought him the decrypted telegram. He agreed with Polk that he should not release the note until he had a chance to talk with Lansing, who was due to come back to town from the West Virginia resort on Tuesday. But Wilson was well aware of the note when, on Monday, February 26, he requested that Congress pass the Armed Ship Bill.

Wilson did not mention the Zimmermann Telegram in that message to Congress. In that speech, however, he explicitly said that, despite the *Housatonic* and the *Lyman M. Law*, as yet, Germany had made no overt act of *war*. The situation was fraught with danger, he noted. If the Zimmermann Telegram was the overt act he had dreaded, he did not treat it as such in this address, nor did he even mention it, although he had had the decrypted version for more than thirty-six hours. Wilson also explicitly said in this same address, two days after receiving the Zimmermann Telegram, "I am not now proposing or contemplating war or any steps that lead to it."[8]

Laconia

As Wilson delivered his address asking approval of the Armed Ship Bill, news arrived that the British Cunard liner *Laconia* had been torpedoed with the loss of life, including three Americans. The *Laconia* was a new liner, built in 1912 by Swan, Hunter & Wigham Richardson. The 18,001-ton liner sailed for Britain from New York on February 18, and was torpedoed a week later, about 160 miles northwest by west of the Fastnet Light, a little after 2100 (local time) on February 25, 1917. A second torpedo hit the engine room, and the ship sank at about 2220. The ship carried 75 passengers and a crew of 217. Six passengers and six members of the crew died, most of them in one lifeboat that was severely damaged when it was hurriedly lowered. Two of the passengers, Mrs. Mary Hoy and her daughter, Elizabeth Hoy, were killed, along with an African American fireman (that is, one who tended the coal-fired steam engines) by the name of Thomas Coffee. Most news stories reporting the sinking focused on the loss of Mrs. Hoy and her daughter, both of whom were socially prominent in Chicago. Details of their lives in Chicago with Mrs. Hoy's husband, Arthur Harris Hoy, who represented an American company in London, abounded. Some news items about the *Laconia* did not mention the loss of Mr. Coffee at all, while others did not record his first name. Six of the passengers had been Americans. Twenty of the crew were also American citizens, mostly African American men stoking the steam engines. They had been signed on in New York to replace British crew members who refused to sail into the war zone.[9]

Floyd Gibbons, an American journalist from the *Chicago Tribune*, was among the survivors. After a night in a lifeboat and his rescue, he was approached by a British fellow-passenger with whom he had many conversations about whether or not the United States would enter the war. As Gibbons stepped ashore, his British acquaintance slapped him on the back, and asked, "Well, old Casus Belli," he said, "is this your blooming overt act?"[10]

Gibbons made no reply, but immediately located a typewriter and began writing a detailed account that he cabled later that night, with the story arriving as congressmen listened to Wilson's appeal for the Armed Ship Bill on Monday, February 26. Over the next few days, some editorialists in both Britain and the United States, like Gibbons's fellow passenger, speculated whether this outright violation of the *Sussex* Pledge, and the death of American passengers aboard an armed British liner would represent the overt act. But within a week, it was clear that the *Laconia*, like the *Falaba*, *Lusitania*, and *Arabic*, and more than twenty other British ships, did not provide a casus belli in the view of Woodrow Wilson.[11] Three Americans, Mary Hoy, Elizabeth Hoy, and Thomas Coffee, had been killed by the Germans, but not from the loss of an American ship. The United States would not go to war over the violation of the *Sussex* Pledge in the sinking of a British liner. Wilson had only promised to break diplomatic relations if the pledge were violated, and he had already done that. The *Laconia* incident demonstrates that it is not correct to view Wilson's decision to go to war as deriving from German acts in violation of the *Sussex* Pledge. Germany would have to take a direct, overt act against the United States before Wilson would be forced to abandon neutrality.

The Armed Ship Bill and the Zimmermann Telegram

On Tuesday, February 27, Wilson showed the Zimmermann Telegram to Lansing, who agreed it should be released to the press. On Wednesday, Lansing called E. M. Hood, of the Associated Press, to his home and gave him a copy of the telegram. The next morning, March 1, the Zimmermann Telegram story was carried across the nation. Even the Hearst newspapers, which had been critical of Wilson for his pro-British form of neutrality, endorsed the Armed Ship Bill. In the House of Representatives, the bill immediately passed by the overwhelming vote of 403 to 13. Hawks and doves could both support it: hawks because they believed it showed more muscle and might provoke an armed clash that would lead to war; some doves because it was conceivable that armed neutrality was better than full-scale war. Furthermore, in the widespread public anger over the Zimmermann Telegram, the position of the die-hard pacifists and pro-German elements had been weakened, as has been well documented by Tuchman, Kahn, and others.

However, in the Senate Foreign Relations Committee, suspicion over the timing of the release of the telegram mounted. The Associated Press erroneously implied that Wilson had the decryption for several weeks, and if that had been true, it appeared that he had timed the release to affect the outcome of the bill. The Senate requested more information about the telegram from Wilson. Lansing helped prepare a careful statement to the Senate and to the press that vouched for the authenticity of the telegram; hinted that for security reasons, the means of obtaining the note could not be revealed; and clarified the fact that Wilson had only had the note since February 24, four days before he released it. Meanwhile, however, Senator Robert LaFollette had gathered together a group of ten senators who were dead-set against the Armed Ship Bill on the grounds that it might provoke war with Germany. He led a filibuster of the bill, which would die without a vote if the filibuster could be continued to the end of the session that was due to end on Sunday, March 4.

On Saturday, March 3, word came that Zimmermann admitted to the press that the transcript of the telegram was accurate and that he had indeed sent it. He thought it was only natural that Germany should, in the event of war with the United States, seek allies, and he was rather surprised at the American indignation over the idea. However, even this admission by Zimmermann and his rather obtuse observations about American public opinion did not change the views of those conducting the filibuster.

According to the rules of the Senate at that time, even a solid majority of two-thirds or three-quarters of the Senate could not bring cloture to a debate. In fact, it was this particular filibuster that led the Senate to later change its rules to allow a two-thirds majority to close off a filibuster.[12] LaFollette and his group spoke all night, fending off points of order and other maneuvers. Finally, at noon on Sunday, the Senate adjourned, without taking action on the Armed Ship Bill. Thoroughly outraged, Wilson issued a rare statement of pique to the press, stating that it was disgraceful that the United States was the only democracy in which the clear majority of the legislature and the will of the people as expressed through that majority could be frustrated by "a little group of willful men." The phrase entered history.

For war hawks like Theodore Roosevelt, the filibuster was disgraceful. But Roosevelt believed that the Armed Ship Bill itself "was practically worthless." Armed neutrality was "nothing but timid war," he wrote to a friend.[13] He later used the same description in a speech to the Union League Club, thoroughly outraged that the United States had done nothing to prepare for war since the announcement of unrestricted submarine warfare, which he regarded as a declaration of war. For Roosevelt, there had been many overt acts, but in Roosevelt's view, Wilson still perversely held to his hope that neutrality could be preserved.[14]

Wilson's moral views dominated his thinking about foreign policy, and he apparently believed that if Germany could operate the submarine blockade within the constraints of propriety as defined by the unratified Declaration of London, the United States would be able to remain neutral. Theodore Roosevelt, Walter Hines Page in London, Lansing, and many of Wilson's closest advisors grew increasingly frustrated at what they saw as Wilson's dilatory manner and refusal to face facts. In retrospect, it is clear that Wilson's persona prevented him from accurately assessing German behavior. By asserting that he could not believe that German submarine officers would do what the German Foreign Office said they would do, and by persisting in that refusal to believe as long as he could, even as events showed that they would do so, he was forced into an untenable position. His moralism continued to blind him to reality through early March 1917.

On Sunday, March 4, Wilson took the oath of office for his second term in a private ceremony in the President's Room at the Capitol Building, and the next day Wilson delivered his public inaugural address. In that speech, Wilson had still another opportunity to claim that the accumulated actions of Germany, including the sinking of *Housatonic* and *Lyman M. Law*, the affront of the Zimmermann Telegram, and a variety of violations of diplomatic immunity by lower-level German and Austrian diplomats engaged in espionage and subversion constituted overt acts of war. He made no such claims. Instead, he said, "We have been deeply wronged upon the seas, but we have not wished to wrong or injure in return; have retained throughout the consciousness of standing in some sort apart, intent upon an interest that transcended the immediate issues of the war itself." As evidence of how strongly he believed in neutrality, the original dictated draft of the speech had said that the United States had been "deeply injured and wronged by the governments of both sides." He had scratched out "by the governments of both sides" at the last minute.[15]

He spoke generally of some injuries to the United States that "have become intolerable," but the United States wished nothing but "fair dealing, justice, the freedom to live and to be at ease against organized wrong." However, he went on: "We stand firm in armed neutrality since it seems that in no other way we can demonstrate what it is we insist upon and cannot forget. We may even be drawn on, by circumstances, not by our own purpose or desire, to a more active assertion of our rights as we see them and a more immediate association with the great struggle itself." Crucial points in Wilson's prose were that he reasserted the fact that the United States chose armed neutrality, and that only unspecified circumstances could draw the nation into some undefined association with the war.[16]

Figure 12. Riding to the inauguration. Wilson and his second wife, Edith Boling Galt, ride in an open car to his second inauguration, held in public on March 5, 1917. He caught a severe cold and was bedridden for about two weeks. (Courtesy of Library of Congress.)

Only a possibility of "a more active assertion of our rights" was as far as Wilson was willing to go, fully a month after the *Housatonic*, two weeks after the *Lyman M. Law*, nine days after getting the Zimmermann Telegram, and a week after learning of the *Laconia*. The overt acts were yet to come. Another full week would pass before another U.S.-registered ship was sunk.

Although assured by Lansing that he had the authority to provide arms and naval crews to merchant ships, Wilson still preferred to obtain a congressional endorsement of the action when Congress came back in session. During the week following his inauguration, on March 9, Wilson, who had caught a severe cold (probably during the outdoor speech) and was confined to bed, announced through his secretary Joseph Tumulty that he intended to go ahead and arm merchant ships on his own authority but would still seek congressional approval of his actions. In response to a request from Speaker of the House Champ Clark, Wilson said he would ask Congress to convene in full session (House as well as Senate) on April 16. In the message conveyed from his sickbed, there was no indication that Wilson would be asking for a declaration of war at that time, but only some form of endorsement for his armed neutrality policy. With the established clear majority in the House, and with new Senate rules allowing cloture to cut off filibusters passed on March 9 as the Senate met separately, some form of the Armed Ship Bill would seem to be on the agenda.[17]

During the week after his inauguration, Wilson made inquiries through Secretary of the Navy Josephus Daniels about exactly how the Navy would go about arming ships, and what policies naval officers would recommend. The exchange about what a later generation would call rules of engagement was not released to the press at the time, although parts were later published in the official State Department publication *Foreign Relations of the United States*. Naval officers reflected on some of the difficulties such a policy might

Figure 13. Cloture. When the Senate reconvened following Wilson's second inaugural, the members—in response to the debacle of the filibuster that prevented passage of the Armed Ship Bill—passed a rule allowing the closing of debate. (Wilson Presidential Library, Staunton, Va.)

entail. Since German submarines would attack an armed ship on sight without warning from a submerged position, it was difficult to imagine how a deck gun on a freighter, even staffed by professionals, would offer much protection. Nevertheless, naval planners worked on the issue. The suggested rules of engagement required the proposed gun crews to exert every effort to avoid an armed clash.[18]

Algonquin

The *Algonquin*, a freighter owned by the American Star Line of 25 Beaver Street in New York, was one of the first American ships to leave port bound for Europe after the German announcement of unrestricted submarine warfare. Together with the *Mongolia*, owned by the Atlantic Transport Company (a subsidiary of International Mercantile Marine), the two ships left New York for British ports on February 20.[19] The *Algonquin* was a single-screw, three-masted steamship of 1,806 gross tons, commanded by Captain A. Nordberg. The owners had agreed to give the officers of the ship a war bonus of 50 percent in wages, and a bonus of 25 percent to the crew. If the vessel were to be captured or destroyed, the crew would be paid the bonus with wages until they could be returned to the United States.[20] Although very few ships departed, the tanker *Healdton*, owned by Standard Oil, was notified that it could depart Halifax after a delay in that port. Standard Oil had ordered such tankers to stand by, and released *Healdton* to resume its voyage from Philadelphia toward Rotterdam on the same day that *Algonquin* departed New York.[21]

The *Algonquin* had been built in 1888 at Yoker yards in Glasgow, by Napier, Shanks & Bell, Limited. Originally owned by the Canadian Northwest Steamship Company, it was later transferred to the St. Lawrence and Chicago Steam Navigation Company, Limited, of Toronto. The Port Colborne and St. Lawrence Navigation Company acquired the ship about 1912 and ran it in the inland waterway grain trade until December 29, 1915, when it was sold to A. B. McKay, in Hamilton, Ontario. In 1916, it entered saltwater trades, under the Nova Scotia Steel and Coal Company with British registry. In December 1916, it transferred to U.S. registry.[22] With the U.S. transfer, it had been sold to William Wotherspoon in New York. By the time it steamed out of New York on February 20, it had been taken over by the American Star Line.[23] The day after it left port, it was sold to John Stephanidis and J. D. Benas of 24 Beaver Street, two participants in the American Star Line. The foodstuffs aboard were valued at $1.25 million. Since the shipping commu-

Figure 14. *Algonquin*. The former grain carrier *Algonquin* was sunk without warning on March 12, 1917. Wilson and Secretary of State Lansing did not treat the event as an "overt act of war" because the ship had just been transferred from British registry to U.S. registry. (Reprinted with permission from Mariners' Museum, Newport News, Va.)

nity was well aware of the German interpretation of rules regarding transfer of flag after the beginning of the war, the voyage was a notably high-risk venture.[24]

The first reports of the sinking of *Algonquin* on March 12 came from Consul Stephens at Plymouth, who wired a brief cable in "telegraphese" to the State Department: "Steamer Algonquin of New York, from New York for London with foodstuffs, sunk by German submarine sixty five miles west of Bishops March 12, 6.AM. Captain reports vessel not warned and sunk by shell fire. Crew of twenty-seven all saved in own boats. Submarine refused assistance. No other boats in sight."[25] Stephens later corrected his report on the cargo, which in addition to foodstuffs, consisted of "copper, tin, machinery, acids, and formaldehyde."[26]

Shipping reporters noted that a total of eight American steamships had sailed since the January 31 pronouncement of the unrestricted submarine policy by the Germans. The seven others had arrived safely in France, Britain, and Italy when the *Algonquin* was sunk.[27]

First reports indicated that *Algonquin* had not been warned, although apparently before finally sinking the ship, the crew of *U-62* waited until all the crew were aboard lifeboats, and then went aboard to place explosive charges to sink the ship. Charles Schultz, the chief engineer of *Algonquin*, in recounting the story to his granddaughter years later, remembered that he had asked the submarine crew in German for directions to land, and they responded by pointing eastward.[28]

Several international law aspects of the *Algonquin* sinking were noted by Washington D.C., Associated Press reporters in discussions with official sources:

> The circumstance that the *Algonquin* carried foodstuffs which are contraband and that it recently was transferred from British to American registry, a transaction Germany might plead it would not recognize, are not taken to outweigh the fact that the ship was reported destroyed without warning. Neither does the fact that apparently no lives were lost mitigate the situation. But the real fact, as officially expressed, is that while the destruction of an American ship in such a manner is very serious the American Government already has taken all the steps it can take to meet such a case, unless it wishes to take the last step and declare war. . . . It is generally accepted on first reports as not being the "overt act."[29]

On the other hand, the owner, John Stephanidis, in an interview quoted in the *Christian Science Monitor* three days after the attack, gave the opinion that the sinking of the *Algonquin* was indeed the required "overt act." Several other newspapers emphasized the negative aspects of the incident, such as the *Atlanta Constitution*, which headlined its story: "Germans Merciless to Algonquin Crew after Sinking Ship—Submarine Commander Gruffly Refused to Tow Boat in Which American Captain and Sailors Took Refuge."[30]

The avowedly neutralist Hearst press headed the story: "U.S. Ship Shelled and Sunk without Warning—*Algonquin*, Innocent Freighter Is Victim." Despite the use of value-laden terms such as "innocent" and "victim" in the headline, the Hearst papers featured a very evenhanded evaluation of the situation by noted Hearst writer John Temple Graves. Graves, a former Atlanta, Georgia, columnist who was well known for his avowedly segregationist views and who had run for vice president on the Hearst-created Independence Party ticket in 1908, offered this assessment of the situation, which was a careful rewrite of the Associated Press version printed by the *New York Times* and other papers.

> The sinking of the American steamship *Algonquin* by a German submarine in the German war zone is the most exciting incident of a week of international tension and strain.
>
> The circumstances which permit the view that this was not yet the "overt act" are these:
>
> FIRST—That the *Algonquin* was recently transferred from British to American registry, a transaction which Germany may plead she could not recognize.
>
> SECOND—That the *Algonquin* carried a cargo of foodstuffs, which were contraband of war.
>
> THIRD—that the ship was sunk by shell fire and not torpedoed.
>
> FOURTH—that no lives were destroyed.
>
> The circumstances which are unusually aggravating and look dark are:
>
> FIRST—that the *Algonquin* was destroyed without warning.
>
> SECOND—that the first report that the submarine made no effort to save or assist the passengers to safety.
>
> In the absence of any official statement from the White House or the State Department, the unofficial view is that in the arming of American ships and the establishment of an armed neutrality the American government has already met this action by Germany, as far as it is possible to do so this side of an actual declaration of war.[31]

Graves went on to observe that the sinking of the *Algonquin* was "more nearly the overt act" than the attacks on *Housatonic* or *Lyman M. Law*. Even so, he reported, it seemed the loss of the ship would "not lead to immediate developments in the situation between the United States and Germany."[32]

The official leaks to the press reflected the fact that the *Algonquin*, although not warned, did not quite fit the definition of an overt act. Most significantly, as demonstrated in the *Pass of Balmaha* case, Germany was not about to recognize a transfer from British registry to American registry that took place after the war had begun. State Department spokesmen, shippers, and reporters all knew that the British, French, and German governments regarded such transfers as evasions, unless proven otherwise. Article 56 of the Declaration of London was explicit in treating such transfers as spurious: "The transfer of an enemy vessel to a neutral flag effected after the outbreak of hostilities, is void unless it is proved that such transfer was not made in order to evade the consequences to which an enemy vessel, as such is exposed."[33]

The United States had only sought to defend the rights of ships transferred to the American flag, if the ship had been previously owned by an American firm, as in the case of Standard Oil ships transferred from Germany. Even in those cases, the British noted that the firm, Deutsche Amerikanische Petroleum Gesellschaft (DAPG), was incorporated in Germany, despite American protests that it was wholly owned by Standard Oil of New Jersey.[34]

The British-built *Algonquin* had been transferred more than two years *after* the war began. It would have been difficult, if not impossible, to demonstrate that the ship was truly a neutral ship, if looked at strictly in terms of prevailing international law as interpreted by the European naval powers. The quick transfers of ownership just as the ship sailed suggested that Wotherspoon, then Stephanidis and Benas had acquired title as a speculation, perhaps in the hope of collecting insurance, or at the very least, making a good profit on the supplies in dire need in Britain.

As the incident with the *Pass of Balmaha* had demonstrated, the United States was not in a good position to claim that an attack on a ship transferred in flag and in ownership just before its current voyage, was an offense against the United States, no matter the nationalities of the crew. The transfer of the ship, in the language of Article 56 of the Declaration of London, had clearly been to avoid the consequences of its belligerent status. Lansing, who watched all such developments closely, did not list the loss of the *Algonquin* as an attack on the American flag.[35] The loss of *Algonquin* would not be the overt act.

Meanwhile in Mogilev

Three days after the sinking of the *Algonquin*, in Russia, Czar Nicholas II reluctantly took the advice of members of the Duma, and signed an abdication while at his military headquarters in Mogilev. Dated March 2 under the old-style calendar still in effect in Russia, the date was Thursday, March 15, in western Europe and the United States. To many Americans, the abdication of the czar in favor of a government chosen by an electoral process seemed to represent a fundamental shift. Suddenly, one might be able to claim that all the major Allies were democracies, while the Central powers were autocracies.

On closer examination, the alignment of democracies versus autocracies might not have seemed quite so clear-cut. The Central powers—Germany, Austria-Hungary, Bulgaria, and the Ottoman Empire—although formally monarchies with parliamentary systems, were all widely viewed as autocracies in the United States. Considering the degree to which the military had taken over administration in those nations, calling them autocracies was fair enough. For the purpose of making the distinction, it was convenient to avoid recognizing that several of the Allies even after the conversion of Russia to "democracy," especially Japan and Serbia, were monarchies dominated by autocratic, intensely nationalistic military regimes. Despite such quibbles, for those who saw the war as a clash between types of regimes, the movement of Russia from autocratic monarchy to an elected provisional government seemed highly significant. In March 1917, no one in the United States could foresee that within a year, Russia would be transformed into a harsh dictatorship under the Bolsheviks, descend into civil war, and withdraw from the war. Of course, the change of status of one of the belligerents from autocracy to apparent democracy was not a casus belli, but like the Zimmermann Telegram, the several American flagged ships lost already, and the continuing loss of American lives aboard belligerent ships, it was part of the context of events nudging the balance of opinion from neutrality toward war.

The events of the next weekend, however, provided the overt acts and the tipping point.

8

The Tipping-Point Ships

Vigilancia, City of Memphis, Illinois

From Friday, March 16, 1917, through Sunday, March 18, 1917, three more U.S.-registered ships were sunk by German submarines. The news of the three losses arrived in the United States on Sunday and was widely published on Monday, March 19. *Vigilancia* was sunk at ten in the morning on the 16th, the *City of Memphis* on the 17th, and the *Illinois* was sunk on the 18th.[1]

The details of these ship losses explain why the three events together constituted the long-awaited set of overt acts, and constituted the tipping point in the decision for war. The facts make it clear why they were different from all the others that had preceded them that had *not* brought the United States into war. The group, *Vigilancia, City of Memphis,* and *Illinois* were American-registered ships carrying the United States flag, in contrast to the passenger liners *Falaba, Lusitania, Arabic, Sussex,* and *Laconia*. More than 130 Americans had died aboard those four ships, but the United States had not gone to war over those incidents. The three tipping-point ships of March 16 to March 18 also stood in contrast to *Armenian, Eavestone, Marina,* and about six other Allied-registered freighters on which some 45 American crew members or mule tenders had been killed. Again, in those cases, the ships flew the flags of belligerent nations, and the loss of American lives, while of concern and an affront, had not been an attack on American sovereignty at sea.[2]

Furthermore, a close review of *Vigilancia, City of Memphis,* and *Illinois* shows that they also stood in contrast to the loss of American ships before February 1, 1917, namely *William P. Frye, Gulflight, Nebraskan, Pass of Balmaha, Leelanaw, Chemung,* and *Columbian,* none of which constituted a casus belli. An even finer point is that the three tipping-point incidents of March 16 to March 18 also varied in their particulars from the three that had already occurred during the period of unrestricted submarine warfare following February 1, 1917: *Housatonic, Lyman M. Law,* and *Algonquin.*

Understanding those differences is essential to understanding why the United States did *not* go to war over any of the prior ship losses, and why Wilson and his cabinet *did* decide for war after the news came in on March 19. Although Wilson and his cabinet could not declare war, as that was the prerogative of Congress, the cabinet could advise the president, and the president could request Congress to make the declaration. Thus, what the president and the cabinet knew and when they knew it turned out to be very crucial indeed.

Vigilancia

The 4,115-gross-ton *Vigilancia* had been built in 1890 in Chester, Pennsylvania, by the Delaware River International Ship Building and Engine Works. It had been built for and operated by the American-owned Ward Line, engaged in passenger and freight service between New York and Cuban ports, then sold in 1915 to engage in the cotton trade with Germany. In early 1916, the ship was purchased by Gaston, Williams & Wigmore, Inc.[3]

At the beginning of the war in 1914, Gaston, Williams & Wigmore, Inc., with connections in Canada, had set up business in New York to act as a purchasing agent for the British government, and in February 1916 had expanded by purchasing ships in which to export the goods. The Canadian branch, Gaston, Williams and Wigmore, Ltd., was organized to operate ships flying the British and Canadian flags, while the American branch would operate ships under American registry. Two of the ships that the American office of Gaston, Williams & Wigmore, Inc., bought had been registered abroad, including the *Lord Duffer* (Canadian) and the *Okasan* (Russian). However, the *Vigilancia* and some of the other ships of the company fleet were American-built and had been in American ownership for years. The *Vigilancia* and the other U.S.-registered ships of the company were operated by Globe Steamship Company, a wholly-owned subsidiary of Gaston, Williams & Wigmore, Inc.[4]

George Gaston, who had been president of the Ashtabula Steamship Company at the outbreak of the war in 1914, had interested Charles Sabin, of the J. P. Morgan affiliate Guaranty Trust Company, in getting orders for trucks from the Allies. Between August 1914 and April 1916, he had built the business very rapidly. In 1915, the company did over $47 million in gross, with net profits about $4.8 million. Considering the value of the dollar in that period, such figures represented a major enterprise. The company became the exclusive agency in Britain for Packard, Locomobile, Pierce, and Jeffery automobiles. Other goods shipped to the Allies in 1915 included 100,000 tons of railway supplies, including 450 locomotives to Russia, and $10 million worth of assorted goods including shoes, typewriters, cotton goods, and machinery to other Allies. The company was closely tied to Guaranty Trust Company, which owned $5 million in shares of Gaston, Williams, & Wigmore, Inc. The chairman of the Board of Directors of Gaston, Williams & Wigmore, Inc., was Charles H. Sabin, who was also president of Guaranty Trust Company.[5]

Gaston, Williams & Wigmore, Inc., developed a worldwide network of related firms very quickly, and one of their major lines of business was the export of automobiles and auto parts from the United States to other countries. The company had offices in London, Paris, Rome, and Havana. The company also established an office in the Far East. The American shipping branch, the Globe Steamship Company or Globe Line, was set up to carry freight to "Archangel, Vladivostok, London, France, Spain, Portugal, Cape Town, and other ports," said George Gaston, who served as head of the purchasing agency as well as president of the shipping company.[6]

Gaston, Williams & Wigmore's *Vigilancia* departed for Havre, France, from New York, on February 28, 1917, after signing on a full crew at Wilmington, Delaware. The sailing had been delayed three days by an impromptu strike, during which the crew demanded a 75 percent bonus on top of their regular wages for traveling through the war zone. The demand was compromised at a 50 percent bonus, and the crew agreed to sail, with a mixed cargo, containing some provisions, valued at between $750,000 and $1 million. Besides provisions, the cargo included machinery, steel rails, and railroad equipment. The captain was instructed to proceed via the Azores to stop for coal if needed. As a demonstration of the ship's nationality, the ship flew a large illuminated American flag and had its name and a large American flag painted on both sides, quite a common practice by this time.[7]

Captain Frank A. Middleton supervised a crew of forty-five men of a variety of nationalities. Including himself, nineteen were American citizens, including two from Scandinavia who had been naturalized and four from Puerto Rico whose American citizenship was established by act of Congress on March 2, 1917, two days after the ship left port. A Canadian aboard had taken out naturalization papers. There were at least five men from Spain, two from Greece, and one each from Peru and Venezuela. Others whose nationalities were not noted in news reports had surnames suggesting Greek, Scandinavian, Spanish, or Spanish American national identity.[8]

It was ten in the morning on Friday, March 16, in clear weather 150 miles west of the southwest tip of Britain, when the *Vigilancia* was stuck by a torpedo on the starboard side, near the No. 3 hatch. The torpedo was fired by *U-70*, under the command of Otto Wünsche.[9] Another torpedo, observed by some aboard, had just passed behind the ship. After the detonation near No. 3 hatch, the ship foundered very rapidly, in seven to ten minutes. The engineer was unable to shut off the engines, and the ship continued to plow ahead, going down under way, bow first. Middleton had four lifeboats quickly lowered into the water, but in the swell and with the forward motion of the ship, twenty-five men were capsized into the water from two of the boats. Nine were quickly pulled out, but fifteen drowned, and one, assistant engineer Walter Scott, swam an estimated mile to one of the drifting lifeboats before being hauled to safety. The survivors began navigating the 150 miles toward the Isles of Scilly, rowing and sailing for two days.[10]

During the night, as they held flares aloft to provide warmth, and in the hope of attracting a rescue vessel, survivors thought they spotted the submarine trailing them. They assumed the U-boat was hoping their flares would attract another ship that could be sunk. The lifeboats arrived at the Isles of Scilly on Sunday, March 18.[11]

News accounts of the deaths from *Vigilancia* and the names of the survivors varied in accuracy and detail, but a close reading revealed that among the fifteen dead were two officers: third mate Neils P. North (naturalized American citizen born in Denmark); and third engineer Carl Aderholde, also an American citizen; and four other Americans: carpenter F. Brown; quartermaster J. Siberia (possibly "Loeria"); mess boy Estphan Lopez; and oiler Alexander Rodriquez. The *New York Times* and other newspapers reported five Americans killed, not including Alexander Rodriquez, as Puerto Rican. The nine others who died were Julio Montera from Peru and T. Rondon from Venezuela; A. Galitos and E. Dmitrios from Greece, and Joseph Livio, G. S. Sparrow, Juan Nesz, M. Vasquez, and R. Gonzales from Spain.[12]

Several aspects of this incident clearly set it apart from the ship losses that had preceded it. Despite the fact that the Globe Line and its owner, Gaston, Williams & Wigmore, Inc., were closely associated with the British war effort, the ship herself was American-built, American-owned, and American-registered. It had never transferred from another registry, as had the *Pass of Balmaha* and the *Algonquin*, nor was it in the process of transfer to another flag, as *Lanao* had been. Unlike *Gulflight* and *Nebraskan*, the attack was intentional against a ship that was very clearly marked with the U.S. flag. Unlike *Frye, Leelanaw, Chemung, Columbian, Housatonic,* and *Ly-*

man M. Law, the cargo and ship papers were never examined, but instead, the ship was torpedoed without any warning whatsoever and with no concern with the nature of the cargo. The cargo was contraband by the German definition, but Otto Wünsche had no way of knowing that.

Perhaps most importantly from an emotional point of view, *Vigilancia* was the first American ship ever intentionally sunk by Germany on which there were any fatalities at all. That six of those fatalities were American was noteworthy, even though they were commonly reported as five. By itself, the sinking of *Vigilancia* constituted, in the definition that had been narrowed down and established by precedent, an overt act of war by Germany against the United States, whether or not there had been any fatalities at all. The deaths of the men, however, made the event not only more shocking, they added to the affront. The lives of the men aboard, both American and foreign, had been under the protection of the American flag. Even if all those killed had been noncitizens of the United States, or even if all aboard had survived, the sinking of a ship flying the American flag was a casus belli.

The fact that the fatalities occurred from an accidental swamping of the lifeboats during the evacuation did not diminish the affront to American sovereignty at sea. Almost all fatalities from submarine attacks on merchant vessels came, not from the explosion of the torpedo or shelling of a ship, but from drowning during or after the ship sinking. Nearly all the 1,198 deaths on the *Lusitania* had been from drowning, and most of the deaths from *Laconia* had been from one lifeboat that was swamped. Furthermore, in the case of the *Vigilancia*, because the ship had been torpedoed without warning, the great haste in evacuating, with the ship under way, had directly contributed to the deaths of the seamen. Thus the deaths, although apparently somewhat accidental, were clearly the result of the decision to attack without warning.

German diplomatic notes over 1915 and 1916 had often stressed the compliance of German submarine commanders with the Declaration of London. Article 50 of that Declaration clearly stated that an unarmed merchant ship would not be sunk by a warship until all the crew and passengers had been "placed in safety." *Vigilancia* demonstrated that Otto Wünsche interpreted ruthless submarine warfare to mean that he need no longer adhere to several provisions of the Declaration of London, including warning, safety of those aboard, and inspection of papers and cargo. Wünsche sank at least thirteen ships during his brief cruise in February and March 1917. He went on to sink another ship, the British steamer, *Norma Pratt*, on the same day as *Vigilancia*.[13]

News of the loss of *Vigilancia* arrived almost simultaneously with the news of the loss of the other two American-flag vessels on the weekend, resulting in news stories covering all three together on Monday, March 19.

City of Memphis

Compared to some of the other American-registered ships sunk up to this date, *City of Memphis* was a relatively new ship. Built in 1902 in Chester, Pennsylvania, by John Roach, it remained in the coastwise trade, mostly in cotton. It was owned by the Savannah Line, founded in 1873, also known as Ocean Steamship Company, which regularly operated a freight service between Savannah, Boston, New York, and Caribbean ports. The *City of Memphis*, at 5,225 tons, and with a double hull, was larger than the older "City" ships in the Savannah Line and represented the first of an effort to modernize the company. Several older ships had been sold off to help finance the construction and purchase of both *City of Memphis* and *City of Macon*, a "sister ship" of the *City of Memphis*. In 1907, E. H. Harriman purchased a controlling interest in the Central Georgia Railway that owned the Savannah Line, but he sold his interest to the Illinois Central Railway before his death in 1909.[14]

In 1914, *City of Memphis* was chartered by the U.S. government during the Tampico crisis with Mexico, and used to transport supplies from Galveston to Vera Cruz in Mexico. The significance of the American flag in the period had been clearly demonstrated when the Tampico incident occurred because Mexican forces in that port failed to properly salute the U.S. flag aboard a warship. The symbolism of the flag was further noted when a German freighter fired a salute from a brass signal gun mounted on the deck to the American-flagged *City of Memphis* as that ship departed Boston on the 1914 mission to Galveston and Veracruz.[15]

As the ship completed its charter for the government in December 1914, the *City of Memphis*, under Captain Lewis P. Borum, was loaded with cotton and sailed for Germany during the brief period when Germany was able to import cotton from the United States. *City of Memphis* sailed with its hatches sealed to ensure that nothing besides cotton had been loaded in a Gulf of Mexico port in January 1915. Unaware that the Weser River was mined, Borum took the *City of Memphis* into the port of Bremerhaven, earning a rebuke from the local authorities for not getting a pilot aboard.[16]

In common with other ships of the Savannah Line, *City of Memphis* continued trade with both sides and with other neutrals during American pe-

Figure 15. *City of Memphis*. Before the outbreak of war, *City of Memphis* had carried passengers and freight on regular runs to the Caribbean for the Savannah Line. It was sunk without warning on March 17, 1917. The crew all survived, although for several days, they were feared lost. (Reprinted with permission from Mariners' Museum, Newport News, Va.)

riod of neutrality in the war, with five trips to Italy, one to Rotterdam, and three to France. Several of the trips to Italy had been to deliver horses for war use. During one of the trips to Italy, Borum took on a charter from a Philadelphia company to steam to Scalanova, Turkey, to pick up a cargo of licorice. Since Turkey was a Germany ally, the voyage entailed its own special risks. Escorted by British and French warships into the harbor of Scalanova, he had to withdraw while the ships bombarded the town. He then returned, entertained the local authorities, picked up the licorice, and sailed out during a second bombardment, during which the Allied gunfire slightly damaged *City of Memphis*. Captain Borum earned quite a reputation for fearlessness after these adventures.[17]

On the voyage in 1917, the *City of Memphis* had American flags painted on either side, with the name of the ship in six-foot letters, illuminated with lights and reflectors at night. The officers of the ship were all U.S. citizens, either native-born or naturalized. The Savannah Line had made sure that every officer aboard had an American license, and that any naturalized citizen carried his naturalization papers. The crew of fifty-seven or fifty-eight (the reports varied) included twenty-five Americans, found among the galley and mess staff as well as the officers. Most of the able-bodied seamen were

Danish, while the coal-passers and firemen were Hispanic. The ship sailed from New York on January 23, with a load of more than nine thousand bales of cotton. On January 30, off the Isles of Scilly, the ship was hailed by a German submarine. This encounter, it will be remembered, was one day before Germany announced the unrestricted submarine warfare policy.[18]

When a mate from *City of Memphis* went aboard the sub with the ship's papers in that encounter, the German commander informed him that, since the ship carried contraband, it should be sunk. However, since the two countries were on friendly terms, he released the ship with an ominous warning: if caught again, it would be sunk without warning. The German commander no doubt realized that unrestricted warfare was to begin on February 1. *City of Memphis* proceeded and safely delivered the cotton cargo at Havre, France.

After leaving Havre, the *City of Memphis* returned to British waters, directly through the war zone, and put in at Cardiff in Wales to load bunker coal for the passage to New York. The ship departed Cardiff with no cargo ("in ballast") on Friday, March 16, the same day that *Vigilancia* was torpedoed. At four in the afternoon of March 17, steaming west, it was accosted about thirty-five miles south of Fastnet by *UC-66*, under Herbert Pustkuchen. He was the same officer who, in command of *UB-29*, had torpedoed *Sussex* almost exactly a year before, on March 24, 1916, precipitating Wilson's threat to break off diplomatic relations with Germany. Pustkuchen, ironically enough, was less "ruthless" during the sinking of *City of Memphis* in 1917 than he had been in the attack on *Sussex* in 1916.[19]

From a distance estimated at three miles, Pustkuchen fired a gunshot and signaled Borum with flags "AB," which meant "abandon ship," and then approached and fired another shot to hurry along the process. As the sub neared the ship, the flag signals could be made out clearly, and Borum ordered a long blast on the whistle, indicating "order understood." Quickly, the crew scrambled into four lifeboats, and Borum signaled with four blasts, indicating "crew in boats." Then *UC-66* approached the freighter, and with the sub's decks awash, fired the deck gun at point-blank range, with eight to twelve shots. The American freighter went down, stern first, after twenty-five minutes.[20]

Pustkuchen went from lifeboat to lifeboat in search of the freighter's captain. An interview from submarine to lifeboat with a ship's officer had become a common practice to get further information for the official report. The lifeboats were separated, and two of them were picked up at sea on Sunday morning by a British Admiralty vessel, about eleven hours after

City of Memphis went down, with thirty-four of the survivors. Another lifeboat, with fifteen aboard, landed at the port of Schull in Ireland at seven in the evening on Sunday, March 18. The survivors from the British ship and those from Schull were taken to Queenstown, Ireland, where they were turned over to U.S. consul Arthur C. Frost. Consul Frost had overseen the care and handling of American survivors of *Lusitania*, and knew the importance of detailed reporting. Frost immediately wired the State Department of the safe arrival of the known survivors. Altogether, Frost could account for forty-nine of the crew, but nine—including Captain Borum—were still missing.[21]

The separation of the lifeboats and the distribution of the survivors among them led to some confusing reports in the American press. Considering the interest of relatives in the United States in the fate of the merchant mariners, newspapers tried to determine where exactly the survivors landed, whether all had been accounted for, and whether all the American citizens aboard had reached safety. In some of the shorter news accounts, the surviving Americans were identified by name, while those of foreign citizenship were not.

When Borum's lifeboat was found empty, with a tin containing the ship's papers stowed under one of the seats, speculation mounted as to whether he and those with him had been rescued, had fallen overboard, or had been captured by the submarine. Some merchant ship masters had been taken as prisoners aboard submarines in the past (as in the case of Captain Curtis of *Columbian*), and it seemed possible that Borum had been seized.[22] Doctor Robert Shea, the ship's surgeon, told newspaper reporters: "Captain Borum's boat got separated from us in the darkness. I know the occupants hailed a rescue ship, but they were mistaken for fishermen and left to their fate."[23]

The adventures of Borum and those of the crew in his lifeboat were cleared up on Wednesday, March 21, when they arrived in Glasgow, Scotland, having been picked up by another freighter. That news arrived at the State Department on March 21, and was published in the United States on Thursday, March 22. Relatives of the survivors in Borum's boat were relieved to learn that the missing men were safe. In addition to Borum, they were H. O. Bevill, N. P. Clausen, Charles Walker, David Jackson, Fred Prutting, S. Ludvigsen, Manuel Lopez, and Manuel Barbrito.[24]

Some news stories regarding the sinking of *City of Memphis* were carried in the same item with accounts of the loss of *Vigilancia*, sometimes with headlines implying greater loss of life than in fact had occurred. Further sensational aspects included the fact that Pustkuchen reportedly refused to aid the lifeboats, and the fact that Borum and his crew members were not reported safe until nearly four days after the sinking. Thus, between March 19, when the first headlines appeared, and March 22, after word of the safe arrival of Borum in Scotland flashed across the undersea cables, it appeared quite possible that a total of twenty-four men had been lost—the fifteen aboard *Vigilancia*, and the nine in the missing lifeboat from *City of Memphis*.

Only a close reading of the accounts would reveal the degree to which Pustkuchen had varied from cruiser rules. In conformity with the rules, he had warned the ship with gunshots and signals, and had provided time for the crew to evacuate. They had done so, and Borum had saved the ship's papers, as appropriate, although he apparently forgot them in a biscuit tin under the lifeboat seat when rescued by the passing freighter. There had been no casualties. On the other hand, Pustkuchen made no effort to determine the cargo of the ship. The fact that the ship was empty of all cargo and was in ballast meant that as a neutral ship, it should have been immune from destruction under cruiser rules, as it was not carrying contraband. Although the crew all survived, Pustkuchen had made no direct effort to ensure their safety. Thus, in these less dramatic ways, Pustkuchen demonstrated that the Declaration of London no longer governed German U-boat practices. Some later assertions that the ship had been sunk without warning were incorrect, although the fact there was no contraband, nor even any cargo aboard, meant that the submarine had not followed Declaration of London rules.

These finer points of law, while noted by some observers, were hardly as important to most of the public than the more sensational facts. Those were that the ship loss came almost simultaneously with the *Vigilancia* tragedy, it was covered in the same news accounts with that loss, and that for several days, it seemed that Borum and his crew had died as a result of the German attack. Those ominous aspects of the events were further driven home by the sinking of the third of the tipping-point ships, *Illinois*.

Illinois

The tanker *Illinois* was one of the growing fleet of tankers owned by Texaco, the Texas-based oil company that had burgeoned into a major producer of crude oil and petroleum products in the first decade of the twentieth century. The oil company, founded in the 1890s, got a boost with a spectacular oil gusher in 1901, at Spindle Top, Texas. With another find at Sour Lake, a health resort, in January 1903, the company was well on its way. By 1913, the Texas company's assets were about $60 million. By the end of the war, with the increase in demand for petroleum from the war and from the beginning of the automobile age, the company had quadrupled its assets. The Texaco fleet of tankers, started before the war, was expanded in 1913, with the completion of the 5,225-ton tanker *Illinois* in Newport News. The tanker had been built to order for the company beginning in 1912 and launched in 1913. Only four years old in 1917, *Illinois* was by far the newest of the American ships sunk by Germany in this period.[25]

Under the command of Captain H. Iverson, *Illinois* left Port Arthur, Texas, on February 17, headed for London with a cargo of oil. The officers and eight of the crew were American citizens, for a total of sixteen out of the total crew of thirty-two. The other sixteen were five Russians, three Spaniards, and two each from Sweden, Denmark, Norway and Britain. After unloading the cargo in London, *Illinois* sailed out on its return trip for Port Arthur on Friday March 16, at 7:45 a.m., a couple of hours before the *Vigilancia* attack.[26]

Captain Iverson stated that the tanker was sunk on Sunday March 18, a date confirmed in the German records.[27] In the southern reaches of the English Channel, north of the Channel Island of Alderney, Iverson spotted a submarine, *UC-21*, commanded by Reinhold Saltzwedel, bearing down from the southwest, about three miles off. The submarine then submerged and came closer. At about two miles off, the sub opened fire. After backing the engines for two minutes, W. Osenber, chief engineer of *Illinois*, brought the ship to a stop. The second shot from the submarine knocked down the wireless antenna. After all the crew had gotten into lifeboats, the submarine approached one of them, and Saltzwedel ordered five of the men out onto the deck of the U-boat. He then put five of his own crew in the lifeboat. The boat pulled for the ship, and the German sailors placed some fourteen bombs "alongside the ship and in the engine room," according to Iverson. He believed the bombs were timed for seven minutes.[28]

The ship sank bow first, but some 150 feet of the stern remained above water. The Germans photographed the ship in a sinking position, with the ship's name and painted American flags still visible, and the photograph was widely reproduced in Germany as proof of the success against American ships.[29] According to later reports, a British destroyer came along the next day and fired on the hulk, sinking the vessel on March 19.[30]

After the tanker men were put back in the lifeboat, Iverson asked for a tow toward land, but Saltzwedel replied, "I have no time." Setting the lifeboat sails, the survivors then began sailing and rowing toward Alderney.

Figure 16. *Illinois* sinking. As the *Illinois* was sinking, its picture was taken from the deck of *UC-21*, and the image was later published in Germany as evidence of the success of the unrestricted submarine campaign. Together with *Vigilancia* and *City of Memphis*, the loss of three ships convinced even the doves in Wilson's cabinet to support a declaration of war. (Reprinted with permission from Mariners' Museum, Newport News, Va.)

When they got within ten miles of the island, they were taken in tow by two motorboats. They arrived on shore six and a half hours after the shelling of their ship began.

Iverson pointed out that the commander of the submarine had taken no measures for the safety of the crew, and that the submarine guns had fired continuously as the crew got into the boats. One man was injured by fragments from the shells. Iverson also noted that the submarine did not show a flag when first observed.[31] Although the crew were all safe, the attack, like that on *City of Memphis*, further demonstrated that "ruthless"— that is, unrestricted—submarine warfare had indeed begun.

Although news stories about the three ship losses contained some exaggerations and errors, on the whole, the accounts did convey the facts, and on close reading, showed how the attacks represented a new German submarine policy. The distinctions between the sinking of *Vigilancia*, *City of Memphis*, and *Illinois*, and the sinking of all the ships that preceded them become even more clear when examined dispassionately from a distance of nearly a century.

But at the time, it was extremely difficult for most readers of the press to follow the reasoning that would treat the deaths of *Vigilancia* crew and the three ship losses as more significant than the deaths of the women and children passengers aboard *Lusitania*, or the loss of the more than ten American flag vessels that had been sunk before. Even though the distinctions in policy were not entirely obvious, the ways in which the news reached the American public, the cabinet, and the president added to the picture of a suddenly enhanced and more ruthless form of warfare. Some news stories combined the details of the three separate incidents into a single, detailed report, creating the impression of a suddenly increased intensity of attacks on American ships. The fact that the news of three ships sinking came at once contributed to the sense that the awaited "overt acts" were occurring regularly. On March 19, no one knew but that three or more ships would be sunk later in the week, which would seem quite possible if the rate of sinking continued at the new pace.

Other aspects of the incidents had both legal and emotional significance. All the ships were U.S. registered, all had been built in the United States, and none had ever been registered abroad. All were officered and partly staffed by American citizens. In the case of the *Vigilancia*, there had been no warning. The *City of Memphis* was warned and its crew given a few minutes to evacuate, but the crew of the tanker *Illinois* got into the lifeboats under fire. All seamen aboard the second two ships survived the attacks, but both of those ships had been in ballast—that is, neither was carrying a contraband cargo, and there had been no effort on the part of the German submarine officers to determine the nature of their trade. They were simply sunk for being in the declared war zone. As the public anxiously awaited the fate of Captain Borum and the eight sailors in his lifeboat between March 19 and March 22, it certainly seemed apparent that Germany had begun a war on America at sea.

It was not incidental that these three ships were owned by major, well-established American corporations. Gaston, Williams & Wigmore, Inc., funded by the J. P. Morgan subsidiary Guaranty Trust, operated *Vigilancia* through their Globe Line. The long-established Savannah Line, now under the control of the Illinois Central Railway, ran the *City of Memphis*. E. H. Harriman's son, W. Averell Harriman, inherited his father's interests in Illinois Central and other rail lines, and owned a controlling interest in the American-Hawaiian Line (whose ships were also exposed to attack through this period) as well as the Savannah Line. The rapidly expanding major producing and refining oil company Texaco owned and operated *Illinois*.[32]

By contrast, the first three American flag ships earlier destroyed after the announcement of unrestricted submarine warfare had all been owned by small, independent firms. The German-built *Housatonic* was operated by a one-ship company; *Lyman M. Law* by a traditional New England joint stock company common in the schooner business, which had just acquired the ship from a similar New England company; *Algonquin*, a former lake steamer, had been transferred immediately before and after sailing to what appear to have been shipping speculators taking on a clear risk in the hope of a quick profit. The owners of that ship, like the other two companies, were not the operators of a regular ocean transport line or major corporate fleet.

Although larger American firms had at first hesitated to send their vessels into the war zone, several factors appear to have been at work to convince executives of the Globe Line, the Savannah Line, and Texaco to take the risk to send these newer and more valuable ships through the war zone by mid-March. *City of Memphis* had departed on January 23 for Havre, before the announced change in German submarine policy. It began its return voyage on March 16, after the arrival of several American ships safely in France, and after *Housatonic*, *Lyman M. Law*, and *Algonquin* had all been evacuated before being sunk. Even though Captain Borum had received a friendly warning on the trip from Savannah to Havre by a submarine off Britain, with his reputation as an experienced blockade runner, the risks no doubt seemed acceptable.

When *Illinois* departed Port Arthur on February 17, and *Vigilancia* left New York on February 28, only *Housatonic* and *Lyman M. Law* had encountered submarines under the new unrestricted warfare policy, and both of them had been warned and safely evacuated. The fact that Hans Rose had graciously towed the crew of *Housatonic* toward the Isles of Scilly in a widely published account may have been on the mind of Captain Iverson when he asked Reinhold Saltzwedel to tow the *Illinois* boats towards Alderney. Iverson and Texaco executives had a chance to read about both the *Housatonic* and *Lyman M. Law* incidents before the *Illinois* departure from Port Arthur. Certainly the treatment of the crews of *Columbian* and *Chemung*, who had returned to United States a few weeks earlier, in January 1917, testified to the prior careful and relatively humane treatment of merchant mariners by the German U-boat crews. The three tipping-point ships, all owned by large American corporations, had been dispatched through the war zone with apparently the same faith in German good behavior that dominated the thinking of the president. Of course, it would have been a good line of argument for those opposing the war on the grounds that it was being fought for the interests of capital if contemporaries had taken the time to note that the three ship losses most prominently affecting the decision to go to war were all owned and operated by major, modern U.S. corporations. However, even the committed Marxists of the era, like other politicians, tended to argue on the plane of generalities, and not seek specific evidence for their arguments in the mundane and detailed facts of ship-owning.

On Monday morning, March 19, one of the first orders of business for the day for Lansing was to discuss the sinking of the three ships with his advisor, Frank Polk. Wilson's secretary, Joseph Tumulty, called Lansing about the possibility of summoning Congress to meet early to discuss the new crisis. But when Lansing went to see the president later in the morning, between 11:10 and noon, Lansing noted in his diary that Wilson "opposes action now." That evening, between 11:00 p.m. and 1:00 a.m., Lansing wrote a long letter to the president on the "advantages of entering the war *now*."[33]

Cabinet, March 20, 1917

When Wilson convened his cabinet on Tuesday, March 20, the only confirmed loss of life from attacks on U.S. ships since the German declaration on January 31 had been from the swamped *Vigilancia*'s lifeboats and the loss of the fifteen men, including the six Americans. Secretary of State Lansing noted in his memoirs, regarding the *Vigilancia, City of Memphis,* and *Illinois,* that "there could be no question but that the three sinkings manifestly constituted 'actual overt acts,' which Mr. Wilson had emphasized in his address announcing the severance of diplomatic relations."[34] In this statement, he agreed with the overwhelming judgment of the press. As it turned out, even the doves in the cabinet agreed that the overt acts had finally occurred.

Lansing, who had a good knowledge of the mind of Woodrow Wilson, understood that Wilson did not like facts to alter his preconceived notion of correct policy, and that he would find this episode very disturbing. When the cabinet met and unanimously agreed that a state of war existed on that Tuesday, March 20, the loss of the three ships was at the core of the crisis. From the records left by the participants, it appears that no one raised the specific point that six Americans had died. Secretary of State Robert

Lansing, Secretary of Agriculture David F. Houston, Secretary of Interior Franklin K. Lane, and others recorded the substance and specific content of the cabinet discussion, and their accounts substantiate each other. Although the *Vigilancia* and the other two ships were not mentioned in their notes, it was clear from the discussion that the death of American seamen aboard an American-flagged and the attacks on the other two ships were the events that had changed the minds of even the most convinced neutralists in the cabinet, Secretary of the Navy Josephus Daniels and Postmaster General Albert Burleson. But the ship names and the exact numbers of casualties were not mentioned.[35]

The meeting faced a crisis because, as Lansing had said, Germany had finally committed the overt acts that they had all anticipated or dreaded. All of the memoirists describing the cabinet meeting saw the March 20 meeting as momentous, and as convened in the atmosphere of a crisis that had reached a head. Wilson listened to their opinions respectfully, as each remarked that now the United States and Germany were in a state of war, but Wilson kept his own views to himself. The next day, March 21, Wilson decided to convene Congress at the earliest practical date, April 2. In the statement calling Congress to convene, Wilson did not reveal his intentions, but stated only that he wanted Congress to consider the serious situation that had arisen. Over the next few days, he would struggle with the question of exactly what to say to Congress.

9

The Agony of Woodrow Wilson

Although it is clear that the cabinet was convinced at their meeting on March 20, 1917, that a declaration of war was needed, the second party to the decision process for war in 1917, the president, presented a far more enigmatic response to his associates and to the press. Wilson left no memoir of his time in office, nor any personal diary or daily account. The memoirs and notes of two of his closest advisors that might provide clues to his thought processes—his personal secretary, Joseph Tumulty, and his "minister without portfolio," Edward House—have both proven to be highly controversial. Both men appeared to be very impressed with themselves and their place in history, and their observations must be weighed very carefully to discount for self-aggrandizement and dramatization. For such reasons, among others, the nature and timing of Wilson's response to the ship losses has remained difficult to analyze.

Between March 20, the date of the cabinet meeting at which the members unanimously recommended that Wilson call Congress into session and ask for a declaration of war, and the time when he actually addressed Congress, Wilson studiously refrained from informing anyone, including his close advisors, of his decision. He concealed the timing and nature of his decision because he believed it was constitutionally improper to leak his intentions and have them printed in the press prior to informing Congress. As in the past with other important announcements, this legally and constitutionally very correct practice had the effect, which he may have cultivated, of heightening the drama of his presentation. It also had the effect of concealing from contemporaries and later researchers exactly when and how he made his own decision.

When Germany had announced the unrestricted submarine warfare policy in a note delivered by Ambassador Bernstorff on January 31, Wilson had not finalized his decision to break relations until the night of February 2–3, keeping Lansing and others on edge as they tried to interpret his conversations and remarks to find out whether he had made a decision. A very similar, but much more dramatic and drawn-out period of apparent indecision troubled Wilson's advisors between March 20 and March 30. Robert Lansing, Edward House, and William Gibbs McAdoo, who by this time all agreed that war with Germany was in fact already under way and that it should be declared, spoke with each other several times about Wilson's silence.

The actual date of his decision is a matter of some importance. If he decided for war by March 21, then the ship losses that convinced his cabinet to ask for war were also the losses that convinced him to follow their advice. However, if he did not decide for war until the following weekend, then his decision was informed by the loss of another ship, the *Healdton*, which was mistakenly believed to have been torpedoed by a German U-boat, but which, in fact, was lost to a British mine.

There were some indications—none of them very clear to his advisors—that Wilson was working through the decision process. Wilson did decide on March 21 to issue a proclamation convening Congress on April 2. He had earlier issued a proclamation convening the Senate on March 6, and that body had already acted to revise its rules regarding cloture. Wilson had already issued one proclamation convening both houses of Congress on April 16, but the March 21 proclamation, issued on the advice of the cabinet, superseded that earlier call and advanced the convening date to April 2. He could not address Congress until it met and organized, and the first opportunity would be on April 2 or April 3. As it turned out, Congress, despite some difficulties, organized quickly and was ready for him by 8:00 p.m. on April 2.[1]

A close review of the evidence helps narrow down when Wilson came to his decision, and exactly what facts he had at hand when thinking about what he would say. What he knew and when he knew it, although somewhat concealed from our view nearly a century later, can be inferred from several established facts.[2]

The president's preserved correspondence of the crucial period gives very little direct evidence of his thought process as he politely responded to petitioners and congratulations from friends and relatives who had either attended or missed his recent inauguration, and as he read through the gratuitous advice offered by advocates of peace or war.[3] From the mass of material that he collected from around the country in various repositories, diaries, and archives of official documents and put on deposit at Princeton, the historian Arthur Link culled out and reproduced about ninety documents covering the ten-day period, March 21 through March 30, in his multivolume edited collection, *The Wilson Papers*. A review of those published documents and the larger collection from which Link selected the documents does not firmly establish the exact day when Wilson decided for war. But documents in the broader collection and in the published volume help show what information he had at hand at the different stages of the decision process.

From the date of his inauguration (March 5) through about March 21, Wilson did not respond to routine correspondence, offering as an apology, when he got to the letters, the fact that he had suffered from a severe cold (the "grippe," as he called it) and that the press of events had prevented a more prompt response.[4] This correspondence and other sources indicate that Wilson was seriously ill from the cold he caught at the inauguration, and that he was bedridden for several days. Lansing visited the White House on March 12 and found the president in bed.[5] Despite his cold, as noted in the previous chapter, he attended the Tuesday, March 20, cabinet meeting that recommended an early call to Congress and a declaration of war, in response to the loss of *Vigilancia*, *City of Memphis*, and *Illinois* over the prior weekend. Then, on March 21 and 22, he busily responded with dozens of dictated short formal notes to the piled-up incidental correspondence. From other evidence, it appears he was in the pattern of using Thursdays to catch up with such letters in this period. Also on March 21, he issued Proclamation #1360, calling Congress into session to convene on April 2.

On the evening of March 22, at 7:30 p.m., Lansing received word from the Associated Press that the ESSO tanker *Healdton* had been lost. The cabinet met on Friday, March 23, for an hour and three-quarters, and the discussion apparently did not include the loss of that ship, but focused instead on drastic legislation by various departments to improve preparedness for war, should it be declared.[6] On the 24th, the *New York Times* and other papers carried detailed stories of the loss of *Healdton* and the suffering of the crew. Germany denied the ship had been torpedoed by a German submarine, and subsequent investigation shows that denial to have been correct. The ship was probably lost to a British mine, as detailed in appendix A. At the time however, the press, the State Department, and the president all assumed the ship had been lost to another German attack.

On Saturday, March 24, Wilson asked for and received from Secretary of the Navy Josephus Daniels materials explaining how the Navy would cooperate with the British in the event of war. Wilson's request also indicated that the communications should be done confidentially "until Congress acted." Also on Saturday, March 24, he signed an executive order increasing the enlistments in the Navy to eighty-seven thousand. From his note to Daniels

Figure 17. Colonel Edward House. Three days after hearing of the loss of the *Healdton*, Wilson told his close friend and informal advisor Edward House of his decision to seek a declaration of war with Germany. Wilson assumed the ship was lost to a German submarine. (Courtesy of Library of Congress.)

and his signing of the executive order expanding the Navy, it seems correct to infer that he had decided to ask for a declaration of war by that date, although there appears to be no direct evidence that he had decided for war by then, a view supported by prior analysts of Wilson's decision process.[7] Colonel House came to Washington and stayed at the White House that weekend. On Saturday, Lansing had a conference with Colonel House at noon, and then dinner with him at the Colony Club, with a large gathering.[8]

Wilson met with Colonel House on Tuesday, March 27, and asked House's opinion then as to whether he should ask Congress for a declaration of war or a declaration that a state of war existed. Despite problems with the accuracy of the House diary, there is no reason to doubt that Wilson did in fact ask that question on March 27. A further indication that Wilson had come around to favoring war by that time was a note in Lansing's diary for the day after the Tuesday, March 27, cabinet meeting, "Prest. evidently going strong." By Wednesday, March 28, Wilson wrote to Key Pittman that "my leadership will be very definite," a further indication that he had fully decided on asking for a declaration of war by midweek.[9] From these indications, it seems quite reasonable to conclude that Wilson had already decided to ask for a declaration of war (of one of the two sorts) by March 27, probably no earlier than March 21.[10]

The Silence of the President

In the newspapers, little word leaked of the presidential thought process between March 20 and March 30, although there were some interesting rumors. The press of course, was frantic to get any hint of what was going on. News stories carried rank speculation over exactly why even Wilson's closest advisors on the cabinet were so strangely reticent about his thinking.[11]

Newspapers that favored entry on the Allied side, like the *New York Times*, published several stories from Washington correspondents that hinted that Wilson had decided for war as early as March 22. Such accounts represented creative writing at its best, combining wishful thinking, rumors, and speculation about likely outcomes, along with scraps of facts. For example, on that date the *New York Times* carried a story pointing out that "All the records relating to the prosecution of Germany's ruthless submarine warfare since February 1 were carried to the White House this morning and the President dictated long passages in a tentative way." Information regarding the sinking of the Standard Oil tanker *Healdton* on the night of March 21 would not have been available that morning so the documents "carried" made a fairly light folder, including the consular reports on the survivors of six ships. The March 23 story about information sent to the president went on to speculate that the "extended consideration of the submarine records begun by the President confirms what had previously been expected—that he would lay before Congress, as a basis for its action, a full history of the more recent German outrages, with reference to former misdeeds." The report also suggested that the president would ask Congress to declare that a state of war existed since the date of "the recent sinking of three American ships."[12]

Wilson met with the cabinet on Friday, March 23, but newsmen were disappointed to learn that, although he was working on his address to Congress, he had not discussed it with cabinet members, and no leaks as to its themes were forthcoming. The *New York Times* noted that Wilson and his advisers were taking the attitude that it would be improper to indicate the war policy of the administration until Congress could be consulted. Again, reflecting a mix of leaks and guesswork, the Washington correspondent of the *New York Times* speculated that Wilson would not address the details of how the war was to be conducted, rather, he would be "devoting himself largely to a statement of principles." As it turned out, that guess was right on the mark. Knowing Wilson's style, it was not difficult to predict that his speech would be high-minded and based on principles, rather than presenting a litany of administrative details and specifics.[13]

Lansing suggested to Wilson on March 26 a memo to the press explaining the constitutional reasons why Wilson could not reveal his intentions. Lansing's proposed statement explained that since it was the right of Congress to make the decision, it would be improper for Wilson to attempt to bring pressure on Congress by making a prior announcement; the proposed press release would have explained the public silence during these few days. Wilson suggested to Lansing that such a statement would have indicated that the criticism of his inaction "was getting under my skin," and he rejected the idea of the press release on March 27. Despite the fact that the statement was not given out officially, the sentiment that it would be inappropriate constitutionally to be explicit about war plans had already been reflected in news items published on March 24, possibly as the result of unauthorized leaks from some members of Wilson's inner circle.[14]

All of these considerations about the period between March 20 and March 30 are pertinent to the larger issue of the relationship of ship losses to Wilson's decision, precisely because of the problematic nature of the sinking of *Healdton*, the seventh American-flagged ship lost since the declaration of unrestricted submarine warfare. The likelihood that it played at least some part in the president's decision makes the circumstances of that merchant ship incident particularly important.

The *Healdton* Mystery

It is certain that Wilson was aware of the loss of *Healdton* when he prepared the final draft of his speech because the final draft was not prepared until the weekend of March 31–April 1, after press reports detailed the loss and after Lansing provided Wilson with a memorandum listing *Healdton* among ships attacked by Germany.

The Standard Oil tanker *Healdton* had been built in 1908 by the Greenock and Grangemouth Dock Yard Company, in Greenock, Scotland, a seaport near Glasgow. The tanker, formerly known as *Pure Light*, was wholly owned by Standard Oil of New Jersey, home-ported in Bayonne, New Jersey. It had been owned before the war by the Pure Light Oil Company of Hamburg, and was one of several Standard Oil ships transferred from German companies to United States registry quite properly and legally early in the war. As *Healdton*, it had departed Philadelphia on January 26, 1917, carrying $2.15 million worth of petroleum, bound for Rotterdam. Under the command of Captain Charles Christopher, with a crew consisting of thirteen Americans and twenty-eight seamen of other nationalities, the 4,489-gross-ton tanker had an interrupted voyage. Standard Oil issued a call by wireless to all its tankers to return to a port after the German announcement of unrestricted submarine warfare, and *Healdton* put into Halifax, Nova Scotia, on February 9. At the beginning of March, Standard Oil released the ship and directed it to take the northern route to Bergen, Norway, before proceeding on to Rotterdam. Like Texaco, the Savannah Line, and the Gaston firm financed by Morgan, Standard Oil had decided to risk the trip. The tanker left Halifax on March 2 and called at Bergen on March 17. It departed Bergen for Rotterdam on March 20, steaming southward through the narrow neutral or safe zone in the North Sea between Britain and the European continent toward the Netherlands.[15]

The next night at 8:15 p.m., about twenty-five miles north by east of the Terschelling Light (according to the later report of Captain Christopher) on the approach to Rotterdam, the ship suffered two explosions. At the time, Christopher was certain that his ship had been hit with two torpedoes from a submerged submarine. The ship immediately caught fire, and flames from the tanker were so bright that distant fishermen thought they were observing the Northern Lights. Hastily, the crew evacuated, many of them still in their underwear, into the cold March night. One boat overturned, and counting those trapped on the ship, those who drowned, and those who died from exposure, there were twenty-one fatalities.

Among the dead were seven of the thirteen American citizens in the crew: W. Chandler, second mate, from Brooklyn; C. F. Hudgins, third mate, from Norfolk; Walter Johnson, third engineer, from Hoboken; E. Leveaux, oiler, from Hoboken (more probably Henry Lee Veaux, from Michigan, as reported in a later account); George Healey, second steward from San Francisco; R. W. Smith, able seaman from Chicago; and John Steiner, able seaman from Pittsburgh. After a twelve-hour night of suffering from both burns and cold, the survivors were picked up by two vessels, the fishing boat *Java*, and the Dutch torpedo boat *G-13*. They arrived on land on March 22, and reports of their ordeal reached the American consul by March 23. As already noted, the story of the sinking reached Lansing on the evening of the 22nd and was published in American newspapers on the 24th.[16]

Captain Christopher later claimed that he saw the conning tower of a

Figure 18. *Healdton*. Built in Scotland and launched as the *Pure Light*, the *Healdton*, a U.S.-registered Standard Oil tanker, sank on March 21, 1917, just as Wilson was deciding to convene Congress early. Germany denied sinking the ship, as it was probably lost by striking a British mine. (Reprinted with permission from the University of Glasgow Archives.)

submarine briefly surface as if surveying the damage. He saw no identifying marks on the submarine. He was surprised that the submarine did not approach and ask for papers or other information. Exactly what he saw, if anything, has never been clarified, and remains a mystery more than ninety years later.[17]

Although the American press reported the loss of the *Healdton* as another case of a loss to a U-boat, the German government denied that a German submarine had sunk the tanker. That denial in itself is significant, since the German authorities *always* confirmed losses to their submarines based on the logs of the submarine commanders. For this and other reasons, it appears that the tanker struck one or two mines and sank as a consequence. Later investigation of the event suggests that the loss may have been due to striking mines from a minefield laid two nights previously by the British. The detailed and somewhat contradictory evidence regarding the loss of *Healdton* is presented and evaluated in appendix A.

None of the minefield information was known to the public at the time, nor, to the best of the author's knowledge, has this explanation for the loss of the *Healdton* been published prior to his research into the topic. These facts raise the questions: Did Woodrow Wilson decide to go to war on the basis of erroneous information? Did the loss of an American ship destroyed by a British mine convince Wilson to go to war with Germany because he thought the loss was due to a German torpedo?

When considering these issues, it is well to remember that before *Healdton*'s loss, the cabinet had already recorded its unanimous recommendation for war. Wilson had already called Congress, even before the detonations that sank *Healdton*. Even if Wilson had been fully aware of all of the details of what actually happened to *Healdton*, he was in fact justified to ask for a declaration of war based on *Vigilancia*, and to a lesser extent on *City of Memphis* and *Illinois*. Those losses did in fact meet his requirement for the "overt acts." The information available at the time seemed to indicate that *Healdton* had been lost to a German submarine, and it was only natural to disregard German denials.

However, it is also true that as part of the cumulative loss of American ships, *Healdton* was the seventh American-flagged ship lost since the declaration of unrestricted submarine warfare, and the second one on which there were known American fatalities. When added to the loss of *Vigilancia*, *Healdton* could very well have contributed to Wilson's reluctant recognition of the fact of German unrestricted warfare. The close examination of the timing of Wilson's decision process shows that the news of the loss of *Healdton* did in fact *come after the cabinet had recommended war, but before Wilson told even his closest advisors that he had decided for war. Thus it is altogether likely that Wilson's final decision was influenced by the false assumption that Healdton had been a victim of a German U-boat*. Although he had apparently already decided to convene Congress early before hearing of the loss of *Healdton*, there is no evidence that he intended to ask for a declaration of war until several days after the news arrived. The news arrived on March 22, and the first clear record of his decision for war is that of Colonel House on March 27. *Healdton* seemed to Lansing to be part of the casus belli, and it probably seemed to Wilson to be one of the overt acts that he had said would be required for further action. The loss of *Healdton* was certainly on the minds of members of Congress, and several would mention *Healdton* in the following week during debates over the war resolution. The seven American deaths aboard the tanker brought the total number to thirteen U.S. citizens killed at sea as the result of the sinking of American ships between February 1 and March 31 (counting all of the Americans lost aboard *Vigilancia*).

During the press speculation about Wilson's speech and over the question of whether he had reached a decision on March 24, the Washington correspondent of the *New York Times* offered a perceptive observation:

> The sinking of the Standard Oil steamer *Healdton* caused scant comment here today, and that was in the line of emphasizing the belief of officials that the country was rapidly becoming a unit in favor of a war with Germany. It was regarded as a peculiarly aggravated case of murder on the high seas because it was committed outside the barred zone, but it was pointed out that it could do little more than constitute another point in the whole indictment against Germany's ruthless disregard of all consideration for neutrals.[18]

Building the Case for War

Wilson understood that the public sentiment had shifted somewhat in favor of war, although it was by no means a "unit in favor of a war with Germany," as the *New York Times* had averred. In the age prior to public opinion polling, there was no objective way to measure that shift. From anecdotal evidence, it appeared that the mood of much of the public and Congress, including those from the West, had indeed changed with the Zimmermann Telegram, with abuses to American diplomats and others in Germany since breaking relations, with the Russian Revolution, and with the tipping-point ships.[19] Wilson understood that, even if he viewed the case for war narrowly and legalistically as based on the loss of three or four ships, the public and Congress viewed it much more broadly, and he planned to speak to that broader set of reasons. In addition, it seems that while public opinion might have shifted, a large sector of the public and members of Congress did not believe that a declaration of war was called for. For that reason, Wilson had to marshal a very powerful and comprehensive indictment of Germany to help convince at least some of those who wanted to hold out for continued neutrality. As many historians have noted, Wilson had a habit of construing all his decisions, even those taken for practical or political reasons, as matters of high ideals and morality.[20]

At the Friday, March 30, cabinet meeting, Wilson read part of his speech to the members of his cabinet and apparently hinted that it could benefit from the addition of some further specifics. Although still hesitating to be too explicit with the press, some of the cabinet members let it be publicly known on that Friday before Congress was to meet that Wilson intended to ask for a declaration that a state of war existed. Extracts from the address, "read at a regular meeting of the cabinet this afternoon, brought satisfaction to his official advisers who have insisted that the national honor and dignity demanded a resort to arms." Since the most consistent advocates of such a position had been McAdoo, Lansing, and Houston, it would seem that one or more of them provided the source for the leak. Secretary of the Navy Josephus Daniels, who had very reluctantly come around to support a declaration of war, noted that Wilson said that he wished "to present facts, convincing from evidence, justifying position."[21] After the meeting, Lansing or his staff put together four separate memoranda into a single memo outlining different categories of specific offenses committed by Germany. The details in the memo, signed by Lansing, let us know precisely what the president knew after he had decided for war, but before he completed the final draft of his address.[22]

Lansing's note prepared late on March 30 provided a great many specifics. It appears that afternoon when Wilson read to the cabinet the parts of the speech, he indicated he needed some facts to flesh out his presentation, which is clearly implied by Lansing prefacing his compiled memo with, "in view of certain remarks which you made at the meeting of the cabinet this afternoon I thought you might find helpful the enclosed memoranda in regard to violations by German officials of the laws of this country and the practices of mankind."[23]

The memo from Robert Lansing, dated on the afternoon or evening of March 30, was a detailed accounting of the affronts to American sovereignty and violations of American rights committed by Germany. Arthur Link did not include this lengthy memo in the published *Wilson Papers*, nor did he reference it in his detailed account of the Wilson decision process, but it is in the collection that Link compiled and that is housed at Princeton. Selected elements of this memorandum were employed in Wilson's address.

When Lansing took the hint for more specifics on March 30, Lansing and his staff had most of this information at their fingertips; the fact that the memo contained four separate memoranda indicates that the lists had been prepared separately, perhaps in anticipation that they would be requested. The fact that two of the lists mentioned *Healdton* demonstrates that the final drafts of those lists were prepared no earlier than March 22 or March 23.

This Lansing memo offers the best evidence of what the president knew and when he knew it. It also reveals by its omissions what facts regarding ship incidents the president did *not* have when he prepared his final speech.

The Lansing Memo of March 30, 1917

In his memo of March 30, Lansing included a great many offenses by Germany, bringing together four separate lists under the cover note and the general rubric: "violations by German officials of the laws of this country and the practice of nations." The four lists were as follows:

- improper activities of German officials in the United States (22 cases);
- violations of American rights by Germany since the suspension of diplomatic relations (8 cases, including the Zimmermann Telegram);
- ships sunk with loss of American lives (22 cases, mostly British ships, but including three American ships: *Gulflight*, *Vigilancia* and *Healdton*, with a total of 225 American lives lost);
- American ships damaged or sunk by German submarines: 17 cases (also including *Gulflight*, *Vigilancia*, and *Healdton*).

Although the memo was prepared along the lines of providing evidence that Germany had already taken acts of war against the United States, when examined closely, very few of the sixty-six specific facts represented what Wilson had called overt acts of war, or incidents that would meet a strict definition of a casus belli.

The twenty-two violations by German officials in the United States had already been partially dealt with by the recall of some of them, by the arrest of others, and by breaking diplomatic relations. Numerous German officials had violated their diplomatic status, but such actions were not a casus belli. Furthermore, most of those abuses had occurred long before the current crisis, and the United States had taken other actions, such as declaring particular individuals as persona non grata and requiring that they be sent home to Germany. Such earlier actions, far short of war, were the appropriate responses.

The violations of the rights of American citizens in Germany after the suspension of diplomatic relations certainly were offensive, but again, under the law of nations, such abuses did not represent attacks on American sovereignty, but rather violations of the rights of individuals. The United States was correct to protest such violations vigorously, and asked the Spanish legation, which represented the United States in Germany after the severance of relations, to intercede and protest. Again, those protests had been lodged and the angry American response was correct, but the abuses did not represent acts of war against the United States. The Zimmermann Telegram had been released earlier without comment, except for an assertion of its authenticity. Although there had been an extensive uproar in the press over the telegram, as has been seen, the telegram in itself did not constitute an overt act of war, and had not been so treated by the administration.

Lansing provided a list of twenty-two ships on which American passengers and members of crews had perished as a consequence of German attacks. His total of 225 American lives lost included two from *Gulflight* (there had been three, if one counts the subsequent heart attack of the Captain Gunter); five from *Vigilancia* (there had been six, if one counted Mr. Rodriquez, whose American citizenship had been established by act of Congress); and seven from *Healdton* (despite the lack of confirmation that the ship had been lost to a German submarine). Some of the figures of American losses aboard foreign ships also appeared inaccurate, but the actual total was probably very close to 200. With the exception of *Gulflight*, *Vigilancia*, and *Healdton*, all the losses of life had been under foreign flags. Many members of Congress and much of the public had rejected the notion that the loss of American lives aboard foreign ships represented a cause for war. Furthermore, the State Department had already taken the position that such losses were matters for diplomatic protest over the abuse of American citizens' rights, and were not in themselves acts of war.

The fourth category of detailed information presented by Lansing was a list of seventeen American-flagged ships that had been sunk or damaged by German submarines. Eleven of these events had happened before February 1, 1917, and had been dealt with through diplomatic channels. Included in the eleven were the admitted accidents, *Gulflight* and *Nebraskan*; the admitted transferred ship, the *Lanao*; and two that had reflected careful German adherence to cruiser rules, *Leelanaw* and *Columbian*. The eleven included one that had been lost to a mine (*Seaconnet*). Five were very minor incidents of ships being hailed by gunfire and damaged: *Owego* (misspelled by Lansing as "Oswego"), *Rebecca Palmer*, *Sacramento*, *Golena*, and *St. Helen's*. The last two incidents were so minor that no record of them surfaced in the *New York Times* or in the published diplomatic correspondence of *Foreign Relations of the United States*. Notably, his listing did not include the *William P. Frye* or the *Pass of Balmaha*, neither of which had been "sunk or damaged by a submarine." It will be remembered that *William P. Frye* was sunk by a surface ship, and *Pass of Balmaha* had been confiscated by a submarine crew. Furthermore, those two incidents had been more or less resolved through diplomacy. Nor did Lansing include *Chemung*, apparently because the submarine was presumed to have been Austrian. Even with these omissions for very logical reasons, the list of ship losses prior to February 1 does appear to have been an attempt to inflate a number of previously resolved or extremely minor incidents into a set of grievances.

Most relevant from the point of view of the current analysis, Lansing's list also included six of the seven ships lost since February 1: *Housatonic, Lyman M. Law, Vigilancia, City of Memphis, Illinois,* and *Healdton*. Since President Wilson had specifically said that *Housatonic* and *Lyman M. Law* did not represent the "overt act" in his speech of February 26, their inclusion was somewhat dubious. It will be remembered that they had been sunk with full and careful application of accepted cruiser rules and had so been treated by the State Department and by Wilson. In common with the press (and with historians who have dealt with the issue since that time), Lansing also included *Healdton* even though it was not clear how that ship had been sunk. He did *not* include *Algonquin*, apparently because of the issue of transfer from the British flag made its inclusion as an American ship in the list problematic. Neither was *Algonquin* included in the list of foreign and American ships on which Americans had been killed since the whole crew had evacuated safely.

In the long list of sixty-six German offenses presented by Lansing, therefore, the *only* offenses that constituted actual "overt acts" of war by Woodrow Wilson's own definition were three ship losses: the tipping-point ships *Vigilancia, City of Memphis,* and *Illinois*. Even though later evidence suggests that *Healdton* was not lost to a German submarine, its inclusion in the list at the time made good sense based on the preliminary reports. In a very real sense, the three confirmed losses of American ships represented real and overt acts of war by Germany against the United States in the form of attacks on American sovereignty at sea. They were in fact a sufficient and legitimate reason for the Congress to declare that a state of war existed between the United States and Germany, even under Wilson's own earlier very narrow definition of overt acts as spelled out in his February 3 address to Congress. By including those three incidents in the mass of other German abuses and offenses of various degrees of accuracy, magnitude, and significance, Lansing had somewhat obscured their significance. But they were on the list, and their presence was appropriate.

Wilson, Mass Psychology, and Just War Doctrine

If the most appropriate evidence that Germany had initiated war against the United States was the sinking of the three ships *Vigilancia, City of Memphis,* and *Illinois*, it seems at first somewhat puzzling that the president did not mention those incidents and the specifics surrounding them in his address to Congress. Rather, he couched his denunciation of Germany in his April 2 address in very broad terms, ranging over some of the offenses Lansing had mentioned in his memo and covering even broader issues, such as the autocratic form of German government and their brutal methods of conduct of the war. As a speech, his address to Congress has often been cited as an example of Wilson's idealistic view of the world, as well as a major achievement of oratory.

The fact that the three specific ships (or the names and particulars of any ships at all) did not show up in Wilson's address can be attributed not only to Wilson's preference to deal on a higher, more idealistic plane, but to a problem that had both psychological and international law aspects. Psychologically, it would seem inappropriate to ask the Congress to throw the resources of the United States into war over the confirmed loss of three ships and fifteen seamen, six of whom were American. From the point of view of international law, it would also seem that the action was out of proportion to the cause.

From a psychological point of view, the much longer list of abuses by Germany presented by Lansing in his memorandum, and the even broader idealistic values enunciated by Wilson in his address, were more likely to seem convincing to members of Congress and the public. The German plot to involve Mexico against the United States, as revealed in the Zimmermann Telegram, was clearly hostile. The other offenses did indeed show a ruthlessness, arrogance, and disregard for the practice of nations on the part of Germany, including the mistreatment of American detainees, diplomats, and civilians; the killing of civilians who traveled aboard foreign passenger ships; and the active abuse of diplomatic privilege by German officials in the United States through espionage and subversion. While not strictly legal reasons to go to war, all of these abuses added up to a picture of a ruthless, hostile, and inhumane threat to America. Public opinion had been aroused by many of these events and in the broader psychological sense, the events were part of the context. Those abuses and attitudes had certainly helped provoke a wide public sentiment for war, even among many in the traditionally neutralist and isolationist Midwest and West.

Lansing, Wilson, and others were well aware of the psychological requirement that the cause of the war be broad, not narrow. Lansing revealed his insight into the need for Wilson to present a convincing case in an exchange of personal correspondence. A longtime friend of Lansing's, the newspaper publisher and attorney Edward N. Smith, of Watertown, New York, had written to Lansing during the difficult weeks after the German announcement of unrestricted submarine warfare, congratulating Lansing on a strong stand regarding American shipping, but complaining about the narrowness of the apparent concern:

> If as it seems we must, we get into this war, I hope that events will shape themselves that it will not be done on a question of international law alone, but that our people will be inspired with a consciousness of the menace of German philosophy of government . . . and [a] more inspiring basis of action than the mere fact that Germany would not heed the President's warning.[24]

On February 28, Lansing had written a long, heartfelt, confidential reply to Smith that he later preserved in his files, no doubt because he believed it captured his thinking. Lansing addressed the issue raised by Smith about narrow and broad causes:

> The psychology of the situation is the real problem that has to be solved. I wish this was not so and that no question existed as to the attitude of all the American people in the present crisis. . . . If we enter this war—and we seem to have been drawn very "near to the verge of war" . . . it must be on the general recognition that modern civilization is threatened by military Absolutism. . . . When the time comes, as it seems to be coming, the indictment will not contain only a single count. It will be an indictment of many counts, there are many, very many which may be presented to the judgment of the world.[25]

The fact that Lansing had been thinking about an "indictment" with "many counts" at least since the end of February for what he deemed "psychological reasons" helps explain why he had several lists of such reasons ready for Wilson. His exchange of confidential correspondence with E. N. Smith also shows how he and others had developed an understanding of the psychological need for presenting the cause of war to the American people, not as a narrow legal case, but as one based on broader, more idealistic grounds. It is noteworthy that Lansing himself used the term "psychological" in explaining the need for a broad indictment.

In addition, there was a more abstract theoretical or legalistic reason for avoiding a short list of specific overt acts and instead referring to a broader range of misdeeds. In many ways, Wilson was scrupulous in conforming his actions to principles of international law and the Constitution. From the point of view of international law, there had evolved several principles that defined a just war, that is, principles that defined whether or not a war was legitimate. If Wilson were to move the United States from what he saw as the proper, peaceful, neutral role to a state of war, he was certain to want to ensure that it would be seen by his contemporaries and by future generations as a just war.

Four of the principles that defined whether or not a war was just had been enunciated by Saint Augustine himself in the work *Civitas Dei* (*City of God*) early in the fifth century C.E.:

1. the war should be initiated on proper authority;
2. it should derive from a proper casus belli;
3. it should not be undertaken without probable success;
4. the action should be in proportion to the offense.

Wilson very clearly understood these principles and applied them as he crafted his speech. There is no direct evidence that he had such abstract principles in hand, but the degree to which his address met these principles is quite striking.[26] At the very least, Wilson had an intuitive sense of what constituted a just war; it is quite likely, with his background in history, law, and political science, that he was very familiar with the precepts. A review of his speech with the just war principles in mind shows the following.

Wilson sought proper authority by coming before Congress and asking them to make the declaration. The sinking of the ships constituted a legitimate casus belli. Wilson warned Congress that sufficient resources would have to be devoted to ensure probable success. The fourth Augustinian principle, that the action should be in proportion to the offense, helps account for the failure to mention the three ships or the specific number of lives lost. If the war were initiated on the narrow casus belli of the three ships, and more particularly on the casus belli of the loss of six Americans aboard *Vigilancia*, it would result in *an action out of proportion to the offense*. Only by seeing the war in the broader context of a great many offenses by Germany would the principle of proportionality be preserved. If Wilson had given emphasis to this rather small-scale cause of such a great endeavor, it would have been to suggest that at least on this one count, the war would be unjust.[27]

Wilson met other requirements for a just war with the later famous phrase in this speech that it was to be "a war to make the world safe for democracy." Only in retrospect did it become obvious that the war fell far short of achieving anything like that goal, and much of the postwar criticism of Wilson's policy centered on the charge that this ideal was rather naïve. Once the realization of the ideals appeared impossible or unlikely, Wilson's effort to define his action as a just war seemed at best misguided, and at worst, an extremely grave error. The well-known postwar disillusionment of the 1920s and the revival of American isolationism in that decade have often been traced to the widespread recognition that Wilson's idealistic war goals had not been realistic.

The three ships that formed the specific casus belli could be alluded to only obliquely by Wilson, for to have placed emphasis or focus on them would have made the war seem far out of proportion to the offense and would have meant that the nation was not entering a just war. However, when those three ship losses were submerged in the broader picture of German offenses against all of mankind, as well as in the general behavior of Germany in its manner of conducting the war, no such problem arose. Rather than mentioning three ships and six or fifteen deaths, the broader bill of particulars raised by Wilson in his speech made for a far more psychologically convincing and legally appropriate plea for declaring that a state of war existed.

As we shall see in the next chapter, the tendency to conflate the specific casus belli with broader offenses was carried out with less finesse by members of Congress as they debated the issue. Following information supplied by the State Department, many maritime events that the United States State Department and the president had already accepted as *not* being overt acts of war were listed by some members of Congress, apparently out of a similar desire to broaden the causes of war to a wider set of grievances.

The confusion, inaccuracy, and lack of specificity in later historical reports about the ships that brought the United States into the war probably also have roots in the instinctive need to preserve the sense of proportionality. When presenting a narrative of events, a writer has a natural desire to present a consequence as in proportion to a cause. For those who saw the war as justified, the broader set of causes have provided a greater sense of legitimacy than does the narrowly defined precipitating incidents of the loss of *Vigilancia*, *City of Memphis*, and *Illinois*. For those critical of the decision to go to war, the aspects of Wilson's neutrality that contributed to Germany's final decision to unleash unrestricted submarine warfare have been rich fields of research, as have been the roots of his idealistic (and, most have argued, naïve) vision of a world made safe for democracy. So the ships themselves, at the core of the causation, sank into the murky waters of history, while the atmospherics of broad and sweeping issues continued to rage as a lasting storm.

On April 2, 1917, Wilson's speech was well received by a majority of, but not all, members of Congress. Between April 1 and April 4, before Congress could respond to his speech and come to a vote, three more U.S.-flagged ships were sunk by German submarines. Some of the information about these three losses was available to members of Congress as they debated the war resolution, the subject of the next chapter.

10

Aztec, Missourian, Marguerite, and Congress

As Woodrow Wilson delivered his address to Congress on the evening of April 2, word spread through the chamber that another U.S. ship—the freighter *Aztec*—had been sunk, off Brest, on the north coast of France. The president had already made up his mind before reports of this loss arrived, so *Aztec* was not part of *his* decision process. However, members of Congress were quite aware of the news of the sinking of *Aztec* as they debated the war resolution over the next three days.

The *Aztec* was the first ship armed under the president's order to provide guns and gun crews to merchant vessels. The regular merchant marine crew consisted of thirty-four seamen and officers, of whom seventeen were American citizens and seventeen foreign citizens. Among the American citizens serving in this crew were five from the territory of Hawaii, at least three of whom were apparently of native Hawaiian ancestry, citizens of the United States since 1900. The gun crew consisted of thirteen men, including a naval lieutenant in charge. All the Navy sailors were U.S. citizens, bringing the total number of American citizens aboard to thirty.

Aztec was a 3,727-ton freighter built in 1894 in Newcastle, England. *Aztec* was owned and operated by the Oriental Navigation Company, a firm that also owned the ship *Orleans*, one of the first ships to sail from an American port after the German announcement of unrestricted submarine warfare. *Orleans* had successfully made it to France, arriving with great fanfare on February 26. *Aztec* left New York March 18 with a cargo of "foodstuffs and general supplies," bound for Le Havre.[1]

Early on April 1, some of the crew spotted a periscope, and later that evening, about 2130, when it was nine miles west southwest of the Ushant Light off the coast of France, the ship suffered a detonation. It was quite unusual for submarines to torpedo ships at night, although the British liner *Laconia* (lost on February 25, 1917) had reported being struck by a torpedo at night, and the *Healdton* suffered two detonations, at about 2015 at night on March 21. The loss of *Healdton*, as noted in the previous chapter, was almost certainly due to striking two mines.

Figure 19. *Aztec*. The freighter *Aztec* was one of the first merchant American ships to be provided with naval guns and crews before sailing. Nevertheless, it was sunk on April 1, 1917. Among the casualties was boatswain's mate John I. Eopolucci, the first American serviceman killed on duty in World War I. (Reprinted with permission from Mariners' Museum, Newport News, Va.)

Because *Aztec* sank at night, and because no survivor in the ship crew or gun crew reported seeing a submarine, American newswriters speculated that the ship might have struck a mine. German records published years later showed that *Aztec* had been torpedoed by *U-46* under the command of Leo Hillebrand.[2]

The loss of life aboard *Aztec* was the most serious aboard any American-registered ship up to that time in World War I. Ten minutes after the detonation that knocked out the lights and the wireless, the forward end of the ship was entirely underwater, and Captain Walter O'Brien ordered evacuation in lifeboats. The captain had intended to get into boat No. 2, launched on the port side, but after retrieving the ship's papers, he returned to find that boat, loaded with survivors, had broken up in getting away. The two other boats were lowered successfully from the starboard side, away from the weather, and he hurriedly scrambled into Boat No. 1. The presence of the disciplined Navy sailors in that lifeboat no doubt contributed to his survival. That boat, containing the captain, twelve of the thirteen members of the Navy guard, and six other officers and members of the ship's crew, was rescued by a French patrol boat later in the night. Boat No. 3, although it had gotten away from the ship, was never found. Altogether there were twenty-eight lives lost, including one of the Navy sailors in the gun crew, boatswain's mate John I. Eopolucci. Eopolucci was apparently the first American serviceman killed in World War I while on duty with the U.S. armed forces.

Among the dead were ten other American members of the ship's crew and all of the seventeen merchant sailors of foreign citizenship. Lieutenant William Fuller Gresham, in charge of the naval gun crew, later wrote a report with several recommendations for greater safety aboard merchant ships traveling in the war zone, and was decorated for his part in the action. He urged that crews sleep in their weather clothes, that lifeboats be stocked with different provisions, that ships come to a full stop before the launching of lifeboats, and that the lifeboat lines, pulleys, and davits be kept in good working order. Some of his recommendations were later implemented.[3]

Two other American ships were lost before the final vote in Congress. Word of the *Missourian*'s loss on April 4 arrived in time to be mentioned in the congressional debates. At 7,914 gross tons, the *Missourian* was by far the largest of the American ships lost during the period of neutrality. It was built in 1903 by the Maryland Steel Company in Sparrows Point, Maryland. Home-ported in New York City, the ship had a crew of fifty-three, including thirty-two American citizens. In her earlier career, like the *City of Memphis*, it had served briefly as a transport ship for the U.S. government in the operation against Mexico in 1914.

Owned and operated by the American-Hawaiian Line on a charter for the France and Canada Steamship Company, it departed New York for Genoa with a general cargo on March 5. It left Genoa for New York on April 4, in ballast. Steaming to the southwest from Genoa, off Porto Maurizio, a small coastal town some twenty-five miles east of the Italian border with France, it was torpedoed about 1630 and then shelled by *U-52*, under the command of Hans Walther. The attack came without warning, but all of the members of the crew were able to evacuate to lifeboats as the submarine shelled the ship. The boats were picked up by an Italian vessel and towed into Porto Maurizio, where Captain Lyons wired a brief report on April 5 to the American consul at Genoa, David F. Wilber, who immediately sent word of the loss to Washington.[4]

Quite unnoticed in the flurry of news surrounding the heated debates in Congress and the next week's preparations for war was the fact that one more ship, the relatively small American schooner *Marguerite*, was stopped, evacuated, and burned thirty-five miles southwest of Sardinia on April 4. Lothar von Arnauld, in command of *U-35*, who had burned the schooner *Lyman M. Law* not far from the same spot on February 12, accosted *Mar-

guerite, and then made sure that the crew of twelve got away safely before setting the wooden ship afire. However, he refused to tow the lifeboat, and after nearly two full days at sea, the survivors were finally picked up by a French torpedo boat off the coast of Tunisia and landed at Bizerta. Although the loss of *Marguerite* was not part of the decision process of the cabinet, the president, or Congress, the ship's loss later demonstrated that the German policy of unrestricted warfare was in full swing in the Mediterranean as well as the Atlantic before the American declaration of war. Von Arnauld, like Hans Rose, continued to adhere to cruiser rules when he could. *Marguerite* was the last of the ten American ships lost after the German announcement of unrestricted submarine warfare and before the declaration of war by the United States.[5]

The Congressional Debates

After Wilson delivered his speech, but before the vote in Congress was taken, editorialists speculated that in the Senate there would be several opposed to the war, but not enough to launch a successful filibuster, especially considering the new cloture rules in effect. Trying to anticipate the vote in Congress, the prowar *New York Times* optimistically estimated that only six in the Senate and fewer than twenty in the House of Representatives would oppose the war measure. The lone Socialist in the House, Meyer London of New York, along with pronounced neutralists like Dorsey Shackleford, were expected to oppose the measure. As it turned out, there was more opposition in the House of Representatives than anticipated.[6]

A parliamentary maneuver by Senator Robert LaFollette delayed immediate action by the Senate for one day. LaFollette was well-known in maritime circles for his backing of the Seaman's Act of 1915 (long advocated by maritime labor leaders), as well as for his staunch neutrality. Nevertheless, the Senate was able to complete its deliberations and come to a vote on April 5, while it took until the early morning hours of April 6 for the lower house to complete the debate. Speeches in the House were at first limited to twenty minutes, then to ten minutes, and then to five minutes, as one hundred representatives sought to make remarks.[7] With soul-searching comments and charges of disloyalty, appeals to logic, and tortured explanations of why their minds had changed, the members of the House continued to make speeches past midnight on April 5, not recording the vote until a little after 3:00 a.m. on April 6.[8]

An odd mix of Democrats, Republicans, Progressives, pacifists, convinced neutralists, and pro-German or anti-British legislators and members of the public had a variety of arguments against war. Although various sectors of organized labor were strong neutralists, particularly those unions with large Irish American membership, such as New York longshoremen, their views appeared not to be considered in any explicit way during the congressional debates. The American Federation of Labor, once the United States joined the war, adhered to a no-strike policy and generally supported the war effort, as did even some of the more radical independent unions, such as the American Clothing Workers, led by Sidney Hillman.

Some congressional opponents of the war, like Robert LaFollette and Democratic congressman Albert Cummins, pointed out that Germany had not directly attacked America, but only sought to destroy American aid to her enemies. It was not the American people who demanded war, said those on the Left, but Wall Street. Other members of Congress, like Claude Kitchin, the Democratic majority leader, simply believed that efforts at diplomacy had not been exhausted. Jeannette Rankin, the lone woman in Congress, opposed the war on moral grounds.

In Congress, as in the public, there was no single antiwar "dove," or neutralist position. Rather, those who opposed the war varied greatly in their motives and concerns, just as did those who came around to supporting the call for war. Neither side was "organized" in any sense during the hectic weeks between February 1, 1917, and April 6, 1917, and the "public mind," if there ever was such a thing, was characterized then, as it often has been, by chaos, not by clear alignments.

Senators and representatives spoke several times, both directly and indirectly, of the ships that represented the final cause to go to war. Some of those references were exaggerated, inaccurate, incomplete, or lacking in specifics, but nevertheless, the maritime causes of the war were on the minds of many of the members of Congress.

The Senate

The Senate began discussions on April 3, postponed for a day because of LaFollette's request, and then completed the discussion and vote on April 5. Senator Hitchcock of Nebraska introduced the war resolution to the Senate with a speech in which he pointed out he had been bitterly opposed to war. He had favored armed neutrality, and was disappointed to see the armed ship bill filibustered. He went on to refer to the ship losses, not directly by name or with specifics, but indicating that they were indeed a central cause for the current debate. Like many others in both houses, he was not too concerned to have the names and numbers exactly right, but like others he saw the ship losses as part of the casus belli. He made his lack of specific information very explicit: "Five or six, possibly seven, American vessels, upon innocent errands of commerce upon the high seas, have been sunk. Some of them were not even upon the way to a neutral port but were returning to the United States in ballast, and in three of the cases, at least, the lives of American citizens have been lost."[9]

The best-known of the opponents of the war, Robert LaFollette, delivered the most well-known, and oft-reported, speech denouncing the war and those he believed were behind it. He knew very well that his speech would not convince his colleagues, and with the passage of the cloture bill, he knew that a filibuster would be impossible. Nevertheless, he took the opportunity to argue against American participation in the war.

A review of his speech shows that he, like the president, chose to argue on the high plane of ideas and ideals rather than on the basis of facts, evidence, or the small scale of the specific casus belli. He pointed out that both Germany and Britain had violated American neutral rights, but that Germany, through the exchange of diplomatic notes, had sought to resolve the differences. Britain, he said, had never yielded to American protests, except for a short time, by allowing cotton imports to Germany. As to the argument that German submarines were sinking ships without warning, he pointed out that British mines of course never warned their victims, and that German submarines did nothing worse. Although the United States had not protested the mines, the United States proposed to go to war with Germany for "identically the same action on her part," that is, sinking ships without warning.[10]

The fact that *Aztec* was armed and was nevertheless sunk was not lost on members of Congress. Both those who favored the president's call for a declaration of war and those who opposed it saw that the loss of the *Aztec* demonstrated the futility of attempting to protect merchant ships by arming them. LaFollette, who had led the filibuster against the Armed Ship Bill, believed that arming the ships only made them more likely targets and subject to complete surprise attack rather than subject to the cruiser-rule practices of captains like Hans Rose and von Arnauld who would dutifully see to the safe evacuation of crews before sinking an unarmed target ship. LaFollette briefly mentioned the loss of this single ship in his speech.[11]

Senator Paul Oscar Husting, a supporter of the war resolution, gave details of the loss of belligerent ships on which Americans had traveled: *Falaba, Lusitania, Arabic, Sussex,* and *Ancona.* Then he went on to list attacks on some fifteen American ships, all of which had occurred before the January 31 announcement, and none of which had represented a casus belli or "overt act" from the point of view of Woodrow Wilson or the State Department. Many of the incidents were minor confrontations between German submarines and American merchant ships that resulted in no casualties whatsoever, and two of the cases were the admitted accidents, *Gulflight* and *Nebraskan.* Nevertheless, following the same practice used by others who blurred the distinctions between minor and major events, and between those incidents resulting in ship losses and those resulting in mere damage, Husting listed: *Cushing, Gulflight, Nebraskan, Leelanaw, Petrolite, Seaconnet, Oswego (Owego), Kansan, Lanao, Columbian, Galena, Chemung, St. Helen's, Rebecca Palmer,* and *Sacramento.* By stating that they had been "attacked or sunk," Husting left unclear that only four of the fifteen had been sunk, that all four of those sunk had been evacuated in conformity with cruiser rules, and that the entire list involved only three fatalities. Husting went on to mention three ships that had been lost after the German announcement of unrestricted submarine warfare: *Housatonic, Lyman M. Law,* and *Algonquin.* Making his argument, of course, he did *not* point out that the State Department and Wilson had *not* chosen to treat the loss of any of those ships as the "overt act," or casus belli. Husting's argument regarding all of these ships conformed in some of its details to the memorandum prepared by Lansing's staff for Wilson on March 30. Husting, unlike Lansing, included the loss of *Algonquin,* despite the fact of her recent transfer from Canadian registry.[12]

Even though blurring distinctions, Husting did cover some of the maritime facts: "On February 13, 1917, the American ship *Lyman M. Law* was burned by a submarine. As soon as the facts could be ascertained and the matter considered at all, the President did go before Congress on February 26." Husting suggested that the loss of the *Lyman M. Law* contributed to the decision to ask for armed guards, which seemed to be true, and it had been treated in that fashion in the press.

Several facts about the prowar presentation by Senator Husting and others in Congress were noteworthy. Apparently relying on documents provided by the State Department that contained a tally of the ship losses (including even the very minor and inconsequential encounters), Senator Husting and Representative John Thomas Watkins both mentioned the same fifteen incidents involving American ships that had occurred over the two years from early 1915 through January of 1917. Without distinguishing between those that had been merely stopped for inspection, those accidentally attacked, and those evacuated and sunk under cruiser rules, the fifteen incidents were simply listed as affronts to the American flag at sea. Furthermore, Husting and Watkins also listed the attacks on Allied-flagged ships that carried American passengers or crew as part of their reasoning for their vote. By providing a long list of ships confronted, damaged, or sunk, almost all of which had not represented a cause for war, Husting and Watkins obviously sought to make a strong case for war, without worrying too much about the finer points of international law or the actual details of the incidents.[13]

The blurring of some distinctions did not go unchallenged. For example, when Senator James A. Reed of Missouri asserted that women and children had been killed at sea, progressive Republican Senator George W. Norris of Missouri pointed out that none of those kinds of casualties had occurred during the loss of an American ship.[14]

In violation of the rules of the Senate, which prohibited charging a fellow senator with motives unworthy of a senator, Senator Reed accused Norris of "giving comfort to the enemy," one of the grounds for treason. During the Senate debate, Senator Norris of Nebraska aroused the ire of the prowar majority by claiming that if Congress declared war it would be because of commercial reasons. Most Americans who had died at German hands, he said, had "taken their dangerous voyages for the sake of profit." Norris went on: "We are going into war upon command of gold. We are about to do the bidding of wealth's terrible mandate and make millions of our countrymen suffer and untold generations bear burdens and shed their life blood, all because we want to preserve our commercial right to deliver munitions to the belligerents. I feel that we are about to put the dollar sign on the American flag."[15]

Norris commented that American exports to the Allies had caused the Germans to turn their blockade against the United States.[16] Norris's remark about putting the dollar sign on the flag raised the ire of other members of Congress and some in the press. Norris, said Reed, "grazes the edge of treason.... The President calls for war, not to save a few paltry dollars, but to vindicate the sovereign rights of the United States."[17]

The heated exchange between Norris and Reed, although implicitly referring to the maritime origins of the war, went forward without any specific mention of any single ship or specific incident involving a German submarine and an American vessel. Indeed, Norris overlooked the opportunity to clinch his argument with the facts of the corporate owners of *Vigilancia*, *City of Memphis*, *Illinois*, and the Standard Oil tanker *Healdton*.

Some of the other prowar senators were highly irritated at the suggestion that the cause of American loss of neutrality was the influence of capitalists. Senator John Sharp Williams, a Democrat from Mississippi, made his point succinctly and did explicitly mention one of the ships sunk since February 1, 1917, and obliquely refer to three more: "Wall Street did not sink the *Sussex*. Wall Street did not sink the *Algonquin* with the American flag on her main staff, nor did Wall Street sink the last three American ships with flags flying that were sunk in the same way. I am tired of lies like that."[18]

One of the senators voting for the war measure, Claude Swanson, Democrat from Virginia, who later served as Franklin Roosevelt's secretary of the Navy from 1933 to 1939, specifically mentioned the deaths aboard the *Vigilancia* and the *Healdton* as among the acts of war by Germany against the United States. His comments showed that he did not have the numbers of casualties precisely right. Even so, with his concern for the specifics, Swanson was a rarity among the members of Congress, many of whom dealt in larger generalities rather than particular facts. Lansing's desk diary showed that he had had several conferences with Swanson over the prior week, both in person and by telephone, and Swanson's rare command of the details can probably be attributed to those communications.[19] Swanson said, in part:

> We have almost forgotten the wrongs of the past in amazement at the outrages of the present. Germany has shown a fixed determination to enforce by ruthless warfare the infamous purposes indicated in her proclamation of January 31. On March 16 last the American steamer *Vigilancia* bearing the American flag, having a cargo consisting of dried fruit, straw, and other merchandise, sailing from New York for Havre was torpedoed and sunk by a submarine without warning, and 15 American citizens were lost. The ship was flying a United States flag and so marked that there could be no doubt of her nationality. On March 17 last, 44 miles off the Irish coast, the American steamer *City of Memphis*, flying the American flag and sailing from Cardiff to New York in ballast, was torpedoed by a submarine and sunk, the crew escaping in their own small boats and enduring great hardships and suffering before they were landed ashore. The *City of Memphis* was unarmed and did not use wireless. It was on her way to New York, contained no contraband or illegal cargo, and could not have been considered in any way as aiding Germany's enemies.

> The nationality of this boat could not have been mistaken. On March 17 last the American tanker *Illinois*, flying the American flag and sailing from London to Port Arthur, Tex., was torpedoed by a submarine and sunk within 10 miles north of Alderney. This ship was shelled by the submarine without warning and one of the crew wounded. No measures were taken by the submarine for the safety of the crew. The crew were for more than six hours in small boats and encountered much danger and suffering. . . . *Healdton* . . . was sunk and 21 of her crew were lost, including many American citizens.
>
> Shall we permit our flag, the emblem of our honor, our power, and our aspirations, to be lawlessly and deliberately assaulted upon the high seas, and then not strike with all the force possessed by us the arrogant assailant?[20]

In his attention to detail and his account of the crucial ship losses, Swanson was more accurate and specific than any of his Senate colleagues. Swanson erred only in asserting that the fifteen deaths aboard *Vigilancia* were all those of American citizens. Otherwise his account was quite factual, reflecting the consular reports and news reports of the events, and no doubt reflecting his consultations with Lansing over the previous few days.[21]

The vote in the senate was 82 in favor and 6 opposed. Eight other senators who could not attend indicated that they would have voted for the resolution. The speeches in the House of Representatives took much longer.[22]

House of Representatives

In the House of Representatives, the chairman of the Foreign Relations Committee, Henry de la Warr Flood, from Virginia, opened the discussion of the war resolution,[23] asserting: "War is being made upon our country and its people. Our ships are being sunk. Our noncombatant men, women, and children are being murdered. Our merchantmen are being denied freedom of the seas."[24]

The debate itself simply consisted of short statements as to why various members of Congress voted as they did, rather than a true debate in which arguments were framed to match opposing lines of argument. Although the committee promised a report, and it was later printed, both as a separate document and as part of the reported discussion in the *Congressional Record*, Flood did not introduce it into the minutes until midafternoon on April 5.

The committee report was quite detailed, and its language provides some indication of what facts members of Congress had available regarding the maritime issues, as well as the other charges brought against Germany. The report opened with a comment that suggested that a cause of war lay not in any specific offense, but in a more general German rudeness: "The conduct of the Imperial German Government toward this Government, its citizens, and its interests has been so discourteous, unjust, cruel, barbarous, and so lacking in honesty and fair dealing that it has constituted a violation of the course of conduct which should obtain between friendly nations."

The authors of the report immediately moved on from this general and scolding tone to much more solid ground: "the German Government is actually making war upon the people and the commerce of this country, and leaves no course open to this Government to accept its gauge of battle, declare that a state of war exists, and wage that war vigorously." The report then took up the crux of the matter, by describing the January 31 announcement of unrestricted submarine warfare, and then giving these points of fact: "Since that day seven American ships flying the American flag have been sunk and between 25 and 30 American lives have been lost as a result of the prosecution of the submarine warfare in accordance with the above declaration. This is war. War waged by the Imperial German Government upon this country and its people."[25]

The count of American lives lost as "between 25 and 30" was fair enough. A total of 24 American lives had been lost aboard *Vigilancia*, *Healdton*, and *Aztec*, and three others had been lost on the British *Laconia*, so the number given was quite accurate as far as anyone could determine from the publicly available information at the time. It is noteworthy that the House Committee on Foreign Relations did choose to address what was the specific maritime cause of the war in this report. Behind all the grand issues raised by Wilson and discussed by various members of Congress, and behind all the obfuscation that came with the listing of submarine activities, there was a sound and basic awareness that the actual overt act, or casus belli, was the sinking of several ships registered in the United States. The House Committee placed this cause directly after its general statement of German rude misbehavior, and it constituted the first actual cause for war mentioned in the report.

The report then went on to review earlier losses of American lives aboard belligerent ships and the losses of, or damage to, American ships, reporting with relative accuracy the events surrounding *Falaba*, *Cushing*, *Gulflight*, *Lusitania*, *Nebraskan*, and *Armenian*. The report also listed 1916 losses of

Allied ships in which it reported twenty-three Americans lost their lives, including crew or passengers aboard the British liner *Orduna*, the Russian steamer *Leo*, the American steamer *Leelanaw*, the British passenger liner *Arabic*, the British mule ship *Nicosian*, and the British steamer *Hesperian*. The dates and losses were accurate, but the report did not quite make it clear that none of the losses of life were aboard the American ship (*Leelanaw*) in the list. In compiling these listings, the committee report did not repeat in identical language the similar, but slightly different, listing in the memorandum prepared by Lansing's staff for the president on March 30.

The committee report described other ships carrying American passengers, with some casualties. These ships included the French passenger steamer *Patria*, the Norwegian bark *Silius*, the Dutch passenger steamer *Tubantia*, and the British steamer *Berwindale*. Others listed included the British steamer *Englishman*, the French steamer *Sussex*, the British liner *Manchester Engineer*, and the British steamer *Eagle Point*. The report detailed some of the diplomatic notes exchanged between the United States and Germany over the submarine and shipping issues, and reviewed Wilson's decision to break diplomatic relations after the January 31, 1917, announcement.

In reference to the specific American ships sunk and American casualties during the period since the announcement, the report stated: "On February 3 one American ship was sunk, and since that date six American ships flying the American flag have been torpedoed, with a loss of about 13 American citizens. In addition, 50 or more foreign vessels of both belligerent and neutral nationality with Americans on board have been torpedoed, in most cases without warning, with a consequent loss of American lives."

By mentioning a total of seven "American ships," the report appeared to be including *Housatonic, Lyman M. Law, Algonquin, Vigilancia, City of Memphis, Illinois,* and *Healdton*. The total deaths of thirteen would represent the six aboard *Vigilancia* and the seven aboard *Healdton*. Clearly *Aztec* was not included in the basis for this statement, as her loss would have increased the number of ships to eight and the death toll of U.S. citizens to twenty-four. Reports of that loss on April 4 came too late for inclusion in the committee report, which apparently had been prepared on April 3 or 4.

The committee report then went on to repeat the list of "improper activities in violation of the laws of the United States and of their obligations as officials in a neutral country" committed by German diplomatic representatives. This list of twenty-one specific violations followed, word for word with one notable exception, the list compiled by Lansing on March 30, and referred to obliquely by Wilson in his address. It is noteworthy that the list of twenty-one offenses by German officials followed the exact language in the list of twenty-two offenses that Lansing had prepared, omitting only number 20 ("XX") from Lansing's list: "German agents in this country aided in plans for the Irish rebellion in cooperation with Berlin officials." Perhaps, considering the sensitivity of Irish American voters to this issue, Flood's committee report declined to include it, out of deference to those voters and the members of Congress who depended on their vote. Other offenses listed included attacks on relief ships destined for Belgium, and "indignities" suffered by American officials since the break in diplomatic relations, again repeating, word for word, the memorandum prepared by Lansing or his staff for the use of the President on March 30. An English steamer, the *Yarrowdale*, had been brought into Swinemunde, Germany, as a prize, and aboard were 469 detainees taken by German auxiliary cruisers. Some 72 of those crew members and passengers claimed American citizenship, and after several delays and some mistreatment, the Americans reached Zurich, Switzerland, on March 11. Furthermore, the American diplomats in Germany had a number of complaints about their treatment after the severance of relations. The specifics of the Zimmermann Telegram were repeated. All of these details were identical in order and in wording to those listed by Lansing in the compiled memorandum to the president on March 30, suggesting that the House Committee had been provided with the memorandum from the State Department. Lansing's desk diary indicates several opportunities for the informal delivery of the memorandum to Flood between the date of its preparation and the date of Flood's remarks.[26]

From the identical wording in the Lansing memorandum and portions of the House report, it is clear that through this means, Congress had available to it several parts of Lansing's compiled indictment of German offenses. His memorandum had consisted of four parts. The section "Improper Activities of German Officials in the United States" appeared in identical language in the House committee report, with the noted exception of the heading regarding support for Irish rebels. The section of his compiled memo, headed "Violations of American Rights by Germany since the Suspension of Diplomatic Relations," was also replicated in the House committee report, as was the summary of the Zimmermann Telegram affair, and the treatment of the *Yarrowdale* detainees. Clearly, Lansing had worked with Flood to provide the details that would make the case for war. The close similarity of the information in the House report and in the earlier documents prepared by Lansing for Wilson make it virtually certain that the State Department memos had been made available to Flood's committee.²⁷

There was overlap, but there were also a few very significant differences in the listing of ships on which Americans had perished. Both Lansing and the committee had placed emphasis on the sinking of the American ships *Housatonic*, *Lyman M. Law*, *Vigilancia*, *City of Memphis*, and *Illinois*. The apparent inclusion of *Algonquin* in the count of ships by the House committee and her exclusion by Lansing, however, suggests that at least in some regards, the sources of the information were not identical. The exclusion of *Algonquin* from Lansing's list of affronts to American rights was probably due to Lansing's recognition that as a recently transferred ship, it would be difficult to make a claim for its loss, a rather fine point of international law not bothering Flood's committee. The inclusion of *Healdton* casualty figures in both lists was due to the common assumption it had been torpedoed, not mined. And the failure to include *Aztec*, *Missourian*, and, of course, *Marguerite* in either the Lansing memorandum or in the House report, was certainly due to timing, as those events all occurred after Lansing had prepared his March 30 memorandum, and word of the losses arrived too late for inclusion in the Foreign Relations Committee report delivered on April 5. Representative Flood delivered the report, and it was published in the *Congressional Record* as part of his presentation.²⁸

Two members of the committee dissented from the report's recommendation to vote for the war resolution. One of the dissenters, Congressman Dorsey W. Shackleford (D., Missouri) stated that he was "not what, in common parlance, is called a pacifist." He was not "for peace at any price." He went on to say: "I would unhesitatingly vote for war in any case where such a course, consistent with justice, would be to our interest. I would not vote for war for any other reason than to promote our country's interest. Both sides of the European conflict have flagrantly violated our rights, but they were striking at each other and not at us. When the struggle is over, both of them should be required to make such reparation as they are able to make."²⁹

Shackleford included in his minority statement a relatively rare challenge to Wilson's call to make the world "safe for democracy." He doubted America's ability "to accomplish much for the cause of democracy in an alliance with the King of England, the King of Servia, the King of Roumania, the King of Montenegro, the King of Belgium, the King of Italy, and the Emperor of Japan." Citing Washington's Farewell Address, he thought it wrong to abandon America's traditional abstention from the "intrigues and alliances with European countries whose jealousies keep them in constant conflict."³⁰

Shackleford's statement against joining the war did not address the maritime issues, except to indicate that American financial losses incurred by the actions of both sides could be adjusted by postwar claims, as indeed they had been in previous cases. Indirectly, he was suggesting that the affronts to American sovereignty and attacks on American interests were of too small a scale to require war, but he did not choose to explore those losses closely in support of that argument.³¹

Seventeen other members of the committee voted in favor of the committee report, while Henry Allen Cooper of Wisconsin, the ranking Republican on the committee, joined Shackleford in voting against the report and the resolution, although he did not cosign Shackleford's minority statement. In committee, Cooper objected that the English blockade was responsible for the crisis, and that the United States should not blame Germany.³²

In other presentations in the House of Representatives, some members mentioned one or more ships. Congressman William LaFollette, from the state of Washington (apparently not a close relative of Senator Robert LaFollette), mentioned that three American ships had been destroyed by British mines with loss of life, and that the United States had made no protest about them. A total of four lives had been lost on the mined ships *Evelyn* on February 19, 1915, and the *Carib* on February 22, 1915. There had been at least five other ships lost to mines as well. Like the more famous Senator LaFollette, the namesake congressman argued that the United States had not been truly neutral or impartial in its dealing with the two major belligerents. He went further, pointing to the profits of J. P. Morgan and other capitalists as lying behind the cause of the war, and suggesting a resolution that would compel newspaper editors and businessmen to volunteer for service.³³

A colloquy between two members broke out over the case of the *Evelyn*, with Republican representative Henry Allen Cooper of Wisconsin, the second dissenter from the majority on the House Foreign Relations Committee, asking, "Wasn't the *Evelyn* sunk by a British mine?" Committee chairman Flood replied, "The *Evelyn* was sunk by a German mine in a German field near the German coast."³⁴ The disagreement over the loss of *Evelyn* and *Carib* was probably due to early press reports that had suggested the losses might be due to British mines, and then a later note from German ambassador Bernstorff that pointed out that the ships had not adhered to German shipping instructions as to safe lanes, suggesting that the losses were due to German minefields.³⁵

News reports of the loss of *Missourian* on April 4 were published on April 5, and Chairman of the House Committee on Foreign Relations Flood mentioned it on the floor in a colloquy with Democratic Representative William P. Borland of Missouri, who was arguing for the declaration of war: "If the gentleman will permit me to interrupt him for a moment. I want to call his attention to the fact that there was an unarmed American merchant steamer sunk today, the *Missourian*, probably belonging to some of the gentleman's constituents. I want to call his attention to the fact that it was bound to this country and had nothing aboard but ballast and it was sunk without warning, and American lifes [sic] were probably lost on it."[36]

Flood had mistakenly assumed that the *Missourian* was at least partially owned or crewed from Missouri, but Missourian Borland was unimpressed. None of the crew were from Missouri, owners of the American-Hawaiian Line were not residents of Missouri, and all the crew survived, although not all of those facts were known until more information came in.

Representative Scott Ferris of Oklahoma, apparently one of those allowed a longer period to make his presentation, built a long presentation in favor of the war resolution, with what he regarded as sixteen causes to go to war. Four of his sixteen points of indictment of Germany had to do with maritime issues. and one of them was relatively accurate, both factually and from the viewpoint of international law: "We go to war this day because on January 31, 1917, the Imperial German Government notified us in writing that it would sink on sight any ships in certain areas, and later, on March 16, it did sink three American merchant ships—the *Vigilancia*, the *Illinois*, and the *City of Memphis*—engaged in legitimate commerce."[37]

Although he erred in stating that the ships were all sunk on March 16, he was one of very few members of Congress to pinpoint the actual cause that had decided the cabinet and the president for war. Although accurate enough regarding those three ships, Ferris's other comments showed he had not reviewed the facts carefully, and he made several gross mistakes. The arguments made by Ferris regarding other maritime points reflected the tendency to conflate or inflate events that had represented attacks on American sovereignty with those that had no relevance whatsoever. He mentioned the loss of American lives aboard *Lusitania*. He reflected the same error as Husting when he said that "we go to war today because fifteen American ships engaged in legitimate errands upon the high seas have been sunk without warning, without cause, and without mercy."[38] He further exaggerated by saying that "on the fifteen ships, 224 American lives were lost." In this regard, he erred by assigning the total assumed number of American lives lost on belligerent ships and those on the fifteen American-flagged ships, only a few of which had been sunk, and which had a much lower total of fatalities, all to the American ships. Ferris, who was somewhat correct regarding the three ships that constituted the tipping point for the cabinet, certainly confused the issue with garbled statistics. The errors and exaggerations of Ferris went unchallenged.[39]

Congressman John Rogers of Massachusetts, who voted for the war resolution, had most of the specifics regarding recent ship losses quite right, apparently familiar with the details in the House Committee on Foreign Relations report. He described the German unrestricted submarine warfare policy, and stated: "Germany persisted in this course, and in the next two or three weeks sank at least two American ships, the *Housatonic* and the *Lyman M. Law*. Many other ships she also sank with Americans on board, whose lives were lost as a result. Accordingly, on February 26, President Wilson came before Congress" to ask for the Armed Ship Bill. Rogers further mentioned two more of the ships sunk after the German announcement, the *Vigilancia* and the *Healdton* and reported correctly the number of Americans lost on those ships.[40]

Jeannette Rankin, the only woman member of Congress at the time, voted against the war resolution. Her heartfelt vote sprang not from any examination of the maritime issues or other grievances against Germany, but from a straightforward opposition to war itself. She knew she was risking a lot, as numerous women leaders had urged her to vote for the resolution rather than leaving the impression that women would automatically vote emotionally, rather than rationally, feeding into male preconceptions and prejudices, and endangering the chances of women to be enfranchised and to run for office in the future. Nevertheless, she voted her conscience.

The final tally of votes for the resolution among members of Congress was 373 in favor of the resolution, with 50 opposed. Some later observers speculated that if the members of Congress had not been obliged to record their votes, the number opposing the war might have been somewhat higher.[41]

Although the majority for war was overwhelming, observers were surprised that as many as fifty members of Congress finally voted against the resolution. Some observers believed that many of the fifty were convinced to cast their vote against the resolution by the speech of Claude Kitchin (D., North Carolina), who, as House majority leader, surprised many by his plea for continued neutrality and his opposition to Wilson. Kitchin admitted that Germany had violated American rights by sinking American ships, but believed the United States could forgive such affronts if it had forgiven affronts by Britain and Mexico. Kitchin, like a few of the others who opposed the war, stated that he knew he would be outvoted, but that he had to vote his conscience even if it was unpopular and would subject him to heavy criticism.

Debates and Facts

This close review of the congressional debates over the declaration of war reveals that most members of Congress did not mention the ships sunk specifically or at all, and when some of them did so, they usually did not have their facts exactly right. In several cases, following the lead of Chairman Flood and the memoranda prepared by Lansing's staff, the members of Congress conflated the losses aboard the American ships with the losses of American lives aboard ships of foreign registry or with damage to American ships by German surface ships and submarines over the period of 1915 and 1916. In sum, four senators and four congressmen made specific mention by name of some of the ten ships sunk since February 1, 1917. All of the speakers who mentioned specific ships, except Robert LaFollette, were among those favoring the declaration, and they listed the ship losses as among the many affronts to American sovereignty and principles that required a vote in favor of the resolution.

Although some of the senators and members of Congress who mentioned the ships were either vague on the details or tended to blur them, it was clear that many were very aware of the ships, either through the direct references mentioned here, or through their allusions to the acts of war by Germany on the high seas, without specific facts. Some of the exchanges on the floor of Congress—for example, one in which Congressman Flood erred as to a date and was corrected by a fellow member—suggested that others who did not give speeches or who spoke on other topics regarded the ship losses as a casus belli. It was clear that at least some of the members of Congress had State Department documents in hand to provide some facts and figures. And of course, the major daily newspapers had carried news, usually on the front page for at least a day, of all of these events as they had happened.[42]

The degree to which Republicans and Democrats joined in the prowar vote was remarkable. Three members of the "little group of willful men" who had opposed the Armed Ship Bill made it clear they now supported the president's war measure. Albert B. Cummins and William S. Kenyon, both Republicans from Iowa, were quick to announce their support for the war

Table 10.1. Congressional mentions of U.S. ships sunk, debates over declaration of war, April 4–6, 1917

Senator or congressman	Party, state	Vote on war	Ships mentioned	Page
Sen. Claude Swanson	D., Virginia	Yes	*Vigilancia, City of Memphis, Illinois, Healdton*	206
Sen. Robert LaFollette	R., Wisconsin	No	*Aztec*	224
Sen. John Sharp Williams	D., Mississippi	Yes	*Algonquin*	236
Sen. Paul Oscar Husting	D., Wisconsin	Yes	*Healdton, Lyman M. Law*	244–45
Rep. John J. Rogers	R., Massachusetts	Yes	*Housatonic, Lyman M. Law, Vigilancia, Healdton*	334
Rep. Henry DeLaWarr Flood	D., Virginia	Yes	*Missourian, Vigilancia, City of Memphis, Illinois*	340 310
Rep. Scott Ferris	D., Oklahoma	Yes	*Vigilancia, City of Memphis, Illinois*	392
Rep. John Thomas Watkins	D., Louisiana	Yes	*Housatonic, Lyman M. Law, Vigilancia, Healdton*	395

Source: Congressional Record, 65th Cong., 1st sess., April 1917, page numbers as shown.

resolution, even before it passed. They were joined by William F. Kirby (D., Arkansas), who had also joined in the filibuster to oppose the Armed Ship Bill. Opposition to the war tended to be centered in the Midwest and West, and most, but not all, of the senators and congressmen opposing the vote came from those regions.[43]

Opponents of the war did not raise the issue that, as noted in the Foreign Relations Committee report, *only twenty-five to thirty* American citizens had died under unrestricted submarine warfare; only seventeen or twenty-four Americans had died on American ships (depending on whether or not *Healdton* casualties were included in the total); or that *fewer than ten U.S. ships* had been sunk. Such arguments would not have carried much weight in the face of Wilson's high-minded line of argument.

Indeed, if opponents of the war had chosen to focus even more than they did on the actual events, they would only have drawn attention to the fact that German submarines had, after all, fired on American-flagged ships without warning, and that as a consequence, six American citizens had died during unannounced attacks on *Vigilancia* and another eleven on the defensively armed *Aztec*. Furthermore, since *Healdton* was assumed to have been destroyed by a submarine, the total number of U.S.-flagged ships assumed lost to German action since the announcement of the policy was nine, with a total tonnage over thirty thousand, and the number of Americans killed while sailing under the American flag would have been assumed to total twenty-four. Looked at in that light, combined with the losses that included the first two that Wilson had not regarded as "overt acts," and the one that even Robert Lansing had neglected to count, the *Algonquin*, the losses of American ships did amount to a significant set of affronts to American sovereignty at sea. Small as the numbers may seem in an age jaded by mass killings, the specific numbers were in fact a perfectly good indication that Germany had made acts of war against the United States. Supporters and opponents were at least vaguely aware of the facts, and although some supporters of the declaration manipulated the figures somewhat, the basic facts were available and were discussed.

The facts were not emphasized or used as an argument against the war by opponents as, considering the values of the era, the facts were more than a sufficient cause for war. And for supporters of the measure, the specific ship losses and casualties were part of the larger picture of offenses, significant items to be sure, but only part of the longer list of indictments of German behavior.

Members of Congress presented their arguments, for the most part, as driven by ideas, ideals, rhetoric and principle, with only a few listing specific events representing German acts of war. For some of those in Congress, as Lansing had observed regarding Wilson, the facts tended to be inconvenient in the face of preconceived notions. Even so, with the presentation of several members of Congress in both houses, the maritime issues had been mentioned, and in more than a handful of speeches the actual casus belli had been raised. Furthermore, as shown, the House Committee on Foreign Affairs report, presented by Committee Chairman Flood, examined both the broader issue of callous German behavior, and the specific facts with a fair degree of accuracy.

The specific ship losses that had represented the cause for war tended to become submerged in broader issues during the congressional debates over the war resolution. Wilson, his cabinet, Congress, and the American people chose to understand the cause of war as a fight of democracy against the brutish policies of autocracy, in which the ship losses and casualties were merely added factors among many.

Epilogue

As the nation moved into the war and into the well-known period of suppression of civil liberties and the harassment of all who opposed the war, the arguments in the Senate and House of Representatives were largely forgotten. The details of the overt acts, or casus belli, became almost entirely irrelevant to the grand engagements and the high excitement of the war itself. However, in the two decades from the end of the war on November 11, 1918, through the German invasion of Poland on September 1, 1939, that launched World War II, many in the American public and in Congress moved through a cycle of disillusionment with Wilson's war goals to a "revisionist" view of the causes of the war. By the mid-1930s, after the publication of several revisionist historical studies of Wilson's policies, and a lengthy congressional investigation headed by Senator Gerald Nye into the linkage between financial interests and the decision to go to war, the mood had changed. Congress passed a series of Neutrality Acts designed to prevent the United States from being dragged into another war. In several ways, the isolationism, disillusionment, and the Neutrality Acts themselves, represented an effort to draw "lessons" from the causes of American entry into World War I.[1]

Full review of those changes in public opinion and the development of legislation to correct what were seen as the failures of Wilson to be truly neutral in the First World War are beyond the scope of this work, and have been the subject of several excellent historical treatments.[2] However, it should be recognized that although the specific ship losses that brought the United States into World War I tended to be overlooked by both historians and the general public, several lessons derived from the maritime events of the First World War became part of the reasoning behind the new neutrality legislation.

First of all, the Gore Bill and the McLemore Resolution, although they had failed to be passed because Wilson had strongly opposed such congressional interference in foreign policymaking, had both represented means to prevent America from being drawn into war through the loss of American lives aboard belligerent ships. In different ways, each had attempted to outlaw the travel of Americans aboard belligerent ships. The neutrality legislation of 1935, renewed annually through 1939, contained provisions prohibiting Americans from traveling on belligerent ships in time of war. The law also required a complete embargo on the sale and transport of munitions to belligerents.

Secondly, when general war finally broke out in Europe, with the decision of France and Britain to declare war on Germany for its violation of Polish sovereignty in 1939, Congress hurriedly reviewed and revised its existing neutrality legislation. In a remarkable application of lessons learned from World War I, Congress passed, on November 3, 1939, the so-called "Cash and Carry" neutrality legislation. Under this law, belligerent nations could purchase war supplies (direct contraband) and related strategic materials such as petroleum (indirect contraband) in the United States only if they paid for those goods with "cash," that is, with deposits already in the United States. They could not obtain credit to obtain the goods. In this regard, Congress recognized that one of the causes for the German decision to unleash unrestricted submarine warfare in 1917 had been the unequal ability of the Allies in World War I to purchase goods, made possible by extensive loans. In effect, the informal "loan ban" initiated by Secretary of State Bryan in August 1914, but terminated by Lansing a year later, was now made part of statute law.

Confirmed neutralists, including many southern Democrats, applauded vociferously when Representative Sam Rayburn, House majority leader, spoke in favor of the bill. He said that the bill forbade "the things . . . that got this country into the war twenty-two years ago." He pointed out that if there were no such legislation, the country would have "reckless American shipowners sending ships through danger zones with American cargoes and American sailors. I tremble to contemplate what might be the reaction in this country to the sinking of our ships and the destruction of American lives."[3]

The other aspect of "Cash and Carry," the "Carry" side of the law, was that any such goods purchased by a belligerent could not be transported aboard American flag vessels. They would have to be transported aboard either belligerent flag merchant ships or aboard merchant ships registered under the flags of neutral countries other than the United States. The intent of this provision was to prevent the United States from being drawn into the war by the sinking of U.S.-flagged ships such as *Vigilancia*, *City of Memphis*, and *Illinois*, carrying goods to one or the other side of the conflict. The 1939 act, however, was a move away from pure neutrality through a strict embargo on shipments to both sides because it allowed the Allies to import goods aboard their own or neutral ships. In this regard, it represented a compromise between moderate neutralists and pro-Ally members of Congress, and a considerable concession to the mounting pro-Ally sentiment in the United States.

The Cash and Carry legislation passed the Senate by a vote of 55 to 24, and the House of Representatives by a vote of 243 to 172. It was immediately signed into law by President Franklin Roosevelt. Roosevelt, who rankled under congressional dictation of foreign policy through the Neutrality Laws, supported the new law as allowing more flexibility than the prior Neutrality Laws passed from 1935 through 1938. Through several measures and public speeches, he made it clear that he viewed the Axis powers as a threat to freedom throughout the world, and that he favored the Allies.

One policy that quietly got around the Cash and Carry legislation developed during the dramatic events of the twenty-seven-month period between the German invasion of Poland and Pearl Harbor. Led by the United States Line and Standard Oil, numerous companies began taking advantage of the fact that Panama had altered its ship registration laws at the end of World War I to allow for easy transfer of registry, but not ownership, of ships to that country. The transfer of registration could even take place abroad, at a Panamanian consular office. Transfer of registry and flag to Panama would allow an American-owned ship to engage in carrying war goods to the Allies without exposing the American flag to danger. Controversy surrounded those transfers, but they went forward. The use of the Panamanian flag to avoid various other kinds of restrictions had developed over the previous two decades.

During the 1920s and 1930s, an assortment of American shipowners had taken advantage of the modified Panamanian shipping legislation. Those included the Harriman Line, which sought to be able to serve alcohol at sea despite U.S. Prohibition laws, and illegal rum-runners, who sought the slight protection a foreign flag might offer in case of being stopped by the Coast Guard. During the Spanish Civil War, 1936–38, European countries entered into a nonintervention agreement, prohibiting their ships from providing transport for arms to either side in that conflict. Numerous gun-running firms, some based in Greece, registered their ships in Panama in order to be able to carry weapons to the Loyalists in Spain.

Standard Oil, at the end of World War I, had a considerable fleet of tankers registered in Germany. Recognizing that German ships would be confiscated by the Allies under the reparations agreements that followed the Versailles Treaty, Standard Oil quietly transferred most of the ships to registry in Danzig, which under the Versailles Treaty was to be a "free city," locally governed. When the reparations resulted in the confiscation of German-registered ships, the Standard Oil tanker fleet, under the Danzig flag, was safe from the reparations seizures. However, in the mid-1930s, ESSO recognized that the ships were in some danger, as the local government of Danzig was taken over by the local Nazi party, and it was clear that Hitler intended to take over Danzig (as well as other German-speaking areas in Europe). With their German crews, the Danzig ships might very well be lost to Standard Oil in the event of a war between Germany and the United States. The company began transferring ships from Danzig to Panama in 1935.

Then, as the Cash and Carry legislation began to prevent the shipment of petroleum aboard U.S. tankers to Britain in the period 1939–41, Standard Oil and other companies transferred several more U.S.-registered tankers to Panama. All of these developments regarding the origins and evolution of the Panamanian flag of convenience are treated in further detail in the author's monograph *Sovereignty for Sale*.[4]

With the history of these events in mind, it is clear that the loss of the American ships that served as the cause of American entry into World War I had other even longer-lasting impacts on American maritime issues. In the narrow sense of a casus belli, the United States had entered the First World War because its ships exposed the nation's flag to attack. Recognizing that effect two decades later, Congress attempted to prevent further involvement in foreign wars by explicitly preventing the use of American ships in the aid of either side in a conflict in which the United States sought to remain neutral, first through complete embargoes on belligerents, and then through the Cash and Carry neutrality act. As a consequence of the latter decision, flags of convenience began to flourish, in which American companies were able to evade the consequences of neutrality and maintain trade under foreign flags. What had at first seemed a convenient way to avoid the consequences of Prohibition became, by 1939, a convenient way to avoid the consequences of neutrality.

After World War II, transfers to foreign flags became a convenient way to avoid the consequences of American labor laws and other laws that made operation under the American flag an expensive proposition compared to operation abroad. Soon, the Panamanian flag was supplemented with the creation of other flags of convenience, most notably that of Liberia. Meanwhile, the number of ships registered in the United States declined. Companies involved solely in transport between two American ports, such as those in Alaska, Hawaii, or Puerto Rico and the mainland, had to register their ships in the United States by law. But those American-owned ships engaged solely in foreign trade between foreign ports or between foreign ports and the United States could seek the more economical registries abroad, and most did so.

Reviewing the significance of the American-flagged ships that were lost to German submarines in World War I in the light of the questions raised throughout this work, it seems rather surprising that their loss has gone so underreported in the historical literature. The reasons for this oversight, however, are straightforward enough.

First of all, the events themselves, although recorded in detail in the press at the time, were quite minor incidents and episodes compared to the loss of major liners, and compared to the grand events transpiring in Europe. Although front-page news for a few days, each of the events subsided from public consciousness, as was evidenced by the fact that later news stories had to repeat the details of earlier incidents to refresh readers' memories, as in the oft-repeated account of the loss of the *William P. Frye*. Also, as noted, the loss of workingmen aboard merchant ships had far less resonance with Wilson and the public of his era than did the loss of middle-class women and children aboard British liners.

Furthermore, Woodrow Wilson sought to construe his reasons for entry into the war in idealistic terms, rather than in terms of the actual "overt acts" that had convinced his cabinet and members of Congress that Germany was engaged in war with the United States. Thus, historians have rightly enough pursued a deeper understanding of Wilson's idealism, his attempts at neutrality, and the ways in which his neutrality policies ended up favoring the Allies. Even though the ships and their losses were at the heart of the matter, as shown in this volume, Wilson did not choose to present it that way in his address. Once the war began, he continued to promote it, as did his propagandists, such as George Creel, head of the Committee of Public Information, as one of democracy against autocracy. Those ideals and their failure seemed at the core of the disillusionment and isolationism that dominated American public opinion in the interwar decades.

Although Wilson made freedom of the seas one of the "Fourteen Points" in his war goals, nothing was done in the peace treaties to define that freedom or to implement any international agreements that would guarantee the supposed right of neutrals to trade freely with belligerents. Britain strongly opposed any limitation on the use of its fleet to protect its interests through blockades, so the issue was quietly forgotten at Versailles. The Declaration of London was never ratified, and during World War II, its provisions protecting civilian crews of belligerent and neutral merchant ships were almost completely ignored by the combatant navies, including the U.S. Navy.

And lastly, for historians writing about the grand events of World War I, the story is more readily told by concentrating on the major diplomatic and military decision makers and the difficult choices they made. After all, the records of governmental leaders and their decisions are quite accessible through published memoirs and public documents. By contrast, some of the details regarding the lives and deaths of obscure merchant mariners were more casually recorded, with prevalent errors and contradictions, even among those at the time who were concerned, such as news reporters, diplomats, cabinet members, or members of Congress. In addition, historians like to maintain a sense of proportion between cause and effect, and to present a narrative that unfolds in a logical fashion. Grand events on a grand stage, after all, make for a good tale well told.

Sometimes however, small and obscure events are at the turning points of history. *Housatonic, Lyman M. Law, Algonquin, Vigilancia, City of Memphis, Illinois, Healdton, Aztec, Missourian,* and *Marguerite* deserve to be remembered. The loss of those ten American-flagged ships, and the plight of their crews, shaped the future in ways that were rarely perceived then or later.

Appendix A

Loss of the *Healdton*

On March 21, the *Healdton*, a fully loaded ESSO tanker, was sunk off the Dutch coast, with the loss of twenty-one lives, including seven American seamen. Before and immediately after this ship loss, Wilson still did not make his position public. However, we do know from the diary of his advisor Edward House that before any more ships sank, he decided to ask Congress either to declare war or declare that a state of war existed.

The loss of *Healdton* certainly contributed to the decision of Congress, and apparently also to the decision of Wilson. However, Germany denied that any of its submarines had sunk that particular ship (although admitting all the others). And, in fact, that denial was correct, as this appendix demonstrates.

For all of these reasons, the mystery surrounding the loss of *Healdton* ranks with other controversial cases of maritime casus belli, such as the destruction of the USS *Maine* in Havana in 1898, and with the episodes of the USS *Maddox* and USS *Turner Joy* in the Gulf of Tonkin in 1964.

When *Healdton* was lost, the U.S. press and the State Department concluded that it had been lost to a German submarine. The reason for this conclusion was simple enough: Captain Charles Christopher reported to the American consul in Amsterdam that after the ship suffered two detonations, as he was evacuating to a lifeboat, he saw a submarine come to the surface as if observing the destruction. He reported that the submarine then submerged without contacting the survivors. After a night in snowy conditions, with some suffering from burns, the survivors in two lifeboats were picked up by a Dutch trawler and by a Dutch patrol boat and taken to safety in the Netherlands. Among the twenty-one men who died from the loss of the ship were seven Americans. All of this information was reported in the press, including the *New York Times*, from the publicly released consular reports of the U.S. vice consul in Amsterdam. In his statement to the consul, quoted in the newspapers, Christopher reported his position when the ship exploded as about twenty-five miles "north by east" of the Terschelling Light off the coast of the Netherlands.[1]

Several facts make it clear that the tanker was *not* lost to a U-boat:

1. Within a few days of the loss of the ship, the German Foreign Office issued a statement denying that a German submarine had torpedoed *Healdton*. The German official history published years later, Arno Spindler's *Der Handelskrieg mit U-Booten*, contains no mention of an attack on *Healdton*.[2]
2. German submarines rarely attacked at night.[3]
3. German submarine commanders were motivated to report every loss for which they could take credit, and sometimes even reported as sunk, ships that they only damaged. Therefore, had any German submarine even attacked *Healdton*, the commander would have been strongly motivated to report the attack. Indeed, German submarines were required to document their torpedo usage, so there would have been a record of such an attack if it had taken place.
4. German submarines almost invariably fired only a single torpedo, not two, at a target. Should a torpedoed ship show no signs of going under, then sometime later the U-boat may have fired a second torpedo to finish off the job. As the first detonation clearly disabled the ship, a second torpedo would not have been needed to finish off the ship.[4]
5. The area off Terschelling was not a common German submarine patrol area in March 1917. No German submarines were in the area on March 21.
6. There was little German motive for attacking a tanker with an oil cargo destined for Rotterdam, as the Netherlands was neutral and taking a slightly pro-German stand at the time. Goods landed at Rotterdam often found their way to Germany, and Germany did not desire to antagonize the Netherlands. The German unrestricted submarine warfare policy had been expressly moderated toward the Dutch.[5]

Despite these considerations, the early assumption that *Healdton* had been torpedoed by a German U-boat without warning became fixed in the United States both at the time and in most treatments by historians.[6]

In the course of identifying the specific submarines responsible for the loss of each of the ships in this period, the author consulted a wide variety of sources. Among these was an international Web site, "u-boat.net," that hosts a forum specifically devoted to the German submarines of World War I. Inquiries there turned up the suggestion by the U-boat expert Michael

Lowrey that *Healdton* was not sunk by a German submarine, but by a mine, probably one laid by the British two nights earlier on March 19, 1917.

Mr. Lowrey's source for the information was a detailed minefield map included in the official German naval history of World War I, *Der Krieg in der Nordsee*.[7]

Further inquiries on the U-boat Web site revealed that details of that British minefield and other minefields could be obtained by consulting a typescript by Lockhart Leith, "History of British Minefields, 1914–1918," at the Portsmouth, England, naval archives.[8]

The Leith report showed that, indeed, British minefield 156 had been laid on the night of March 19, 1917, by three ships: the *Princess Margaret*, *Angora*, and *Wahine*. The mines had been laid ten feet below "L.W.O.S." (low water ordinary spring tide), and were spaced 200 feet apart. The details of the minelaying route showed that it started at a point 54 degrees 7 minutes north and 5 degrees 11 minutes east, and proceeded in three legs in a generally southwesterly direction ending at 53 degrees 40 minutes north, and 4 degrees 57 minutes 30 seconds east, in a total band about twenty nautical miles in length ending within about twenty miles of Terschelling Island. It would be quite possible for *Healdton*, with a depth of hold of 27.3 feet, and a length of 369 feet, to strike two such mines in rapid succession, one amidships and one at the stern, just as reported by Captain Christopher.[9]

The Leith report also indicated that a "Notice to Mariners" warning of the location of the minefield had been issued on March 20 reporting a change in the safe zone. *Healdton* had left Bergen, Norway, on the early morning of March 20, and thus was at sea when the announcement was published, and Captain Christopher had no way of knowing of the changed safe zone.

All of this information supported the idea that *Healdton* suffered two detonations from mines in British minefield 156 (number 21 on the German chart). Since Christopher reported that he was about twenty-five miles north by east from the Terschelling Light, and since the southern end of minefield 156 was about twenty miles north of the island of Terschelling, the facts support the assertion that the ship hit two of the British mines.

However, there are several important discrepancies raising questions about the minefield explanation. Captain Christopher's reported location for the loss of the tanker could be in *either* of two areas as it is not entirely clear to which of two lights he referred. There was a Terschellingbank Lightship, moored at 53 degrees 30 minutes north and 4 degrees east. On the island of Terschelling itself, there was (and still is) an ancient lighthouse, known as the Brandaris Light, located at 53 degrees 21 minutes 7 seconds north, 5 degrees 12 minutes 9 seconds east. The Brandaris Light can be seen twenty-nine miles at sea. Christopher was quoted as stating his position as north by east from the *Terschelling Lightship* (although its proper designation was the "Terschellingbank Lightship").

Plotting a point twenty-five miles north by east of the Terschellingbank Lightship puts the location of the ship loss nearly fifty nautical miles *west* of the minefield. Plotting a point twenty-five miles north by east from the Brandaris Light on the island of Terschelling puts the location of the ship loss just a few miles *east* of the reported center line of the minefield. If the ship captain confused the two lights at night, and reported his loss north by east of the *lightship* when in fact he was north by east of the Brandaris Light, he could have been in the minefield. However, if he was correct, and his position was correctly reported to the consul and in the press, then the loss was far from the minefield. It is very likely that he was taking his bearing on the Brandaris Light, rather than the lightship.

The Leith report indicates that the ships laying the minefield zigzagged over their course, rather than following it in a straight line, which would account for the minefield being wide, rather than narrow. On a particular "zig" or "zag," mines could have been spread as far as ten miles to the east of the center line of the minefield. It is also possible that Christopher's report of the position as "north by east" of the light was not precisely accurate. If *Healdton* had been twenty-five miles due *north* of the Brandaris Light, the ship would have been right in the minefield.

Lloyd's War Losses: The First World War Casualties to Shipping through Enemy Causes, 1914–1918 simply reports the loss point as "25 miles off Terschelling" (presumably, off Terschelling *Island*). A line drawn twenty-five miles off the island exactly crosses over the center route of the minefield, probably those laid by *Angora*. The center line of the course of *Angora* on March 19, 1917, ran from about thirty miles from the island to about twenty miles from the island.[10]

After the war, a Mixed Claims Commission accepted Christopher's report as accurate and awarded a claim for funds to the American War Risk Bureau based on the assumption that a U-boat sank *Healdton*.[11]

The claim was explicit in repeating the point of loss as north by east from the *lightship*, rather than on a bearing from the Brandaris Light, or, as Lloyd's had reported, at a distance from Terschelling Island. The bureau's evidence, like the consular reports and the newspaper reports, would put the loss far from the minefield. However, the War Risk Bureau report, relying on the consular report, simply repeated earlier sources. In any case, since we know that no German sub torpedoed *Healdton*, it is clear that the award of money by the Mixed Claims Commission was incorrect.

One possibility, of course, is that one or more mines had broken loose from their moorings, and had floated westward with wind and tide. It would not be impossible for one of the one thousand mines laid on March 19 to have drifted thirty or more miles westward over two days. On the other hand, it is extremely unlikely that two mines would have drifted together, and it will be remembered that Captain Christopher noted two detonations, not one.

The bureau claim before the Mixed Claim Commission and the press and consular reports all relied on Captain Christopher's statement that he had spotted a submarine as his ship was sinking. Of course, he could have been mistaken, or he could have fabricated the story of the submarine, either because he felt that steaming into a minefield would be regarded as his error, or because he thought a submarine story would be more dramatic and compelling and perhaps more likely to win the Standard Oil corporation an award from the War Risk Bureau. During this period, it was not uncommon for mariners to mistakenly imagine they saw a submarine, simply because of the fear of, and public clamor over, submarine attacks.

The possibility that there had indeed been a submarine other than German present seemed worth investigating. If it had not been German, it would have had to have been either British or Dutch. British submarine records at the British National Archives at Kew would reveal which British submarines might have been on station on the night of the loss of *Healdton*.[12] It seems that only one British submarine, *E-43*, was on a cruise between March 15 and March 22, in the waters off the Netherlands. The route of that cruise, however, puts it more than thirty nautical miles west from the location of the minefield and well to the north of all the suggested spots of the loss. The report of the British sub's cruise noted smoke on the horizon from steamers in the afternoon, but nothing unusual or remarkable, such as a sinking tanker.[13]

The Royal Netherlands Navy maintained six coastal submarines, numbered O-2 through O-7, during this period of the war. A coastal submarine might have ventured as far out as the various possible loss sites, but of course, the Netherlands had no motivation for sinking a tanker of a fellow neutral nation, destined for a port in the Netherlands. Furthermore, a Dutch submarine beyond the three-mile limit would run the possibility of being mistaken for a German U-boat by a British warship, and of being mistaken for a British submarine by a German warship. For such reasons, it would seem unlikely for one of the handful of Dutch submarines to have been spotted by Captain Christopher on March 21, 1917. A Dutch historian, Johan Joor, was kind enough to check the records of the Royal Netherlands Navy on deposit at the Dutch National Archives at the Hague. He examined the logbooks of the Dutch submarines through this period. Logbooks for two of them began later than the date, and all but one of the others showed that the submarines were in port on March 20 and 21. The one at sea, *O-2*, was accompanied by two torpedo boats along a different, more southerly part of the Dutch coast, from IJmuiden to Den Helder.

Thus, there were no German, British, or Dutch subs in the area, and Captain Christopher's reported sighting of a sub was clearly incorrect.

There are numerous unidentified wrecks off Terschelling, many of which have been located with GPS and sonar equipment. These are reported on a Web site maintained in the Netherlands (www.wrecksite.eu) and frequented by divers. Several wrecks have been located near each of the various points at which *Healdton* might have sunk. Possibly at some future date a dive team will identify the exact location of the loss of *Healdton* and may even be able to verify whether or not it was sunk by mines or by internal explosions.[14]

Looking at all of this evidence and considering the various discrepancies, it is reasonable to conclude that the tanker struck two British mines as suggested by Michael Lowery, that Christopher's quoted report of position was not exactly correct, and that he was either mistaken or deceptive when he reported seeing a submarine. Thus, a major ship loss that convinced President Wilson to request war on Germany in 1917 was the result of a loss to a British mine.

A version of this appendix was presented as a paper at the 2008 conference of the North American Society of Oceanic History.

Appendix B

Casualty Lists

Note that some 20 to 30 American seamen were aboard British ships sunk in this period, and about 186 American seamen were aboard U.S. ships sunk in this period. All except those noted below survived.

Table B.1. Names of Americans lost, by ship, February 5, 1917–April 1, 1917

Date Ship	Persons	How perished
February 5		
Eavestone[a]	Richard Wallace, seaman	Drowned
February 25		
Laconia[b]	Mrs. Mary E. Hoy, passenger Miss Elizabeth Hoy, passenger Thomas Coffee, stoker	Died of exposure in lifeboats
March 16		
Vigilancia	Neil P. North, third mate C. F. Aderholde, asst. engineer Estphan Lopez, mess boy F. Brown, carpenter Joseph Siberia (possibly "Loeria"), quartermaster A. Rodriquez, oiler	Drowned when boat capsized
March 21		
Healdton	W. Chandler, second mate C. F. Hudgins, third mate W. C. Johnson, third asst. engineer Henry Lee Veaux (or E. Leveaux), oiler R. W. Smith, able seaman John Steiner, able seaman George Healey, second steward	Drowned when ship suffered detonation
April 1		
Aztec	John I. Eopolucci, boatswain's mate from naval guard	Presumed drowned

[a] British cargo ship
[b] Armed British liner

Ten other U.S. citizens, not named in consular or published reports, are presumed drowned.

Table B.2. Number of U.S. fatalities, by ship, February 5, 1917–April 1, 1917

Ship	Flag	U.S. fatalities
Eavestone	G.B.	1
Laconia	G.B.	3
Vigilancia	U.S.	6
Healdton	U.S.	7 (from mine)
Aztec	U.S.	11
Total		28

Appendix C Table of Ship Losses

Table C.1. U.S. ship loss details, February 3, 1917–April 4, 1917

Ship Name (type)	Gross tons	Date of incident	Place	Crew	Dead	U.S. killed/ total U.S. aboard	Owner	Captain	Attacked by
Housatonic (freighter)	3,143gt	Feb. 3	Off Scilly Isles	37	0	0/25	Housatonic Co.	Thomas Ensor	*U-53* Hans Rose
Lyman M. Law (schooner)	1,300gt	Feb. 12	Off Sardinia	10	0	0/9	George A. Cardine Syndicate	Stephen W. McDonough	*U-35* Lothar von Arnauld
Algonquin (freighter)	1,806gt	Mar. 12	Off Scilly Isles	26	0	0/11	American Star Line	A. Nordberg	*U-62* Ernst Hashagen
Vigilancia (freighter)	4,115gt	Mar. 16	Off Plymouth	43 or 45	15	6/20	Gaston, Williams & Wigmore	Frank A. Middleton	*U-70* Otto Wünsche
City of Memphis (freighter) In ballast	5,252gt	Mar. 17	Off Ireland	57 or 58	0	0/30	Ocean Steamship Company	L. P. Borum	*UC-66* Herbert Pustkuchen
Illinois (tanker) In ballast	5,225gt	Mar. 18	Off Alderney	34	0	0/16	Texaco	H. H. Iverson	*UC-21* Reinhold Saltzwedel
Healdton (tanker)	4,489gt	Mar. 21	Off Holland	41	21	7/13	Standard Oil	Charles Christopher	Mine (British)*
Aztec (freighter)	3,727gt	Apr. 1	Off Brest	47	28	11/28	Oriental Navigation	Walter O'Brien	*U-46* Leo Hillebrand
Marguerite (schooner)	1,553gt	Apr. 4	Off Sardinia	12	0	0/1	William Chase	Charles W. Willard	*U-35* Lothar von Arnauld
Missourian (freighter)	7,924gt	Apr. 4	Off Genoa	53	0	0/32	American-Hawaiian	William Lyons	*U-52* Hans Walther
Total				360–64	63	24/185			

* U.S. press and State Department assumed loss was due to a German unannounced sub attack; see appendix A.

Notes

Chapter 1. The Voyage of the *Vigilancia*

1. Most of the literature surrounding American entry into the war has dealt with issues of German-American diplomacy, and Wilson's ideals. See, for example, Link, *Wilson the Diplomatist*, or Millis, *Road to War*. Brodie, in *Sea Power in the Machine Age*, recognized that it was the German policy that brought the United States into the war (322), but like most other historians, he provided no details of the episodes. Labaree, *America and the Sea: A Maritime History*, is an exception, accurately listing the individual ships lost (475).

Chapter 2. From *Falaba* to *Sussex*

1. Woodrow Wilson, message to Congress, 63rd Cong., 2nd sess., 1914, S. Doc. 566, 3–4.

2. The story of the American position regarding submarine attacks on passenger liners has been routinely covered in the historic literature. See, for example, Morison, Commager, and Leuchtenberg, *The Growth of the American Republic*, 2: 367–68.

3. U.S. ambassador James Gerard argued with German officials over their analogy to ammunition wagons, pointing out the differences between land and sea travel in law (Gerard, *My Four Years in Germany*, 176, 247). The Germans called American passengers aboard British ships "*Schutzengel*," or guardian angels (ibid., 188). In modern parlance, they would be known as "human shields."

4. Declaration of London, Articles 1–21, dealt with rules of blockade; Articles 22–44, with the nature of contraband; Articles 45–47, with un-neutral service (i.e., supposedly neutral ships serving the interest of a belligerent); Articles 48–54, with destruction of neutral prizes; Articles 55–56, with transfer of flags; Articles 57–60, with defining the neutral character of goods; Articles 61–62 specified rules pertaining to convoys; and Article 63 indicated that resistance or flight from search by a neutral vessel constituted belligerent action. The Senate ordered the Declaration of London printed on August 11, 1914, immediately after the Great Powers in Europe had declared war on each other. For the approval by Senate committee noted by France and it serving as basic approach, see Jusserand to Bryan, September 3, 1914, *Foreign Relations of the United States* (hereafter cited as "*FRUS*"), Supplement: World War, Part II: Neutral Rights, 491; and Lord Lansdowne's comments in the London *Shipping World*, as reported in the *New York Maritime Register*, December 29, 1915, 9. Lord Lansdowne was coleader of the Conservative Party, former foreign secretary, and a minister without portfolio in the British coalition cabinet in 1915–16.

5. Gerard, *My Four Years in Germany*, 248.

6. Brinnin, *The Sway of the Grand Saloon*, provides an excellent and colorful picture of life aboard the great liners.

7. One study reported that Danish, Norwegian, Swedish, and Finnish nationals composed more than 50 percent of the crews on American merchant vessels (Safford, *Wilsonian Maritime Diplomacy*, 109).

8. Although the names of American passengers killed or injured in liner attacks, as well as those of survivors, were widely published, the American consul and the *New York Times* reported only the last names of nine of the twelve muleteers who died aboard the *Armenian* ("Torpedo Mule-Laden Ship," *New York Times*, July 1, 1916). Some accounts placed the total death toll of Americans at twenty-three, but that figure seemed to represent the approximate total number of Americans aboard, including both fatalities and survivors.

9. The list of other passenger liners and merchant ships carrying passengers sunk or attacked by submarines during the period of American neutrality is quite extensive. None of these cases rose to the same level of concern in the United States. They included the following that carried at least some American passengers and/or crew, sunk on (or about) the dates shown.

Armenian	June 28, 1915
Anglo-Californian	July 4, 1915
Iberian	July 31, 1915
Hesperian	September 4, 1915
Sebek	October 12, 1916
Marina	October 28, 1916
Delto	November 18, 1916
Arabia	November 6, 1916
Ancona	November 7, 1916
Russian	December 14, 1916
Persia	December 30, 1916
Laconia	February 25, 1917
Englishman	March 27, 1917

10. The official German published accounts at the time did not usually give the identity of a submarine or its commander, but later published records of the German fleet in World War I substantiated the details. Those records were meticulously gathered from submarine commanders' logbooks and other sources and republished after the war as *Der Handelskrieg mit U-Booten* (The Commerce-War with U-Boats). That volume often provides valuable data missing from the accounts published in the United States (Spindler, *Der Handelskrieg mit U-Booten*, vol. 2, *February–September 1915*, 47–49. Hereafter cited as *Der Handelskrieg mit U-Booten*).

11. Page reported the loss of *Falaba* to Secretary of State Bryan (Page to Secretary of State, March 31, 1915, *FRUS*, 1915, *Supplement: The World War, Part II: Neutral Rights*, File no. 3622.112T41/2, p. 358). Bryan engaged in a lengthy correspondence to determine if the *Falaba* was armed or took evasive action, later followed up by his successor, Lansing. The news was sensational in New York: "Submarine Raid Killed American;

Leon Thrasher, an Engineer, Lost on Falaba, Admiralty Announces; Engaged on Gold Coast; Presumably Returning There When Germans Sank Ship with a Loss of 111 Lives. Shipmasters Want Guns. Demand Right to Arm against Submarines," *New York Times*, March 31, 1915. Doubts as to Thrasher's citizenship persisted, although it was claimed he did have an American passport.

12. Schweiger's comments have been widely quoted. See, for example, Brinnin, *The Sway of the Grand Saloon*, 420.

13. There are many accounts of the *Lusitania* disaster. Perhaps the most balanced remains Bailey and Ryan, *The Lusitania Disaster*.

14. Tumulty, *Wilson as I Know Him*, 237. Some writers saw both the positive and negative aspects of Wilson's comment, as in the editorial "Protests of Little Avail," in the *New York Maritime Register*, June 2, 1915, 9.

15. Josephus Daniels gave a very detailed account of Bryan's meeting with the cabinet when he tendered his resignation (Daniels, *The Wilson Era*, 431–32).

16. In the cases of House, Tumulty, Page, and Lansing, Wilson eventually severed his relation with each of them. House was an honorary colonel in the Texas state militia; he did not promote the use of the title.

17. *Der Handelskrieg mit U-Booten*, 2: 259–60.

18. Bernstorff to Secretary of State (Lansing), September 1, 1915, in *FRUS, 1915, Supplement: The World War, Part II: Neutral Rights*, File no. 753.72/2084, pp. 530–31. It should be noted that, with the proviso that Bernstorff included with the pledge, it would have been perfectly proper for a submarine to attack the *Falaba*, *Lusitania*, and the *Arabic*, as each had zigzagged or attempted to escape. In that sense, the *Arabic* Pledge did not go beyond existing German practice or a strict interpretation of cruiser rules. In fact, Bernstorff openly stated that the policy had been in effect prior to the *Arabic* incident, one more reason why the term "*Arabic* Pledge" is somewhat inaccurate. Gerard explicitly remembered that Bernstorff had stated the pledge was already in effect, as noted in *My Four Years in Germany*, 177. According to Scheer, the policy had been in effect only in reference to large liners, and the *Arabic* Pledge extended the prohibition to all liners. After *Lusitania*, orders had gone out to submarines not to sink any *large* liners. Following the *Arabic* sinking, the orders were altered so as to prohibit sinking *any* liners (Scheer, *Germany's High Sea Fleet in the World War*, 233).

19. Page to Secretary of State, August 29, 1915, in *FRUS, 1915, Supplement: The World War, Part II: Neutral Rights*, File no. 763.72/2078, pp. 528–29. Despite British propaganda suggesting that the German crews regularly killed survivors in the water, the British atrocity against German seamen in the water is one of the very few such events confirmed by neutral witnesses. Page, who was very pro-British, nevertheless dutifully collected and forwarded the affidavits of American witnesses to the event. The literature on Q-ships is extensive. See Bridgland, *Sea Killers in Disguise*.

20. Scheer, *Germany's High Sea Fleet in the World War*, 237.

21. Wilson to Stone, February 25, 1917, in Tumulty, *Wilson as I Know Him*, 205. In the voluminous correspondence of members of the general public giving Wilson advice, there were several continued advocates of the Gore and McLemore approach and variations on it. For example, Lillian Wald, of the American Union against Militarism,

proposed that munitions be sent to the allies only aboard foreign ship (Wald to Wilson, March 16, 1917, Wilson Papers, Seeley Mudd Library, Princeton University, Princeton, N.J.). See the epilogue of this volume regarding the revival of these ideas in the 1930s.

22. *Der Handelskrieg mit U-Booten*, 3: 125. The designation "UB" referred to a class of submarines used almost exclusively in coastal waters, armed with torpedoes and a single deck gun.

23. Gray, *The Killing Time*, 115–16; *Der Handelskrieg mit U-Booten* 3L 125–26; Scheer, *Germany's High Sea Fleet in the World War*, 242.

24. The full text of the "Sussex Note," can be found at *FRUS*, 1916, *Supplement: The World War, Part II: Neutral Rights*, File no. 763.72/2597a, Secretary of State to Gerard [for transmission to German government], pp. 232–34. The quoted passage is at the end of the note on page 234.

Chapter 3. The Flag under Fire: From *Frye* to *Pass of Balmaha*

1. W. J. Bryan to J. P. Morgan, August 15, 1914, *FRUS*, 1914, *Supplement, Part III: Neutral Duties*, File no. 765.72111/484a, p. 580. Bryan resigned in June 1915. Under Lansing, his successor, the loan ban was quietly lifted, and the Allies borrowed some $44 billion in the United States.

2. The full text of the Declaration of London, together with a State Department commentary showing reservations over the document's provisions regarding flag transfer, can be found at *Declaration of International Naval Conference*, 63rd Cong., 2nd sess., 1914, S. Doc. 563; hereafter cited as *Declaration of London*. The question of continuous voyage and American precedents from the Civil War era regarding the doctrine were popularly discussed at the time in both the general press and in more specialized maritime publications. See, for example: "Wilson to Protest; Cites Our Role in '63; Justice Chase's Decision in Matamoras Cases Likely to Be Basis of Message to Allies. President Framing Notes; Will Hold That the Form of Blockade Now Undertaken Is Without Precedent in Law or History," *New York Times*, March 23, 1915; and "Confiscated American Cargoes," *New York Maritime Register*, September 22, 1914, 9.

3. The request by Senator Stone for an explanation and Bryan's reply can be found in *Neutrality: Correspondence between the Secretary of State and Chairman Committee on Foreign Relations, Relating to Certain Complaints that the American Government has shown Partiality to Certain Belligerents during the current European War*, 63rd Cong., 3rd sess., 1915, S. Doc. 16.

4. Hough, *The Great War at Sea*, 169–77; Lambert, *Sir John Fisher's Naval Revolution*; Offer, "Morality and Admiralty"; Doyle, "Danger."

5. Scheer, *Germany's High Sea Fleet in the World War*, 228–32.

6. See the next chapter for incidents of accidental attacks on U.S. ships, particularly the *Gulflight* and *Nebraskan*.

7. The fragmentary news accounts of the Standard Oil tanker *Communipaw* being hailed by gunshot in the Mediterranean on December 3, 1915, with no damage to the ship left it unclear whether it should even be considered a "minor incident." In addition, the *City of Memphis* was hailed by a submarine on January 30, 1917, and then released after a warning. This incident did not engender diplomatic exchanges, and was only recalled

later when the ship was sunk in March 1917 as reported in "Patrol Picks Up Survivors; City of Memphis Crew Is Abandoned at Sea in Five Open Boats; Vigilancia Saw No U-Boat; 29 of Her 43 Men Landed at Scilly Islands after She Is Torpedoed Unawares. Tanker Illinois Is Also Lost; Oil Ship and City of Memphis Were Returning to United States in Ballast," *New York Times*, March 19, 1917. Some listings of minor encounters include one or two events for which no contemporary record could be located. Thus the expression "some ten or twelve" incidents represents the approximate number of minor encounters. The listing of minor encounters is based on newspaper reports and diplomatic correspondence. One or two other minor encounters apparently did not rise to the level of State Department concern.

8. The five lost to mines in the period of neutrality were *Evelyn*, February 19, 1915; *Carib*, February 23, 1915; *Greenbrier*, April 2, 1915; *Vincent*, September 27, 1915; and *Seaconnet*, June 8, 1916. Both *Evelyn* and *Vincent* were owned by Harriss-Irby-Vose. See p. 58.

9. Just such a list, combining most, but not all, of the major and minor incidents, with a listing of mined ships, was compiled by Robert Lansing for Woodrow Wilson in late March 1917. See pp. 132–35.

10. The *William P. Frye* was named after Senator William Pierce Frye, who had served as a senator from Maine from 1881 until his death in 1911. Among his other accomplishments, he was a strong advocate of the merchant marine and had introduced legislation intended to build up the merchant fleet.

11. This account is based upon a lengthy statement in "How the Frye Was Sunk. Capt. Kiene Says His Protests Were Ignored by Germans," *New York Times*, March 18, 1915. See also Cranwell, *Spoilers of the Sea*, 223. The official German History of the War at Sea series, *Der Krieg zur See, 1914–1918*, gives a full account. The volume on the cruiser war in southern waters is *Der Kreuzerkrieg in den ausländischen Gewässern*, ed. Eberhard von Mantey, vol. 3, *Die deutschen Hilfskreuzer*, 131–32.

12. "How the Frye Was Sunk," *New York Times*, March 18, 1915. Upon their return to the United States, his wife agreed with Kiene's assessment.

13. "Sea Rover Prinz Eitel Friedrich Takes Refuge at Hampton Roads. Ends 20,000 mile Raid; Crippled Commerce Destroyer Brings in 342 Persons Taken from Ships She Sank. Likely to Be Interned. Her Arrival Brings First News to Washington of Sinking of the William P. Frye. Starts a Prompt Inquiry. President and All Officials at Capital Stirred by Destruction of American Vessel. Will Demand Reparation. American Captain Says His Nationality Was Ignored and Wheat Cargo Shoveled into Sea" (dateline: Newport News, March 10), *New York Times*, March 11, 1915; *American Journal of International Law* 9, no. 2 (April 1915): 497–98.

14. "The Escape of Paroled Members of the Crews of Interned Cruisers in the United States," *American Journal of International Law* 10, no. 4 (October 1916): 877–82 (see also *FRUS*, 1915, *Supplement: Part III: Neutral Duties*, 839). The *New York Times* reported eleven ships sunk by the German cruiser; but Norman Hamilton, collector of customs of the port, in his report to Secretary of Treasury McAdoo, March 12 1915, stated there were passengers and crews from eight merchant ships sunk (*FRUS*, 1915, *Supplement*, 826). The explanation for the apparent discrepancy in the number of ships sunk is that

Thierichens had already released the crews of three of the ships to other ships at sea or to ports in South America and Easter Island. The "German village" built by the crew is depicted in a collection of photographs in the Sergeant Memorial Room of the Norfolk Public Library.

15. *American Journal of International Law* 9, no. 2 (April 1915): 498–99.

16. "Not to Hurry Gulflight Action; President Wants to Be Sure of Facts about Attack on American Ship; Orders Careful Inquiry; Possibility Seen That Germany May Deny Ship Was Hit by Submarine's Torpedo; Company Files a Report; Chief Officer Says 'Gulflight Submarined.' But More Details Are Wanted; New Theories," *New York Times*, May 5, 1915; "Page Pushes Investigation. Experts Sent to Examine the Gulflight—Crew to Testify," *New York Times*, May 6, 1915. The first names of the two seamen who drowned were not published; Short and Gunter were American citizens; the citizenship of Chapenta, who lived in Port Arthur, Texas, was not established. Second Engineer Crist identified Chapenta as "Spanish," although the press assumed he was American. "Gave No Warning to American Ship; Gulflight Torpedoed without Being Hailed by Submarine Says Second Officer; Saw Craft in the Distance; She Submerged, Launched a Projectile, and Did Not Reappear; Weather Was Only Hazy; President and Bryan Confer over the Affair at Night—Await Official Reports," *New York Times*, May 4, 1915.

17. "Wife of Captain Told; Mrs. Gunter Prostrated at Her Home in Bayonne," *New York Times*, May 3, 1915.

18. "Gave No Warning to American Ship," *New York Times*, May 4, 1915; Consul Stephens to Secretary of State, May 3, 1915, FRUS, 1915, *Supplement: The World War (1915), Part II: Neutral Rights*, 378.

19. *Der Handelskrieg mit U-Booten*, 2: 75–76.

20. Gerard to Secretary of State, June 3, 1915, in FRUS, 1915, *Supplement: The World War (1915), Part II: Neutral Rights*, 431.

21. See discussion of *Lusitania* in chapter 2 of this volume. Some chronologies of events posted on the Internet have asserted that the *Gulflight* was sunk by a submarine. The fact that the *Gulflight* was "torpedoed" but did not sink may have generated some of the confusion, as the term "torpedoed" could lead a casual reader to believe the ship was sunk.

22. "Hit Mine or Torpedo, Captain Reports," *New York Times*, May 27, 1915.

23. "Attacked under U.S. Flag; Nebraskan, Empty and Home-bound, Is Hit off the Fastnet; Attempt to Sink Her Fails; Crew Takes to Boats, but Returns to Vessel, and She Heads for Liverpool; 40 Miles off Lighthouse; News Amazes Washington—Captain Reports Damage Was Done by 'Mine or Torpedo,'" *New York Times*, May 27, 1915.

24. "Washington Awaits Facts; Will Ascertain Whether Nebraskan was Hit by Mine or Torpedo" (dateline: Washington, May 26, 1917), *New York Times*, May 27, 1917.

25. "The Nebraskan Incident," editorial, *New York Times*, May 28, 1915.

26. "Nebraskan Torpedoed; Navy Experts Report; Page Cables Summary of Their Survey—Engineer Swears He Saw Torpedo's Trail," *New York Times*, May 30, 1915; Report: FRUS, pt. 4, p. 87, June 1, 1915.

27. *Der Handelskrieg mit U-Booten*, 2: 106.

28. "Germany Apologizes for Nebraskan Attack; Expresses Formal Regrets and Offers to Pay for Damage to American Ship," *New York Times*, July 16, 1915.

29. Ibid.; Gerard to Secretary of State, July 12, 1915, in *FRUS*, 1915, *Supplement, The World War (1915), Part II: Neutral Rights*, File no. 300.115 N27/17, p. 469.

30. Regarding the *Cushing*, the Germans explained the mistake to Gerard (Gerard to Secretary of State, June 1, 1915, *FRUS*, 1915, *Supplement: The World War, Part II: Neutral Rights*, File no. 300.115G95/31, p. 431.

31. Chatterton, *The Big Blockade*, calls the incident of the *Pass of Balmaha* "one of the strangest sequences of the whole War" (177).

32. The name itself caused considerable confusion at the time and later. Its unfamiliar spelling and perhaps its similarity to "Bahamas" has led to it being listed in various documents as "Pass of Bahama" or "Pass of Balhamas" rather than the correct *Pass of Balmaha*. One *New York Times* columnist, puzzled by the name, confessed to not recognizing the reference ("Must Have Been a Superman," *New York Times*, August 5, 1915). Responding to the editor's puzzlement, an anonymous *New York Times* correspondent from New Hampshire referred the editor to Walter Scott's *Lady of the Lake*, canto 4, that mentions the "Pass of Beal'maha." The passage in the Scott poem is found in *The Poems of Sir Walter Scott* (London: T. Nelson & Sons, 1862), 251–52; "The Haunting Doggerel," *New York Times*, August 8, 1915. A visitor to the region remembered the name of the town in "The Pass of Balmaha," *New York Times*, August 10, 1915. Although the reference seemed obscure to Americans, the scenic town and pass were no doubt well known to the prior shipowners in Glasgow, a city located about thirty-five miles southeast of Balmaha. Today the town of Balmaha is a tourist attraction, as is the hike up to the pass behind the town, in a region noted for allusions by Sir Walter Scott. In 1900, the ship was owned by Gibson & Church Company of Glasgow, which owned three other "Pass of . . ." barks, all named for Scottish passes: *Pass of Branda*, *Pass of Leny*, and *Pass of Melfort* (shipowner information derived from *Record of American and Foreign Shipping*, 1900 ed., 805).

33. "Rival Prize Crews on American Ship—Both British and German Aboard Cotton Vessel Sent to Cuxhaven by Submarine," *New York Times*, August 4, 1915.

34. Chatterton, *The Big Blockade*, 177–79. The rather adventurous tales of the *Seeadler* have been often told. Edwin P. Hoyt, *Count Von Luckner: Knight of the Sea* is a popular retelling of the story. *Der Handelskrieg mit U-Booten*, 2: 118–20, tells of the encounter between *U-36* and *Pass of Balmaha*.

35. "United States Protests to Germany over Seizure of a Transferred Ship," *New York Times*, November 9, 1915; "Condemns American Ship—German Court Treats the Pass of Balmaha as an Enemy Craft," *New York Times*, December 13, 1915; "Germans Pay for Cotton—Owners of Pass of Balmaha Cargo to get $625,000," *New York Times*, December 20, 1915; *New York Times*, January 26, 1916, regarding Harriss receiving the funds.

36. The counselor to the State Department in 1914 developed an extensive critique of the flag transfer issue, reprinted with the Senate Document copy of the Declaration of London, but the Germans remained adamant regarding this issue (Gerard to Secretary of State, December 4, 1914, *FRUS*, 1914, *Supplement: The World War, Part II: Neutral Rights*, File no.195.1/209, p. 502.

37. Lowell Thomas's *Count Luckner, The Sea Devil* was written from Luckner's point of view. For the outfitting and conversion of *Pass of Balmaha*, see 105–28. Pardoe, *The Cruise of the Sea Eagle*, 11–28. Pardoe stated that the British contingent locked below was a total of seven men; his research provided other details that varied from previously published accounts.

38. This precedent, it will be seen, partially helps account for the curiously mild U.S. reaction to the sinking of *Algonquin* in 1917, as discussed in chapter 7 of this volume.

39. Scheer, *Germany's High Seas Fleet in the World War*, 91–92.

Chapter 4. The Flag under Fire: From *Leelanaw* to *Chemung*

1. *Der Handelskrieg mit U-Booten*, 2: 116–17.

2. "Germans Sink the Leelanaw; Destroy Freighter Bearing Contraband, Then Tow Boats toward Land; Give Vessel Full Warning; Hail Her off Orkney Islands, and, Finding Flax Aboard, Shell Her While Her Men Look On; Gravely Viewed at Capital; American Officials Regard the Act as a Contemptuous Disregard of Our Rights," *New York Times*, July 27, 1915.

3. "Americans on Leelanaw; Twenty-three of Her Officers and Crew Citizens of the United States," *New York Times*, July 27, 1915.

4. "Await Captain's Report; Operating Company Wants Details of Vessel's Sinking," *New York Times*, July 27, 1915.

5. "Washington Resents Leelanaw Sinking; Officials Regard It as a Contemptuous Act in Disregard of Treaty Stipulations," *New York Times*, July 27, 1915.

6. Ibid.

7. "Gave Ample Time to Leelanaw Crew; Submarine Captain Quoted as Saying he Couldn't Stop to Throw Contraband Over; So He Had to Sink Vessel; Washington Sees a Clear Violation of Treaty, but without Serious Aspects," *New York Times*, July 28, 1915.

8. Dennison, Consul at Dundee, to Secretary of State, July 28, 1915, in *American Journal of International Law* 10, no. 4, pt. 4, 162–63.

9. Ambassador Gerard to Secretary of State, October 19, 1915, enclosing the Note Verbale dated October 16, 1915, Berlin, *American Journal of International Law* 10, no. 4, pt. 4, 174–75; also in *FRUS*, 1915, *Supplement: The World War, Part II: Neutral Rights*, File no. 462.11 H21/10, pp. 607–8.

10. Secretary of State to Gerard, November 30, 1915, *American Journal of International Law* 10, no. 4, pt. 4, 177; or *FRUS*, 1915, *Supplement: The World War, Part II: Neutral Rights*, File no. 462.11 H21/6, p. 620.

11. "American Steamer Is Sunk by U-boat," *New York Times* (dateline: Washington, November 6, 1916), November 7, 1916.

12. *Der Handelskrieg mit U-Booten*, 3: 326.

13. "Captain Describes the Sinking," *New York Times* (dateline: Barry, Wales), November 7, 1916.

14. Untitled article (dateline: Cardiff, *London Daily Chronicle*, November 6), in *New York Times*, November 7, 1916.

15. Untitled article (dateline: Cardiff, November 6), in *New York Times*, November 7, 1916. *U-63* also sank the Norwegian steamer *Torsdal* and the English steamer *Rio Pirahn*

(probably *Rio Piranha*) on October 28. The rice cargo of *Lanao* was noted by Schultze (*Der Handelskrieg mit U-Booten*, 3: 326).

16. "Germany May Offer to Pay for Lanao; Belief in Washington That She Will Follow the Frye Precedent; Was Flying Our Flag; Decision Hinges on Whether Cargo Was Absolute or Conditional Contraband," *New York Times*, November 8, 1916.

17. Lansing to Grew, November 18, 1916, FRUS, 1916, *Supplement: The World War, Part II: Neutral Rights*, 310.

18. Grew to Lansing, December 11, 1916, enclosing note from Zimmermann, dated December 9, 1916, FRUS, 1916, *Supplement: The World War, Part II: Neutral Rights*, 324.

19. Untitled article, *New York Times* (dateline: Washington, November 11), November 12, 1916.

20. Ibid.

21. "American Ship Columbian Sunk by U-Boat; Crew Saved, London and Washington Hear," *New York Times*, November 12, 1916.

22. "American Skipper U-Boat's Prisoner; Captain Curtis of the Columbian Held for Six Days in Submarine's Brig; Three Fellow-Captives; Shipmaster Statement Contradicts Report That Vessel Was Held Up for Two Days," *New York Times*, November 14, 1916. There were several discrepancies in this story, as it was reported the crews were rescued by the *Varina* on the 9th. Other elements of the tale suggest Curtis was held aboard the submarine for one or two nights, rather than for six days.

23. Ibid.

24. The details in the diplomatic note conformed to the summary report in *Der Handelskrieg mit U-Booten*, 3: 252–53.

25. Grew to Lansing, December 17, 1916, FRUS, *1916 Supplement: The World War, Part II: Neutral Rights*, forwarding the report from Zimmermann (dated December 16), 325–26; *Der Handelskrieg mit U-Booten*, 3: 252–53.

26. Grew to Lansing, December 17, 1916, FRUS, *1916 Supplement: The World War, Part II: Neutral Rights*, forwarding the report from Zimmermann (dated December 16), 327.

27. Gerard to State, FRUS, 1916, *Supplement: The World War, Part II: Neutral Rights*, August 27, 1916, 285.

28. *Chemung* operating company identified as "Harbey Company" in "American Ship Sunk with Flag Flying," *New York Times*, November 29, 1916. The company name was spelled "Harby" in some reports.

29. "Spring Rice Sees Polk; Government to Try Now to Get Some Names off Blacklist; Cotton Firm Demands Act—Exporting House May Quit Business Unless Washington Intervenes," *New York Times*, July 23, 1916. It might seem that British naval intelligence officers had, by some means, provided Germany with information about the sailing and routes of some or all of the Harriss-Irby-Vose merchant ships that were destroyed. To get the Germans to destroy ships of a company that was on the British blacklist for trading with Germany would be quite consistent with British World War I stratagems of using Germany's own policies against her, as evidenced in the employment of Q-ships, in the handling of the Zimmermann Telegram, and in other incidents. It seems more likely that the high casualty rate of this particular firm was simply due to its aggressive effort to trade with both sides.

30. Ibid. Harriss-Irby-Vose apparently made a good income. For example, if the five thousand 500-pound bales of cotton aboard *Pass of Balmaha* had cost between the reported prices of $.055 and $.095 a pound, the cost of the cargo was between $135,000 and $237,000. The price awarded in Germany of $625,000 apparently included a good profit. William Gibbs McAdoo, secretary of the Treasury, had also supported this effort to facilitate cotton exports in the first two years of the war, as noted in Safford, *Wilsonian Maritime Diplomacy*, 38.

31. "Chemung Claim in Doubt; United States May Not be Able to Hold Austria for the Loss," *New York Times*, November 30, 1916.

32. "Harbey" is noted in "Chemung Sunk by Austrians; American Consul at Valencia So Reports to Washington," and "American Ship Sunk with Flag Flying," *New York Times*, November 29, 1916.

33. Ibid.

34. Lansing to Penfield, December 2, 1916; FRUS, 1916, Supplement, *The World War (1916), Part II: Neutral Rights*, 314

35. Untitled article, *New York Times* (dateline: Paris, November 28 [Censored]), November 29, 1916. Note that the *Times* claimed that Harriss, Magill & Co of 15 Williams Street were agents for the owners, in "Chemung Claim in Doubt; United States May Not Be Able to Hold Austria for the Loss," *New York Times*, November 30, 1916; *Der Handelskrieg mit U-Booten*, 3: 334.

36. "Skipper Undaunted by Chemung's Fate; Capt. Duffy, Whose Ship Was Sunk by a U Boat Is Here to Get Another Command; Teutons Let the Flag Fly; Did Not Insist When American Crew Ignored Order to Strike Their Colors—Submarine Towed Lifeboats." *New York Times*, December 29, 1916; "Chemung's Men Imperiled; Almost Swamped by Debris When the Ship Was Torpedoed," *New York Times*, December 9, 1916. Blasting caps mentioned in "140 Survivors Here from Sunken Ships; Officer of the Chemung Told U-boat Commander How to Blow up Steamer; Torpedoed Blasting Caps," *New York Times*, January 2, 1916.

37. "140 Survivors Here from Sunken Ships," *New York Times*, January 2, 1916.

38. Penfield to Lansing, January 23 1917, FRUS, 1917, Supplement 1, *The World War, Part II: Neutral Rights*, File no. 300.115C 42/16, pp. 93–94.

39. Grew to Lansing, November 27, 1916, FRUS, 1916, Supplement, *The World War, Part II: Neutral Rights*, File no. 341.557M331/52, p. 313; "Marina's Gun No Valid Excuse; Washington Holds Germany Cannot Uphold sinking Because Ship Was Armed. So Views German Pledge; Facts Cannot Be Learned Till Next Week—Lansing Goes Home to Vote," *New York Times*, November 3, 1916.

Chapter 5. Meetings at Pless Castle and on Pennsylvania Avenue

1. Tumulty, *Woodrow Wilson as I Know Him*, 254. Tumulty's memoir has been discounted by historians as a dramatization, and this account may be a figment of Tumulty's imagination.

2. Seymour, *The Intimate Papers of Colonel House*, 439.

3. Gerard, *My Four Years in Germany*, 178.

4. Steffen, "The Holtzendorff Memorandum of 22 December 1916," 215–24. Holtzen-

dorff had long advocated the policy, as described in the memoirs of Reinhard Scheer, *Germany's High Sea Fleet in the World War*, 231–38. The *New York Times*, on November 18 and 24, 1916, reported rumors from Berlin that Germany was considering renewing unrestricted submarine warfare. Grew, standing in as chargé d'affaires while Gerard returned to the United States on a visit, reported many rumors regarding the movement to renew unrestricted warfare, including a conversation with the Spanish ambassador on December 12 indicating that Germany would reject the peace overtures and resume unrestricted submarine warfare (*FRUS*, 1916, *Supplement, The World War, Part II: Neutral Rights*, 86). Grew repeated a similar rumor on December 13, from the Danish ambassador (ibid., 89). Grew reported renewed press demands for unrestricted submarine warfare on October 1, 1916 (ibid., 291–92). Before departing Germany in September 1916 for a visit to the United States, Ambassador Gerard had sent many warnings about the likelihood of renewal of unrestricted submarine warfare, as noted in Gerard, *My Four Years in Germany*, 250–58. In his notes, Lansing recorded rumors that Germany intended to "renew ruthless submarine warfare" on January 9, 1917, 37ff; and January 24, 1917, 53ff, Container 64, Private Memoranda, Robert Lansing Papers, MS Division, Library of Congress, Washington, D.C.

5. Houston, *Eight Years with Wilson's Cabinet*, 1: 228.

6. McAdoo to Wilson, September 24, 1916, in Link, *The Papers of Woodrow Wilson*, 38: 260. Considering McAdoo's prowar attitude, his advice to work on the "peace vote" reflected considerable political pragmatism. Illinois voted Republican in any case.

7. Hendrick, *Life and Letters of Walter H. Page*, 217.

8. Gerard, *My Four Years in Germany*, 262–68.

9. An excellent treatment of the internal politics of the German leadership is found in Birnbaum, *Peace Moves and U-Boat Warfare*; for coverage of the Pless Conference, see 315–24.

10. *Official German Documents Relating to the World War*, translated under the supervision of the Carnegie Endowment for International Peace, 2: 1320–21; Görlitz, *The Kaiser and His Court*, 230.

11. Lansing, *War Memoirs of Robert Lansing*, 214; drawn from Container 64, Private Memoranda, February 4, 1917, p. 63, Robert Lansing Papers, MS Division, Library of Congress, Washington, D.C..

12. Gerard, *My Four Years in Germany*, 270.

13. Colonel House believed that Wilson had decided on breaking relations as early as February 1, but Lansing, who participated in the same discussions, was not quite sure that Wilson would stick with the decision (House Diary, February 1, 1917, as cited in Link, *Wilson Papers*, 41: 86–89; Lansing, *War Memoirs of Robert Lansing*, 214; Houston, *Eight Years with Wilson's Cabinet*, 1: 229).

14. Container 64, Private Memoranda, February 4, 1917, pp. 63–64, Robert Lansing Papers, MS Division, Library of Congress, Washington, D.C.

15. "Senators Firm for Action; Majority Want It at Once, But Stone Is Said to Be for Delay," *New York Times*, February 3, 1917; Link, *Wilson Papers*, 41: 89 n. 1.

16. "Senators Firm for Action," *New York Times*, February 3, 1917.

17. "Break with Austria Too," *New York Times*, February 4, 1917; Lansing Desk Diaries,

entry for February 3, 1917 (p. 34 in 1917 volume), Robert Lansing Papers, MS Division, Library of Congress, Washington, D.C.

18. "Text of President Wilson's Address," *New York Times*, February 4, 1917; see also Link, *Wilson Papers*, 41: 111.

19. "Comment of This Morning's Newspapers on President Wilson's Announcement of the Break with Germany," *New York Times*, February 4, 1917.

20. The most notable back-channel negotiations had been through Swiss diplomats (Pleasant Alexander Stovall to Robert Lansing, February 10, 1917, in Link, *Wilson Papers*, 41: 193–94). Stovall discussed the Swiss effort to consult with all the neutrals between February 1 and February 3. See also Paul Ritter to Arthur Hoffman, February 2, 1917, ibid., 41: 102–7; Lansing to Wilson, February 12, 1917, ibid., 41: 201–2. The Swiss effort came to Colonel House's attention on February 12 (Seymour, *The Intimate Papers of Colonel House*, 447).

21. Gerard, *My Four Years in Germany*, 272.

22. Theodore Roosevelt to Hiram Johnson, February 17, 1917, in Morison, *The Letters of Theodore Roosevelt*, 8: 1153–54.

23. Lansing, *War Memoirs of Robert Lansing*, 233.

24. One measure of the usage of the term "overt act" is the fact that over one hundred news stories in the *New York Times* in this two-month period February 3–April 3, 1917, used the term; a year before, the phrase had occurred in only four news stories in the same paper in the same two-month period. Memoirists and correspondents also adopted the phrase as a form of shorthand for an event that would precipitate war.

Chapter 6. *Housatonic* and *Lyman M. Law*

1. A highly readable account of the *Hunley-Housatonic* encounter is Hicks, *Raising the Hunley*.

2. "The Ships List," at www.theshipslist.com, under "Pickhuben." The 1915 date is mentioned in "The Housatonic Case," in *Independent*, February 12, 1917, 89. Information supplemented from *Lloyd's Register*, 1915–16.

3. "First Sinking Reported—London Hears No Warning Was Given Housatonic off Scilly Islands—25 Americans on Board—Armed British Steamer Picks up the Officers and Crew of the Vessel—News Stirs Washington—But if U-Boat Took Precautions Attack Will Not be Adequate Cause for Action," *New York Times*, February 4, 1917.

4. "Captain Says U-53 Sank Housatonic; Returning Here, Ensor Tells of Encountering Craft that Visited Newport; Captor Expressed Regret; American Skipper Comes on Orduna—Rest of Crew Due Today on Philadelphia," *New York Times*, February 21, 1917; Ensor's initials were shown once as "P. A." but "Thomas A." is accurate, as confirmed in an arrival list as passenger aboard the *Orduna* on February 21, 1917. The date of *Housatonic*'s departure is shown in a report by Ambassador W. H. Page to the Secretary of State, reprinted in *American Journal of International Law* 11, no. 4, Supplement: "Diplomatic Correspondence between the United States and Belligerent Governments Relating to Neutral Rights and Commerce" (October 1917): 132–33.

5. "American Steamer from Galveston Was Torpedoed," *Houston Post*, February 4, 1917.

6. *Der Handelskrieg mit U-Booten*, 4: 62.

7. "Sea Visitor Unheralded; Giant U-53 Meets U.S. Submarine Outside and Is Piloted into Port. Ends a 17 Days' Voyage; Capt. Rose, Her Commander, Says He Has Plenty of Fuel and Supplies for Return. Calls on Admiral Knight; Asks for News of the Bremen and Quickly Puts to Sea After Brief Formalities" (dateline: Newport, R.I., October 7, 1916), *New York Times*, October 8, 1916.

8. James, *German Subs in Yankee Waters*, 8. Rose's own account of the visit to Newport and his actions immediately afterward was reprinted in Scheer, *Germany's High Sea Fleet in the World War*, 265–67.

9. James, *German Subs in Yankee Waters*, 8–9. Some of the press thought several submarines were operating off Nantucket, and news stories of the sinking contained some inaccuracies. James noted that the confusion over the number of submarines was due to Rose's own deceptive practice of reporting the losses by using several different U-boat ship numbers over his wireless at the time.

10. "Possibly Three U-Boats; Swift Harvest of Victims Follows the Visit of U-53 to Newport; 4 British, 2 Neutral Ships; Red Cross Liner Stephano is Torpedoed after the Passengers Take to Boats. U.S. Warships Go to Rescue; Seven Destroyers Rushed from Newport—Crew of One British Ship Missing. Nine Vessels Reported Sunk by Three German Submarines" (dateline: Newport, R.I., Monday, Oct. 9, 3 a.m.), *New York Times*, October 9, 1916.

11. "What the Visit of the U-53 Portends to U.S.; Blockade Peril Which Unpreparedness Has Brought Upon Us Graphically Presented by One of Our Foremost Naval Experts, An Authorized Interview with Rear Admiral Bradley A. Fiske, U.S.N.," *New York Times*, October 15 1916. Several of the news reports of the February 3, 1917, sinking reminded readers of Rose's 1916 visit in passing.

12. Gray, *The Killing Time*, 132.

13. "U-Boat Captain Gave Housatonic an Hour's Warning before Sinking; Told American Crew He Had Orders to Sink Every England-Bound Ship, but Tows Men in Boats toward Land—Washington Holds Incident Not the Crucial 'Overt Act,'" *New York Times*, February 5, 1917; "Housatonic's Captain Made Protest in Vain; U-Boat Commander Was Indifferent to Appeals, But Finally Agreed to Tow Boats" (dateline: Penzance, England, February 5), *New York Times*, February 6, 1917.

14. Soap: "The Housatonic Case," *Independent*, February 12, 1917, 256; "U-Boat Captain Gave Housatonic an Hour's Warning before Sinking," *New York Times*, February 5, 1917; "Housatonic's Captain Made Protest in Vain," *New York Times*, February 6, 1917.

15. "Captain Says U-53 Sank Housatonic; Returning Here, Ensor Tells of Encountering Craft That Visited Newport; Captor Expressed Regret; American Skipper Comes on Orduna—Rest of Crew Due Today on Philadelphia," *New York Times*, February 21, 1917.

16. Pages from Rose's log in Scheer, *Germany's High Sea Fleet in the World War*, 271.

17. "U-Boat Captain Gave Housatonic an Hour's Warning before Sinking," *New York Times*, February 5, 1917.

18. Ibid.

19. "The 'Housatonic' Case," *Independent*, February 12, 1917, 256.

20. Gray, *The Killing Time*, 143, 170.

21. See the discussion of *Leelanaw* and *Chemung* in chapter 3 of this volume.

22. "War with Germany," *Outlook*, March 7, 1917, 402.

23. Halsey, *The Literary Digest History of the World War*, 4: 21–25, does not mention the *Housatonic* but, like the earlier Roosevelt-style opinion piece in the *Outlook*, conflates losses aboard American ships with losses of American lives aboard Allied ships, including the *Lusitania* and the *Laconia* as well as with losses of neutral seamen and passengers aboard ships of various registries, both neutral and Allied.

24. "Austrians Sink American Ship, Submarine Puts a Bomb Aboard the Schooner Lyman M. Law Off Sardinia. Crew Saved in Two Boats; Attack Made Near Boundary of Barred Zone—Exact Location in Doubt," *New York Times*, February 15, 1917; *The Record of American and Foreign Shipping*, 1900, p. 686; *Lloyd's Register*, 1916–17.

25. "Law's Cargo Worth $31,200," *New York Times*, February 15, 1917. Stockton Springs is a small town on Route 1 in Maine, just north of Searsport, boasting a small harbor and rail connections.

26. The crew was a total of ten, including the captain; news stories at the time often did not count the captain as a crew member, and thus often referred to a total crew of nine.

27. Tredwell's name was misspelled "Treadwell" and "Treadway" in various reports. In fact, the correct spelling was "Tredwell." Roger C. Tredwell had earlier served as U.S. consul in Bristol, England, and in Turin, before his appointment in 1917 to Rome. "Austrians Sink American Ship, Submarine Puts a Bomb Aboard the Schooner Lyman M. Law off Sardinia," *New York Times*, February 15, 1917.

28. Gray, *The Killing Time*, 171, 224; *Der Handelskrieg mit U-Booten*, 4: 162.

29. "Lothar Arnauld de la Perriere and the Log of the U-35," liner notes, *World War I Films of the Silent Era*, Film Preservation Associates, 2001.

30. Nelson Page to Secretary of State, Rome, February 20, 1917, *FRUS*, 1917, Supplement 1, *The World War, Part II: Neutral Rights*, File no. 300.115L98/10, p. 139.

31. "Austrians Sink American Ship, Submarine Puts a Bomb Aboard the Schooner Lyman M. Law off Sardinia," *New York Times*, February 15, 1917.

32. Ibid.

33. Ibid.

34. For errors, compare "Austrians Sink American Ship," *New York Times*, February 15, 1917; and "Only One Foreigner in Crew," *New York Times*, February 16, 1917.

35. "Six British Ships Sunk by U-Boats, One of Wednesday's Victims Had on Board the Crew of Another Vessel That Was Sunk. Law's Owners Protest; Assert that American Schooner Carried No Contraband and Deserved Protection," *New York Times*, February 16, 1917.

36. "Captain of Submarine Threatened Law's Men.—Said He Would Send Them to Bottom of Sea, Whence They Could Appeal to Wilson" (dateline: February 17, 1917, Cagliari), *New York Times*, February 18, 1917.

37. Ibid.

38. Ibid.

39. Ibid.

40. Nelson Page to Secretary of State, Rome, February 20, 1917, *FRUS*, 1917, *Supplement 1, The World War, Part II: Neutral Rights*, File no. 300.115L98/10, p. 139.

41. "Lyman Law's Skipper Wished for 5-Pounder; McDonough Says He Could Have Sunk U-Boat 'As Easily As Buttering a Piece of Bread,'" *New York Times*, February 19, 1917.

42. Ibid.

43. "The Sinking of the 'Law,'" *Independent*, February 26, 1917, 341.

44. Theodore Roosevelt to Henry Cabot Lodge, February 20, 1917, in Morison, *The Letters of Theodore Roosevelt*, 8: 1156.

45. "Germany's Barred Zones," *New York Maritime Register*, March 7, 1917, 10.

46. Houston, *Eight Years with Wilson's Cabinet*, 1: 233.

47. Ibid., 1: 233–34.

48. *New York Times Current History, The European War*, 10: 980, as cited in Fayle, *Seaborne Trade*, 2: 42.

49. Lansing Desk Diaries, entry for February 21, 1917 (p. 52 in 1917 volume), Robert Lansing Papers, MS Division, Library of Congress, Washington, D.C.

50. Arthur Link, *Wilson Papers*, 41: 283–87, reference to *Housatonic* and *Lyman M. Law* and no "overt act," 284; "Armed Neutrality: The President Asks Authority to Safeguard Our Rights" (dateline: Washington, February 26), *Independent*, March 5, 1917, 396.

51. C. Ernest Fayle, among many others, assumed the Armed Ship Policy was approved as a means of ending the shipping impasse (Fayle, *Seaborne Trade*, 55).

52. Franklin K. Lane to George Whitfield Lane, February 25, 1917, in Link, *Wilson Papers*, 41: 282–83; Daniels, *The Wilson Era*, 594.

53. Lansing, *War Memoirs of Robert Lansing*; for Polk delivery, see 227. Lansing remarked that he had not expected anything important to happen in a letter to Edward N. Smith, February 27, 1917, Container 64, Robert Lansing Papers, Manuscript Division, Library of Congress, Washington, D.C.

Chapter 7. A Telegram, *Algonquin*, and an Abdication

1. As quoted in Beesly, *Room 40; British Naval Intelligence*, 204.

2. Several different translations of the telegram have been published. This is the version from Kahn, *The Codebreakers*, 135.

3. Tuchman, *The Zimmermann Telegram*, 150. Tuchman refers to the telegram as the overt act in other contexts as well, for example on page 149. Beesly, *Room 40*, covers the Zimmerman Telegram episode in pages 204–36; and Kahn, *The Codebreakers*, covers it in pages 129–53.

4. Although Wilson and Lansing were not aware of it at the time, Zimmermann had actually urged Eckhardt, the German minister in Mexico, to go ahead with negotiations with Mexico and Japan, well before the United States declared war, as early as February 5, 1917. As pointed out in the detailed coverage of the episode by Beesly, Tuchman, and Kahn, evidence of this change of strategy from negotiating *in case* war was declared to negotiating *even now* did not surface until the opening of German archives after the war. (Beesly, *Room 40*, 215; Kahn, *The Codebreakers*, 151; Tuchman, *The Zimmermann*

Telegram, 174). If Wilson had learned of that negotiation, given his values, he probably would still not have regarded such negotiations as overt acts of war.

5. Kahn, *The Codebreakers*, 137. Kahn did not assert that the Zimmermann Telegram was the overt act that decided Wilson for war. He did make a strong case, as did Barbara Tuchman, that it convinced much of the American public in the western states to favor war. However, Kahn did assert that American ambassador Page believed that with the telegram, American entry into the war "was delivered into his hands" (147).

6. For "Good Lord," see Lansing, *War Memoirs of Robert Lansing*, 228.

7. Lansing had noted that Wilson already began preparing his address asking for the Armed Ship Bill *before* meeting with the cabinet (Robert Lansing Desk Diaries, February 22, 1917, Robert Lansing Papers, MS Division, Library of Congress, Washington, D.C.).

8. Wilson's address to Congress, February 26, 1917, in Link, *Wilson Papers*, 41: 285.

9. "The Sinking of the Laconia," *Independent*, vol. 89, March 12, 1917, 437; "Chicagoans Lost on the Laconia," *New York Times*, February 27, 1917. The fireman was reported as "F. Coffey" of 44 Gold Street, Brooklyn, in a follow-up story in the *New York Times*: "12 Dead Reported Here," *New York Times*, February 28, 1917. U.S. consul Frost reported that the fireman killed was Thomas Coffee of Baltimore, identified incorrectly in the London press as Thomas Cassey ("Our Consul Sends Details of Sinking," *New York Times*, February 28, 1917). Despite this clarification, many later accounts of the *Laconia* event listed only two Americans killed, Mrs. Hoy and her daughter.

10. Floyd Gibbons, *And They Thought We Wouldn't Fight*, 41.

11. For speculation as to whether *Laconia* could be a casus belli for the United States, see "The Submarine Warfare: An Overt Act," *Outlook*, March 7, 1917, 397. In the foreword to Gibbons's work, Frank Comerford asserted incorrectly that the loss of *Laconia* was indeed the cause of American entry into the war (xiv–xv).

12. That change of rules came the next week, when the Senate, meeting in an extra session convened on order of Wilson, passed the rule change on March 9.

13. Morison, *The Letters of Theodore Roosevelt*, 8: 1161.

14. Union League speech, March 20, 1917, in Morison, *The Letters of Theodore Roosevelt*, 8: 1163 n. 3.

15. Wilson's Second Inaugural Address, March 5, 1917, in Link, *Wilson Papers*, 332–36; quoted passage is on page 333. In the original draft of the inaugural address, Wilson had said, "We have been deeply injured and wronged by the governments of both sides upon the seas," as pointed out by Link, 336 n. 2, and as can be noted in the photocopy of the draft in the Wilson Papers, Seeley Mudd Library, Princeton University.

16. Wilson's Second Inaugural Address, March 5, 1917, in Link, *Wilson Papers*, 332–36.

17. The House of Representatives could only convene earlier than the following fall on request of the president.

18. Correspondence, Daniels-Wilson and Lansing-Wilson, March 9–11, 1917, in FRUS, *The Lansing Papers, 1914–1920*, 1: 618–28.

19. "American Crews Paid Off; Line Abandons Sailings from Here after Many Postponements—Detained for Auxiliaries—Rumor That Guns Received at Navy Yard Will be Used on Steamships—American Freighters Sail—Mongolia and Algonquin First to

Start for England since the German Note.—Berlin's Fresh Warning to Us to Keep Ships Away," *New York Times*, February 21, 1917.

20. Ibid. The 50 percent war zone bonus became standard practice after the United States entered the war, under the rules of the United States Shipping Board (Safford, *Wilsonian Maritime Diplomacy*, 109).

21. "American Crews Paid Off; Line Abandons Sailings from Here after Many Postponements," *New York Times*, February 21, 1917. Reporters at first confused this *Algonquin* with another ship by the same name, owned by the Clyde Steam Ship Company, which was a larger, 3,200-ton vessel. Although Standard Oil reported releasing *Healdton* to proceed as early as February 20, it did not depart until March 2, according to a later statement by the captain (see chapter 9 and appendix A in this volume).

22. Toronto Marine Historical Society, *Scanner* 8, no. 2 (November 1975); *American Register of Shipping*, 1900 ed., 228; *Lloyd's Register*, 1916–17.

23. "Algonquin Sinking Won't Alter Policy; Washington Already Has Taken Last Possible Step Short of Declaring War. Other Americans in Peril. Two Were on Board Steamer East Point When She Was Sunk," *New York Times*, March 15, 1917; "Ship Shelled and Bombed. Crew Rush to the Boats or Jump Overboard on Sudden Attack. Appeal for a Tow Refused. Germans Leave Sailors in the Open Sea to Row 27 Hours to English Coast. Captain 'Too Busy' to Aid. Vessel Was Owned Here and Changed Hands the Day after Sailing" (dateline: Plymouth, March 14, 1917, via London), *New York Times*, March 15, 1917.

24. "Puzzled by Algonquin Trip. Local Shipping Men Thought She Would Arrive March 8," *New York Times*, March 15, 1917.

25. "Algonquin Sinking Won't Alter Policy," *New York Times*, March 15, 1917; Stephens to the Secretary of State, March 14, 1917, File no. 300.115A13, *FRUS*, 1917, *Supplement I: The World War, Part II: Neutral Rights*, 174.

26. Stephens to the Secretary of State, March 15, 1917, File no. 300.115A13/3, *FRUS*, 1917 *Supplement I: The World War, Part II: Neutral Rights*, 177.

27. "Puzzled by Algonquin Trip. Local Shipping Men Thought She Would Arrive March 8," *New York Times*, March 15, 1917. The other ships and the ports of arrival were: *Dochra*, Genoa; *Rochester*, Bordeaux; *Gold Shell*, Bordeaux; *Mongolia*, London; *Rockingham*, Liverpool; *Londonian*, Genoa. However, the report overlooked the fact that two others had departed after the announced policy and had not yet arrived. They were *Healdton* on March 2 and *Vigilancia* on February 28.

28. "Ship Shelled and Bombed. Crew Rush to the Boats or Jump Overboard on Sudden Attack. Appeal for a Tow Refused. Germans Leave Sailors in the Open Sea to Row 27 Hours to English Coast. Captain 'Too Busy' to Aid. Vessel Was Owned Here and Changed Hands the Day after Sailing" (dateline: Plymouth, March 14, 1917, via London), *New York Times*, March 15, 1917; private communication with the author from Emilie McAlevy, granddaughter of Charles Schultz. Schultz was a naturalized U.S. citizen.

29. "Algonquin Sinking Won't Alter Policy," *New York Times*, March 15, 1917.

30. *Atlanta Constitution*, March 15, 1917.

31. *San Francisco Examiner*, March 15, 1917. Ship name not italicized in the original.

32. Ibid.

33. *Declaration of International Naval Conference*, 63rd Cong., 2nd sess., 1914, S. Doc. 563, 18.

34. Since the company owning the ship after registry in the United States had not owned the ship prior to the transfer, the protection of the flag over such a ship was very dubious. Britain, France, and Germany had all indicated that such transfers to a neutral flag were not going to be accepted as establishing the neutral status of the ship under Article 56 of the Declaration of London. The United States had only argued for neutral status after transfer of registry in cases such as those in which the prior ownership had been American, as in the case of Standard Oil ships owned by a German subsidiary. The exchanges over this question had been extensive in late 1914. See *FRUS, 1914, Supplement: The World War, Part II: Neutral Rights*, 485ff. Therefore it is quite likely that Wotherspoon and perhaps Stephanidis and Benas fully recognized that if captured or sunk, the ship would not get official State Department protection.

35. Lansing prepared such a list between March 23 and March 30, and *Algonquin* was notably missing from the list. See pp. 132–35.

Chapter 8. The Tipping-Point Ships: *Vigilancia, City of Memphis, Illinois*

1. Numerous sources indicated the *Illinois* was sunk on the 17th, but both Captain Iverson of that ship, and the German commander of the submarine reported the sinking as occurring on the 18th.

2. The *New York Times* displayed its conscious effort to exaggerate the severity of German attacks that had killed Americans in a news story that described some confirmed 40 to 45 American deaths in addition to the (then) assumed total of 124 aboard the *Lusitania*. ("200 Americans Lost by U-Boat Attacks; How the Tension with Germany Has Ebbed and Flowed since the War Began; Many Cases Unsettled; Lusitania Sinking Brought a Serious Crisis as Did the Attack on the Sussex," *New York Times*, February 4, 1917).

3. *Record of American and Foreign Shipping*, 1900 ed., 973; "Patrol Picks up Survivors; City of Memphis Crew Is Abandoned at Sea in Five Open Boats; Vigilancia Saw No U-boat; 29 of Her 43 Men Landed at Scilly Islands after She Is Torpedoed Unawares.—Tanker Illinois Also Lost; Oil Ship and City of Memphis Were Returning to United States in Ballast" (dateline: London, March 18) *New York Times*, March 19, 1917. Sale of *Vigilancia*, an American-built ship, was made from the Ward Line to an intermediate company, Ward and Armstrong, and only later to Gaston, Williams & Wigmore. The 1915 sale was reported in "Breitung May Buy Liner Sigurancia; Owner of the Dacia Now Negotiating for Another Ship to Use as Cotton Carrier; May Solve Dacia Problem; Transshipment of Her Cotton Cargo to the American Ship Regarded as a Possibility," *New York Times*, January 29, 1915.

4. "Patrol Picks up Survivors; City of Memphis Crew Is Abandoned at Sea in Five Open Boats," *New York Times*, March 19, 1917.

5. "$1,000 Investment rated at $26,000,000; Romance Disclosed in Purchase by Bankers of Interest in Foreign Trade Firm; Gross Business $47,000,000; Gaston, Williams & Wigmore to Be Capitalized with 300,000 Shares of Stock and $5,000,000 Notes," *New York Times*, April 2, 1916.

6. "New $5,000,000 Line in World Sea Trade; Gaston, Williams & Wigmore, Inc., of New York, to Have Fleets on Both Oceans; Ships Fly American Flag; Firm of Allies Buying Agents, Beginning Business with $1,000, Enters Marine Field with 14 Vessels," *New York Times*, February 24, 1916; "Change in Exporting Firm; Two of Three Founders of Gaston, Williams and Wigmore Retire," *New York Times*, May 14, 1918.

7. "U-Boats Sink Three U.S. Ships; No Warnings Are Given; 22 Missing; All Had Names and U.S. Flags Painted Plainly on Sides," (dateline: By cable to the *Chicago Tribune*, London, March 18), *Chicago Daily Tribune*, March 19, 1917; "Patrol Picks up Survivors; City of Memphis Crew is Abandoned at Sea in Five Open Boats," *New York Times*, March 19, 1917. The Globe Line hinted that the crew had demanded higher wages than standard because there were coffins in the cargo, indicating the wage demands were based on superstition. That claim may have been released to the press simply to discredit the wage demand. "Orleans in Port, Lionized by French," *New York Times*, February 27, 1917.

8. Crew identities and nationalities compiled from consular reports and news accounts. "Submarine Trailed Vigilancia's Boats; Hoped to Torpedo Ships Drawn by Their Flares, Survivors at Halifax Assert; Two Life Craft Capsized; Assistant Engineer, Partly Clad in Bitter Cold, Swam a Mile—His Mates Drowned" (dateline: Halifax, N.S., April 1), *New York Times*, April 2, 1917. See appendixes B and C of this volume.

9. *Der Handelskrieg mit U-Booten*, 4: 96.

10. Narrative compiled from: "Patrol picks up Survivors; City of Memphis Crew Is Abandoned at Sea in Five Open Boats," *New York Times*, March 19, 1917; "Fifteen Lives Lost in Sinking of Vigilancia; Captain Says American Ship Was Torpedoed without Warning" (dateline: Plymouth, March 19, via London), *Chicago Daily Tribune*, March 20, 1917; "Lost Ships' Survivors Here; Passengers on St. Louis Describe Submarine Attacks," *New York Times*, April 10, 1917; "Thrown from a Small Boat; Only 10 out of 25 Who Fell Overboard Recovered by Mates; Borum's Party Disappears; Craft in Which Captain Left Sinking City of Memphis Is Found Empty; Five Missing Are American; Indications That Skipper and His Companions Were Taken Aboard a Submarine" (dateline: London, March 19), *New York Times*, March 20, 1917.

11. "Fifteen Lives Lost in Sinking of Vigilancia," *Chicago Daily Tribune*, March 20, 1917.

12. Casualties compiled from news stories cited above. The spellings of Loeria, Livio, Sparrow, and Nesz may have been erroneous, or may have represented family "nicknames" rather than the formal family names. In this period, Spanish surnames were often supplanted by informal nicknames. The author is indebted to Professor Eladio Cortes for this information. See appendix B in this volume for listing of U.S. citizen fatalities.

13. *Der Handelskrieg mit U-Booten*, 4: 96.

14. Mueller, *The Ocean Steam Ship Company of Savannah: The Savanna Line*, 17, 131, 139, 147.

15. "Patrol Picks up Survivors; City of Memphis Crew Is Abandoned at Sea in Five Open Boats," *New York Times*, March 19, 1917. The Veracruz expedition developed because the Mexican government of Victoriano Huerta refused to offer a salute to the U.S. flag after an incident at Tampico. Wilson's bristling at the affront to the flag and Mexican

"insolence" is well documented in Quirk, *An Affair of Honor*. The precipitating flag salute demand is covered pn page 26 of that work.

16. Sealed Hatches after Loading: "Cotton Steamer Seized; Mallory Liner Denver Halted by British—New Shipping Regulations," *New York Times*, January 7, 1915; "Patrol Picks up Survivors; City of Memphis Crew Is Abandoned at Sea in Five Open Boats," *New York Times*, March 19, 1917.

17. Ibid.

18. Ibid. Another source indicated the cargo was fifteen thousand bales of cotton: "Lost Ships' Survivors Here; Passengers on St. Louis Describe Submarine Attacks," *New York Times*, April 10, 1917.

19. *Der Handelskrieg mit U-Booten*, 4: 149

20. "Lost Ships' Survivors Here; Passengers on St. Louis Describe Submarine Attacks," *New York Times*, April 10, 1917. Edward Mueller, in his history of the Savannah Line, asserted that the ship included in the number aboard a few passengers, including women, on its March 1917 voyage, although the press reports, always lurid in such details, mentioned no passengers, nor did the usually scrupulously correct consular reports.

21. Ibid.; "Thrown from a Small Boat; Only 10 out of 25 Who Fell Overboard Recovered by Mates," *New York Times*, March 20, 1917.

22. "Thrown from a Small Boat; Only 10 out of 25 Who Fell Overboard Recovered by Mates," *New York Times*, March 20, 1917.

23. Ibid.

24. "Names Americans Lost on Vigilancia; Plymouth Consul Reports Five and Also Ten Dead of Foreign Nationalities; Tuscania Dodged U-Boat; Passengers Arriving Here Describe Exciting Encounter—Saw a Supposed Raider" (dateline: Washington, March 21), *New York Times*, March 22, 1917.

25. "Sour Lake—the Sweetest Story Ever Told," *Texaco Topics*, November 1950; Bishop, "The American Dream"; "Patrol Picks up Survivors; City of Memphis Crew Is Abandoned at Sea in Five Open Boats," *New York Times*, March 19, 1917.

26. "Patrol Picks up Survivors; City of Memphis Crew is Abandoned at Sea in Five Open Boats, *New York Times*, March 19, 1917. A later story claims there were thirty-four survivors but does not provide the names and nationalities ("The Illinois Sunk by Bombs—Captain, Arriving at Southampton, Describes U-Boat Attack" [dateline: Southampton, March 23, via London], *New York Times*, March 24, 1917).

27. *Der Handelskrieg mit U-Booten*, 4: 131.

28. "The Illinois Sunk by Bombs—Captain, Arriving at Southampton, Describes U-Boat Attack," *New York Times*, March 24, 1917; "Lost Ships' Survivors Here; Passengers on St. Louis Describe Submarine Attacks," *New York Times*, April 10, 1917; *Der Handelskrieg mit U-Booten*, 4: 131.

29. Bishop, "The American Dream."

30. The damage from the destroyer may account for some of the curious damage to the ship observed by divers who frequent the wreck. The destroyer is reported in: "Lost Ships' Survivors Here; Passengers on St. Louis Describe Submarine Attacks," *New York Times*, April 10, 1917. For twenty-first-century divers commenting on the state of the wreck, see Bishop, "The American Dream."

31. "Lost Ships' Survivors Here; Passengers on St. Louis Describe Submarine Attacks," *New York Times*, April 10, 1917.

32. According to a count by Robert Greenhalgh Albion, the American-Hawaiian Line was by far the largest liner fleet of the United States, with twenty-six ships totaling 177,000 gross tons in 1914. The Savannah Line (Ocean Steam Ship Company) that owned the *City of Memphis* was also among the larger lines, with nine ships totaling 43,000 tons. Texaco, which was just starting its line, had only three tankers, with a total tonnage under 15,000 by 1916. The Texaco fleet's great expansion came between 1917 and 1921. Standard Oil, owner of *Healdton*, had sixteen tankers with some 56,000 gross tons in 1914, although that fleet expanded with six more ships, mostly brought in from foreign registries through 1916 (Albion and Pope, *Sea Lanes in Wartime*, 314).

33. Lansing Desk Diaries, entry for March 19, 1917 (p. 78 in 1917 volume), Robert Lansing Papers, MS Division, Library of Congress, Washington, D.C.

34. Lansing, *The War Memoirs of Robert Lansing*, 235–36.

35. Daniels, *The Cabinet Diaries of Josephus Daniels, 1913–1921*, 117–18; Houston, *Eight Years with Wilson's Cabinet*, 241–45; Franklin K. Lane to George Whitfield Lane, February 25, 1917, in Link, *Wilson Papers*, 41: 282–83; Daniels, *The Wilson Era*, 594.

Chapter 9. The Agony of Woodrow Wilson

1. Wilson issued Proclamation no. 1357 on February 23, 1917, calling the Senate to meet on March 5; he issued Proclamation no. 1358 on March 9, 1917, calling the Congress to convene on April 16, 1917; and he issued Proclamation no. 1360 on March 21, calling the Congress to convene on April 2, 1916.

2. Two of the historians who specialized in the study of Wilson and his thought process, Ray Stannard Baker and Arthur Link, explored this question at great length. Both concluded that Wilson decided for war on or about March 21.

3. For the period March 7 through March 31, 1917, two Hollinger boxes (253 and 254) in the Woodrow Wilson Papers at the Seeley Mudd Library at Princeton University contain some 1,500 sheets of correspondence, diary materials, and other primary documents collected from more than twenty repositories.

4. Wilson to Roy Howard, March 22, 1917, Wilson Papers, Seeley Mudd Library, Princeton University. Wilson referred to his illness as "grippe" in this note, while in other apologies, he simply mentioned an illness. Arthur Link saw his long period of seclusion as the period when Wilson gradually came around to accept the idea that war was inevitable.

5. Lansing Desk Diaries, March 12, 1917, Manuscript Division, Library of Congress, Washington, D.C.

6. Ibid., March 22 and 23, 1917, 81–82.

7. Exchange with Daniels in Link, *Papers of Woodrow Wilson*, 41: 461–62.

8. Lansing Desk Diaries March 24, 1917, 83

9. Wilson to Key Pittman, March 28, 1917, Wilson Papers, Seeley Mudd Library, Princeton University.

10. Lansing Desk Diary Tuesday March 27, 1917, 86, in 1917 volume; House in Link, *Papers of Woodrow Wilson*, 41: 482.

11. *New York Times*, March 23, 24, 27, 29, 31.

12. "Mediation Hint Rejected; Germany Can Gain Our Ear Only by Stopping U-Boat Attacks. President Begins Message; Will Sum up Submarine Aggression and Ask Congress to Recognize State of War. To Assess Ways and Means; Conference on Industrial Preparedness Tomorrow—Naval Plans Working Out Rapidly" (dateline: Washington, March 22), *New York Times*, March 23, 1917.

13. "Cabinet Weighs War Plans; Members Agree That It Shall Be No Mere Defensive Conflict. Wilson Frames Speech; Will Devote Himself to Principles, Rather than Details in Appeal to Congress; Push Naval Preparedness; Plans for Raising an Army Also Under Way and Awaiting Legislative Approval" (dateline: Washington, March 23), *New York Times* March 24, 1917.

14. Lansing-Wilson exchange in Link, *Papers of Woodrow Wilson*, 41: 471–72, 475.

15. Captain Christopher gave a detailed schedule of his voyage to the press: "Depicts Suffering of Healdton Crew; Vice Consul Krogh Reports Washington Details of Torpedoing of Tanker; Some Died of Suffocation; Others' Clothing Was Burned Off—Exposure in Lifeboats Caused Two Deaths," *New York Times*, March 27, 1917.

16. Ibid., "Tanker's Lights a Target; Captain Says a Torpedo Struck Where Ship's Name Shone; Oil Cargo Burst in Flame; Trawler at a Great Distance Mistook Glow in Sky for Aurora Borealis; Found Survivors Helpless; Twenty Drowned and One Dead of Exposure—U-Boat Left Crew to Perish," *New York Times*, March 24, 1917.

17. "Depicts Suffering of Healdton Crew," *New York Times*, March 27, 1917. For details, see appendix A of this volume. It will be noted that the few historians who have looked at these events, including the author of the present work, have previously assumed *Healdton* was sunk by torpedo. See, for example, Labaree, *America and the Sea*, 475; and Carlisle, *World War I: An Eyewitness History*, 203. However, further research into the details, as presented in appendix A, demonstrate that the sinking was almost certainly due to one or two British mines.

18. "Tanker's Lights a Target; Captain Says a Torpedo Struck Where Ship's Name Shone," *New York Times*, March 24, 1917.

19. Newspaper reporters noted that congressmen who had returned to their districts after the adjournment on March 4 had noticed that "sentiment had changed" in favor of war ("Message Read to Cabinet—Members Pleased by Decisive Stand the President Is to Take," *New York Times*, March 31, 1917).

20. Wilson's proclivity to construe every decision as based on idealism is noted by, among others, George and George, *Woodrow Wilson and Colonel House*, 176, as Wilson placed his decisions "on the highest idealistic grounds."

21. Daniels, *The Cabinet Diaries of Josephus Daniels*, 125, entry for March 30, 1917.

22. "Message Read to Cabinet; Members Pleased by Decisive Stand the President Is to Take; Believe Nation Is United; Count on Overwhelming Majority in Congress, Despite Pacifist Activities. May Call for Million Men; Huge War Credit Also among First Demands the Executive Is to Make," *New York Times*, March 31, 1917. The need for additional specifics was alluded to in the Lansing to Wilson, memorandum, March 30, 1917, Woodrow Wilson Papers, Seeley Mudd Library, Princeton University.

23. Lansing to the President, March 30, 1917, Container 254, Wilson Papers, Seeley

Mudd Library, Princeton University, enclosing twenty-two pages of listings of German offenses. The original draft of the cover note by Lansing in the Wilson Papers shows that the "a" at the end of the word "memoranda" had been written over the original "um" in "memorandum," indicating that the document was a compilation of *plural* memoranda. Separate internal pagination shows that there were four memoranda included, each covering a separate topic. The erasure on the cover note and the internal pagination suggest that Lansing had the four separate documents already prepared, that he considered sending a single note, but then decided to save time by simply putting them all in one packet. The fact that there was some internal duplication from one list to another supports this line of reasoning. The inclusion of *Healdton* on two of the lists indicates that the final drafts of the lists were prepared after March 22.

24. E. N. Smith to Lansing, February 23, 1917, Container 24, Robert Lansing Papers, MS Division, Library of Congress, Washington, D.C.

25. Lansing to E. N. Smith, February 28, 1917, Container 24, Robert Lansing Papers MS Division, Library of Congress, Washington, D.C.

26. Although Wilson did not cite Augustine, he clearly had a "just war" concept in mind. In his Fifth Annual Message to Congress on December 4, 1917 (State of the Union address), he referred to the cause of the war as "just and holy" and spoke of the "intolerable wrongs done and planned against" the United States by Germany. His later development of Fourteen Points and his advocacy of a League of Nations reflected some Augustinian ideas, spawning a whole literature of debate over the nature of Wilson's ideals.

27. It is also significant that Wilson's approach conformed to other principles of a just war that had been evolved by commentators since Augustine. Other commentators had developed these conditions or requirements of a just war: the war should be undertaken only as a last resort; the war should show the right intent; the war should result in a more just result than continued peace. Whether consciously or not, Wilson certainly sought to show his decision as a moral one, and that the action of going to war was in accord with established principles of what constituted a "just war."

Chapter 10. *Aztec, Missourian, Marguerite,* and Congress

1. "Armed American Steamship Sunk; 11 Men Missing; The Aztec Is First Gun-Bearing Vessel under Our Flag to Be Torpedoed. Surprise Attack at Night. 12 Navy Men and Their Chief Among 17 Survivors Picked up by a Patrol. 11 in a Lifeboat That Sank" (dateline: Paris, April 2), *New York Times*, April 3, 1917.

2. For the loss of *Aztec*, see *Der Handelskrieg mit U-Booten*, 85–86

3. "Aztec's Gun Crew Splendid in Peril; Lieut. Gresham Tells of Bluejackets' Discipline When Ship Was Blown Up; Sunk on a Rough Night; Survivors in His Boat Picked up by a French Patrol after Hours of Suffering," *New York Times*, April 30, 1917. For Gresham's recommendations, see "Lifeboats for All; Government Issues Strict Order on Equipment of Steamers," *New York Times*, May 13, 1917.

4. Consul General Genoa, Wilber, to Secretary of State, April 5, 1917, *FRUS, Supplement: The World War* (1917), 205. For Hans Walther and *U-52* sinking the *Missourian*, see *Der Handelskrieg mit U-Booten*, 167.

5. "Submarine Captures American Schooner; The Marguerite Probably Sunk in Mediterranean—Crew Safe after 46 Hours in Open Boats" (dateline: Washington, April 12), *New York Times*, April 13, 1917. For *Marguerite*, see *Der Handelskrieg mit U-Booten*, 163. Some sources indicated two more American ships were sunk in the neutrality period, the *Edwin R. Hunt* and the *Seward*, both lost on April 7, 1917. Since the declaration of war resolution was actually signed by Wilson on April 6, technically these ships were sunk after the United States was at war. Of course, they had departed before war was declared, and the submarine officers involved had not heard of the U.S. declaration. These two ships are listed in a fugitive publication whose author and date of publication are not shown, apparently published in Britain, entitled "A List of Neutral Ships Sunk by the Germans." The list included those sunk under cruiser rules prior to February 1, 1917, four ships that had been sunk by mines, and both the *Lanao* and *Algonquin*, whose registry in the United States could be questioned. Thus every effort was made to make the list as extensive as possible. Other records confirm the loss of both *Edwin R. Hunt* and *Seward* on April 7.

6. "Senate Presses for Action; Continuous Session Ordered When Action Is Temporarily Halted. Will Begin at 10 a.m. Today; Norris and Gronna May Help LaFollette Filibuster, But Cannot Win, Even without Closure; Only 6 in Anti-War Party; House Almost Unanimous for Declaration, May Act at Once Unless Senate Hurries," *New York Times*, April 4, 1917.

7. "Debate Lasted 16½ hours; One Hundred Speeches Were Made—Miss Rankin, Sobbing, Votes No. All Amendments Beaten. Resolution Will Take Effect This Afternoon with the President's Signature. Kitchin with Pacifists. Accession of the Floor Leader Added others to the Anti-War Faction," *New York Times*, April 6, 1917.

8. Ibid.

9. "Keen Debate for 13 Hours; LaFollette Scourged by Williams as Pro-German and Anti-American. 'Treason' Cry at Norris; Nebraska Senator Denounced for Hinting That Commercialism Prompted Nation's Course. Opponents 'Willful Men'; Three from Each Party—LaFollette, in 4-Hour speech, Assailed Great Britain," *New York Times*, April 5, 1917. Hereafter cited as "Keen Debate."

10. *Congressional Record*, 65th Cong., 1st sess., 224; hereafter cited as *Congressional Record*.

11. Ibid., 224.

12. Ibid., 244–45. Representative John Thomas Watkins (D., Louisiana) presented the same tabular information to the House of Representatives that Husting had introduced in the Senate, with similar conflation of types of losses (*Congressional Record*, 394–95).

13. Document introduced into the *Congressional Record*, 366, showing 226 Americans killed up to March 29, on ships of other nations.

14. *Congressional Record*, 216.

15. "Keen Debate," *New York Times*, April 5, 1917.

16. "Senate Presses for Action; Continuous Session Ordered When Action Is Temporarily Halted," *New York Times*, April 4, 1917; "Keen Debate," *New York Times*, April 5, 1917.

17. "Keen Debate," *New York Times*, April 5, 1917.

18. *Congressional Record*, 236

19. The desk diaries showed numerous meetings and telephone conversations with Swanson on March 27, March 30, and April 2 (Desk logs, Robert Lansing Papers, Library of Congress, Washington, D.C.).

20. *Congressional Record*, 206.

21. Swanson also erred in the date of the loss of *Illinois*, and in assuming *Healdton* had been torpedoed, but in both those cases, he was accurately reflecting what had been stated in the press.

22. For the Senate vote, see *Congressional Record*, 260–61; for the House vote, 412–13.

23. 65th Cong., April 4, 1917, H. Rep. 1, to accompany House Joint Resolution 24. Also reproduced in the *Congressional Record*, 319–22, as part of Flood's statement.

24. *Congressional Record*, 310.

25. Ibid., 319–20.

26. Robert Lansing's desk diaries showed several meetings and telephone conversations with Congressman Flood. Lansing spoke with Flood on March 22 and several times on April 2. It is very likely that the memorandum provided to the president was also provided to both Flood and Swanson (Desk logs, Robert Lansing Papers, Library of Congress, Washington, D.C.).

27. The Lansing memorandum: Container 254, Woodrow Wilson Papers, Seeley Mudd Library, Princeton University. The House Report, as noted above, was printed separately as House Report No. 1, 65th Congress, as well as reprinted in the *Congressional Record*, 319–20. The wording of many passages in the House Report is identical to the wording in the Lansing memo.

28. Ibid. It is not clear from the *Record* whether Flood read the report or simply submitted it. The verbatim nature of the *Congressional Record* suggests that he read it and that it was then transcribed into the *Record*.

29. 65th Congress, H. Rep. 1.

30. Shackelford's minority statement on pages 13–14 of the House Report (published version). The minority statement was not read into the record.

31. Ibid.

32. "House Will Pass Resolution Today; Continuous Session Will Be Held from 10 a.m. until Declaration Is Adopted. Committee for It, 17 to 2; Both Sides File Reports, the Majority Review the Wrongs Suffered at Germany's Hands," *New York Times*, April 5, 1917.

33. Congressman LaFollette quoted in King, *The First World War*, 273–74; *Congressional Record*, 371–72.

34. "Debate Lasted 16½ hours; One Hundred Speeches Were Made—Miss Rankin, Sobbing, Votes No," *New York Times*, April 6, 1917.

35. "Consul Cables Washington," *New York Times*, February 22, 1915. For the colloquy between Flood and Stafford, see *Congressional Record*, 310–11. The Bernstorff memo was introduced in the discussion in Congress (*Congressional Record*, 359–60) by Representative Henry Temple, from Pennsylvania.

36. *Congressional Record*, 340.

37. Ibid., 392–93.

38. Ibid.

39. Ibid.

40. Ibid., 334.

41. For the Senate vote, see *Congressional Record*, 260–61; for the House vote, ibid., 412–13.

42. Ibid., 310.

43. "Senate Presses for Action; Continuous Session Ordered When Action is Temporarily Halted," *New York Times*, April 4, 1917; "Keen Debate," *New York Times*, April 5, 1917.

Epilogue

1. The historical work most noted for capturing the revisionist critique of the failure of neutrality was Millis, *Road to War*, published in 1935.

2. One such work, covering the pro-Ally side in depth is Chadwin, *The Warhawks*. An excellent coverage of the emotional revulsion against war in the 1930s is Osgood, *Ideals and Self Interest in America's Foreign Relations*.

3. Congessman Sam Rayburn quoted in Turner Catledge, "Opponents Routed," *New York Times*, November 3, 1939.

4. Full coverage of the development of the Panamanian flag of convenience is found in Carlisle, *Sovereignty for Sale*, 1–97.

Appendix A. Loss of the *Healdton*

1. "Tanker's Lights a Target," *New York Times*, March 24, 1917.

2. *Der Handelskrieg mit U-Booten*. Spindler's reference is the definitive record of ships sunk by German U-boats in World War I, compiled from a review of the original U-boat logs and other official German records.

3. See Bacon, *The Dover Patrol*, 348–49, referring to the fact that subs rarely operated at night in the period.

4. The author is obliged to Michael Lowrey, U-boat history expert, for these particular details regarding U-boat practices.

5. Fayle, *Seaborne Trade*, vol. 3, *The Period of Unrestricted Submarine Warfare*, 50.

6. Robert Lansing put the list together after the reported loss of *Healdton* by March 30, giving it to Wilson on that day. The list is in the Wilson Papers, Princeton University. Secretary of State Lansing included this ship loss in a list of German offenses that he prepared for Wilson, and the seven American casualties aboard the ship were alluded to by the House Foreign Relations Committee in their report supporting the war resolution in April. Later historical treatments of the U.S. ship losses in this period, although usually very cursory, have often included references to the *Healdton* along with the nine other ships lost to German submarines between February 3, 1917, and April 4, 1917.

7. The map in question is entitled *Minelage und Sperrgebietsgrenzen 1917*, map 16. This volume is held in several American libraries. The author consulted the copy at the Nimitz Library of the Naval Academy in Annapolis, and found that the map indeed showed a British minefield, number 21 on the German map, laid down on March 19, 1917.

8. The researcher Oliver Lörscher referred the author to the Leith report document, from which Curatorial Officer Iain MacKenzie of the Naval Historical Branch, Admiralty Library at Portsmouth, was kind enough to copy and mail the pertinent pages.

9. Lockart Leith, "History of British Minefields, 1914–1918," typescript, 228, with a table on page 433.

10. *Lloyd's War Losses: The First World War Casualties to Shipping through Enemy Causes, 1914–1918*, 107.

11. The report by the American Bureau of War Risk Insurance that paid a claim for the loss of *Healdton* was clearly derived from the original consular reports. The successor to the Bureau of War Risk Insurance brought cases before the international Mixed Claims Commission to recover funds for payments for property destroyed by Germany during the war. The Bureau of War Risk, under a policy issued on January 19, 1917, to Standard Oil, insured *Healdton* for $450,000. The bureau paid the claim and sought indemnity from Germany through the Mixed Claims Commission after the war. The bureau, in its claim, stated: "At about 8.15 p.m. on March 21st, when as near as the Master could judge, 25 miles north by east of Terschelling Lightship, the vessel was torpedoed without warning, *probably* by a German Submarine." After describing the casualties, the claim stated: "In a statement transmitted to the Department of State by the Vice Consul at Rotterdam March 24, 1917, the Master reported that 'from actions Captain and crew believe submarine undoubtedly German.'" The Mixed Claims Commission awarded the claim to the bureau (NARA RG76, Evidence Relating to U.S. Vessels, Docket number 7498, Healdton Policy 1878).

12. Bruce Dennis, a historian conducting his own research at Kew, kindly volunteered to photocopy pertinent British submarine cruising records for the period.

13. The cruise reports are found at ADM 137/1684, British National Archives, Kew.

14. Among divers and other researchers who have searched for specific wrecks, such as the *Titanic*, the *Hunley*, and lesser-known historic ships, it is extremely common to find conflicting data regarding possible locations. The novelist Clive Cussler, who has funded numerous searches for lost ships, details many such problems in his nonfiction treatment *The Sea Hunters II* (New York: Putnam's, 2002), as does the nonfiction author Robert Kurson in his treatment of the difficulties of identifying a submarine wreck off the coast of New Jersey, *Shadow Divers* (New York: Random House, 2004).

Bibliography

Much of the story of the ships that launched the United States into World War I was readily available in the archived files of the *New York Times* and other newspapers. The *New York Maritime Register*, a business periodical of the period, gave some insights into how the ship-owning and shipping business community viewed developments. In addition to the published works listed below, the author consulted several archival collections. Most notably, the Woodrow Wilson Papers, collected by Arthur Link from numerous repositories, housed at the Seeley Mudd Library at Princeton, proved extremely useful. Professor Link published only a selection of those papers in the *Papers of Woodrow Wilson*, and a few of those he chose not to include were of great interest to this study. Furthermore, the papers of Robert Lansing, at the Library of Congress Manuscript Division, were useful, particularly the "desk diaries" that noted specific meetings with members of Congress and with the president over the days of decision. The printed (and Internet-available) *Foreign Relations of the United States* (FRUS) provided access to many of the consular reports of U.S. ship losses. The *Congressional Record* provided full coverage of the debate over the Declaration of War. In addition, kind assistance from international scholars in Britain and Holland, who retrieved documents from the British National Archives, from the Portsmouth Nautical Museum, and from the Dutch National Archives, as noted in appendix A, helped flesh out the missing elements regarding the loss of *Healdton*. See the end notes for specific archival and periodical sources.

Albion, Robert Greenhalgh, and Jennie Barnes Pope. *Sea Lanes in Wartime: The American Experience*. New York: Norton, 1942.
Allard, Dean. "Anglo-American Naval Differences during World War I." *Military Affairs* 44, no. 2 (April 1980): 75–81.
American Journal of International Law 9–11 (1915–17).
American Journal of International Law 11, no. 4. Supplement: Diplomatic Correspondence between the United States and Belligerent Governments Relating to Neutral Rights and Commerce.
American Ship Casualties of the World War, Including Naval, Merchant, Sailing and Fishing Vessels. Washington, D.C.: U.S. Office of Naval Records, 1923.
Augustine of Hippo. *City of God*. Translated by Henry Bettenson. New York: Penguin, 2003.
Bacon, Reginald. *The Dover Patrol 1915–1917*. New York: George H. Doran, 1919.
Bailey, Thomas, and Paul B. Ryan. *The Lusitania Disaster—An Episode in Modern Warfare and Diplomacy*. New York: Free Press, 1975.
Baker, Newton D. *Why We Went to War*. New York: Harper and Brothers, for the Council on Foreign Relations, 1936.

Baker, Ray Stannard. *Woodrow Wilson and the World Settlement.* Garden City, N.Y.: Doubleday, Page, 1922.
Bass, Herbert. *America's Entry into World War One: Submarines, Sentiment, or Security?* New York: Holt, Rinehart and Winston, 1964.
Beesly, Patrick. *Room 40: British Naval Intelligence, 1914-1918.* London: Hamish Hamilton, 1982.
Bernstorff, Erich von. *My Three Years in America.* New York: Scribners, 1920.
Birnbaum, Karl. *Peace Moves and U-Boat Warfare. A Study of Imperial Germany's policy towards the United States, April 18, 1916–January 9, 1917.* Hamden, Ct.: Archon Books, 1970.
Bishop, Leigh. "The American Dream." *Diver* (UK), April 2005.
Bowling, Roland Alfred. "The Negative Influence of Mahan on the Protection of Shipping in Warfare: The Convoy Controversy in the Twentieth Century." Ph.D. diss., University of Maine, 1980.
Bridgland, Tony. *Sea Killers in Disguise: The Story of Q-Ships in the First World War.* Annapolis: Naval Institute Press, 1999.
Brinnin, John Malcolm. *The Sway of the Grand Saloon: A Social History of the North Atlantic.* New York: Delacorte Press, 1971.
Brodie, Bernard. *Sea Power in the Machine Age.* Princeton, N.J.: Princeton University Press, 1941.
Carlisle, Rodney. "The Attacks on U.S. Shipping That Precipitated American Entry into World War I." *Northern Mariner/Le marin du nord* 27, no. 3 (July 2007): 41–46.
———. *Sovereignty for Sale: The Origins and Evolution of the Panamanian and Liberian Flags of Convenience.* Annapolis: Naval Institute Press, 1981.
———. *World War I: An Eyewitness History.* New York: Facts on File, 2007.
Carnegie Endowment for International Peace. *Official German Documents Relating to the World War.* Translated under the supervision of the Carnegie Endowment for International Peace. Vol. 2. New York: Oxford University Press, 1923.
Chadwin, Mark Lincoln. *The Warhawks: American Interventionists before Pearl Harbor.* New York: Norton, 1968.
Chatterton, E. Keble. *The Big Blockade.* London: Hurst and Blackett, 1932.
———. *Danger Zone.* Rich and Cowan, 1934.
Clark, William Bell. *When the U-Boats Came to America.* Boston: Little, Brown, 1929.
Clephane, Lewis P. *History of the Naval Overseas Transportation Service in World War I.* Washington D.C.: Naval History Division, 1969.
Cranwell, John Phillips. *Spoilers of the Sea: Wartime Raiders in the Age of Steam.* New York: Norton, 1941.
Cussler, Clive. *The Sea Hunters II.* New York: G. P. Putnam's Sons, 2002.
Daniels, Josephus. *The Cabinet Diaries of Josephus Daniels, 1913–1921.* Edited by E. David Cronon. Lincoln: University of Nebraska Press, 1963.
———. *The Wilson Era: Years of Peace—1910-1917.* Chapel Hill: University of North Carolina Press, 1946.
DeGaulle, Charles. *The Enemy's House Divided.* Translated by Robert Eden. Chapel Hill: University of North Carolina Press, 2002.

Dixon, William Macneil. *The Fleets behind the Fleet: The Work of the Merchant Seamen and Fishermen in the War*. New York: George H. Doran, 1917.
Doyle, Arthur Conan. "Danger." *Strand Magazine*, July 1914.
Dupuy, R. Ernest. *Five Days to War*. Harrisburg, Pa.: Stackpole, 1967.
Emergency Fleet News. United States Shipping Board Emergency Fleet Corporation. Washington, D.C. [Weekly 1918-?]
Fayle, C. Earnest. *Seaborne Trade: History of the Great War Based on Official Documents*. Vol. 3, *The Period of Unrestricted Submarine Warfare*. London: John Murray, 1920-24.
Fess, Simeon Davidson. *The Problems of Neutrality When the World is at War*. Washington, D.C.: Government Printing Office, 1917.
Film Preservation Associates. *World War I Films of the Silent Era*. DVD. 2001.
Forstner, G. G. Von. *The Journal of Submarine Commander Von Forstner*. Translated by Mrs. Russell Codman. New York: Houghton Mifflin, 1917.
Furringer, Werner. *Fips: Legendary U-Boat Commander 1915-1918*. Translated by Geoffrey Books. London: Leo Cooper, 1999; Annapolis: Naval Institute Press, 2000.
George, Alexander, and Juliette George. *Woodrow Wilson and Colonel House: A Personality Study*. New York: Dover, 1974.
Gerard, James W. *My Four Years in Germany*. New York: Grosset and Dunlap, 1917.
Gibbons Floyd, *And They Thought We Wouldn't Fight*. New York: Doran, 1918.
Gibson, Charles Dana. *Merchantmen? Or Ships of War*. Camden, Me.: Ensign Press, 1986.
Gibson, E. Kay. *Brutality on Trial, "Hellfire" Pedersen, "Fighting" Hansen, and the Seamen's Act of 1915*. Gainesville: University Press of Florida, 2006.
Gibson, Richard H. *The German Submarine War, 1914-1918*. New York: R. R. Smith, 1931.
Gleaves, Albert. *A History of the Transport Service*. New York: George H. Doran, 1921.
Görlitz, Walter, ed. *The Kaiser and His Court: The Diaries, Note Books and Letters of Admiral Georg Alexander Von Müller, Chief of the Naval Cabinet, 1914-1918*. New York: Harcourt Brace, 1964.
Grant, Robert M. *U-Boat Intelligence, 1914-1918*. London: Putnam, 1969.
Gray, Edwyn. *The Killing Time: The German U-Boats, 1914-1918*. New York: Scribners, 1972.
Groos, Otto. *Der Krieg in der Nordsee*. Berlin: E. S. Mittler, 1920-29.
Grotius, Hugo. *The Law of War and Peace (De Jure Belli ac Pacis)*. Translated by Louise R. Loomis. Roslyn, N.Y.: Walter J. Black, 1949.
Hale, William Bayard, ed.. *United States Congress 1915-1916. Peace or War? The Great Debate in Congress on the Submarine and the Merchantman. Compiled from the Congressional Record by William Bayard Hale*. Baltimore, Md.: Organization of American Women for Strict Neutrality, 1916.
Halsey, Francis Whiting. *The Literary Digest History of the World War: Compiled from Original and Contemporary Sources: American, British, French, German, and others*. 10 vols. Vol. 4, *The United States Enters the War, Western Front, December 1916-March 1918*. New York: Funk and Wagnalls, 1919.

Hamilton, Richard, and Herwig Holger, eds. *The Origins of World War I*. New York: Cambridge University Press, 2000.

Hardern, L. H. "The Submarine War on Merchant Shipping." *Brassey's Naval and Shipping Annual, 1919*. London: William Clowes and Sons, 1919.

Hendrick, Burton Jesse. *The Life and Letters of Walter H. Page*. Garden City, N.Y.: Doubleday, Page, 1925–26.

Hezlet, Arthur. *The Submarine and Sea Power*. New York: Stein and Day, 1967.

Hicks, Brian, and Schuyler Kropf. *Raising the Hunley: The Remarkable History and Recovery of the Lost Confederate Submarine*. Novato, Calif.: Presidio Press, 2002.

Higgins, A. Pearce. *Defensively-Armed Merchant Ships and Submarine Warfare*. London: Stevens, 1917

Hoehling, A. A. *The Great War at Sea: A History of Naval Action, 1914–18*. New York: Crowell, 1965

Hough, Richard. *The Great War at Sea, 1914–1918*. New York: Oxford University Press, 1983.

Houston, David. *Eight Years with Wilson's Cabinet, 1913 to 1920*. Vol. 1. Garden City, N.Y.: Doubleday, Page, 1926.

Hoyt, Edwin P. *Count Von Luckner: Knight of the Sea*. New York: McKay, 1969.

Hurley, Edward. *The Bridge to France*. New York: Lippincott, 1927.

Hutchinson, Robert. *Jane's Submarines: War beneath the Waves from 1776 to the Present Day*. London: HarperCollins, 2001.

James, Henry J. *German Subs in Yankee Waters—First World War*. New York: Gotham House, 1941.

Kahn, David. *The Codebreakers*. New York: Signet, New American Library, 1973.

Kemp, Paul. *U-Boats Destroyed: German Submarine Losses in the World Wars*. Annapolis: Naval Institute Press, 1997.

King, Jere Clemens. *The First World War*. New York: Walker, 1972.

Kurson, Robert. *Shadow Divers*. New York: Random House, 2004.

Labaree, Benjamin W. *America and the Sea: A Maritime History*. Mystic, Ct.: Mystic Seaport, 1998.

Lambert, Nicholas. *Sir John Fisher's Naval Revolution*. Columbia: University of South Carolina Press, 1999.

Lansing, Robert. *War Memoirs of Robert Lansing, Secretary of State*. 1935. Reprint, Westport, Ct.: Greenwood Press, 1970.

Lautenschlager, Karl. "The Submarine in Naval Warfare." *International Security* 11, no. 3 (Winter 1956): 94–140.

Lawrence, Babcock F. *Liberty's Victorious Conflict: A Photographic History of the World War*. Chicago: Magazine Circulation, 1918

———. *Spanning the Atlantic*. New York: Knopf, 1931.

Leuchtenberg, William. *The Growth of the American Republic*. New York: Oxford University Press, 1969.

Link, Arthur, ed. *The Papers of Woodrow Wilson*. Vol. 41, *January 24–April 6, 1917*. Princeton, N.J.: Princeton University Press, 1983.

———. *Wilson the Diplomatist: A Look at His Major Foreign Policies.* Baltimore: Johns Hopkins University Press, 1957.
Lloyd George, David. *War Memoirs of David Lloyd George.* Vol 3, *1916–1917.* Boston: Little, Brown, 1934.
Lloyd's Register of Shipping. London: Lloyd's, 1914–18.
Lydon, Kelly K. *The U-Boats of World War I.* New England Seafarer, 1997. West Barnstable, Mass.: New England Seafarer Books, 1997.
Mallison, W. Thomas. *Studies in the Law of Naval Warfare: Submarines in General and Limited War.* Washington, D.C.: Government Printing Office, 1968.
Mantey, Eberhard von, ed. *Der Kreuzerkrieg in den ausländischen Gewässern.* Vol. 3, *Die deutschen Hilfskreuzer.* Berlin: E. S. Mittler & Sohn, 1937.
Marcher, Arthur. *From Dreadnaught to Scapa Flow.* 5 vols. London: Oxford University Press, 1961–70.
Messimer, Dwight R. *The Merchant U-Boat: Adventures of the Deutschland, 1916–1918.* Annapolis: Naval Institute Press, 1988.
———. *Verschollen: World War I U-Boat Losses.* Annapolis: Naval Institute Press, 2002.
Millis, Walter. *Road to War: America, 1914–1917.* 1935. Reprint, New York: Howard Fertig, 1970.
Mombauer, Annika, and Wilhelm Deist. *The Kaiser: New Research on William II's Role in Imperial Germany.* Cambridge: Cambridge University Press, 2003. See esp. chap. 9, "Germany's Last Card," by Holger Afflerbach.
Morison, Elting E., ed. *The Letters of Theodore Roosevelt.* Cambridge: Harvard University Press, 1954.
Morison, Samuel Eliot, Henry Steele Commager, and William E. Leuchtenberg. *The Growth of the American Republic.* 2 vols. New York: Oxford University Press, 1969.
Mueller, Edward. *The Ocean Steamship Company of Savannah: Savannah Line.* Fleischmanns, N.Y.: Purple Mountain Press, 2001.
Natkiel, Richard, and Antony Preston. *Atlas of Maritime History.* New York: W. H. Smith, 1987.
Neureuther, Karl, and Claus Bergen, eds. Translated by Eric Sutton. *U-Boat Stories: Narratives of German U-Boat Sailors.* London: Constable, 1931.
Norton, Grace Fallow. *The Odyssey of a Torpedoed Transport.* Boston: Houghton Mifflin, 1918.
Offer, Avner. "Morality and Admiralty: 'Jacky' Fisher, Economic Warfare and the Laws of War." *Journal of Contemporary History* 23, no. 1 (January 1988): 99–118.
Official German Documents Relating to the World War. Translated under the supervision of the Carnegie Endowment for International Peace. New York: Oxford University Press, 1923.
Osgood, Robert E. *Ideals and Self Interest in America's Foreign Relations: The Great Transformation of the Twentieth Century.* Chicago: University of Chicago, 1953.
Padfield, Peter. *Aim Straight.* London: Hodder and Staughton, 1966.
Pardoe, Blaine. *The Cruise of the Sea Eagle: The Amazing True Story of Imperial Germany's Gentleman Pirate.* Guilford, Ct.: Lyons Press, 2005.
Parrish, Thomas. *The Submarine—A History.* New York: Viking, 2004.

Paxson, Frederic L. *American Diplomacy and the World War: Pre-War Years, 1913–1917.* 1936. Reprint, New York: Cooper Square, 1966.

Peterson, H. C. *Propaganda for War: The Campaign against American Neutrality, 1914–1917.* Port Washington, N.Y.: Kennikat Press, 1968.

Quirk, Robert. *An Affair of Honor: Woodrow Wilson and the Occupation of Veracruz.* New York: Norton, 1967.

Record of American and Foreign Shipping. New York: American Bureau of Shipping, 1900.

Reynolds, Francis Joseph. *The Story of the Great War.* 16 vols. Vol. 12, *The German Retreat, Vimy and Messines, Revolution in Russia, United States at War.* New York: P. F. Collier and Son, 1917.

Rosenberg, Arthur. *Imperial Germany: The Birth of the German Republic, 1871–1918.* Translated by Ian F. D. Morrow. 1931. Reprint, New York: Oxford University Press, 1970.

Rossler, Eberhad. *The U-Boat: The Evolution and Technical History of the German Submarine.* Annapolis: Naval Institute Press, 1981.

Safford, Jeffrey J. *Wilsonian Maritime Diplomacy.* New Brunswick, N.J.: Rutgers University Press, 1978.

Scheer, Admiral Reinhard. *Germany's High Seas Fleet in the World War.* New York: Cassell, 1929.

Seymour, Charles. *American Diplomacy during the World War.* 1934. Reprint: Hamden, Ct.: Archon Books, 1964.

———. *American Neutrality, 1914–1917: Essays on the Causes of American Intervention in the World War.* New Haven: Yale University Press, 1935.

———. *The Intimate Papers of Colonel House.* Vol. 2, *From Neutrality to War.* New York: Houghton Mifflin, 1926.

Shelford, Capt. W. O. *Sub-Sunk.* Edinburgh, Scotland: Harrap, 1960.

Showell, Jak. *The U-Boat Century: German Submarine Warfare, 1906–2006.* Annapolis: Naval Institute Press, 2006.

Smith, Daniel. "Robert Lansing and the Formulation of American Neutrality Policies, 1914–1915." *Mississippi Valley Historical Review* 43, no. 1 (June 1956): 59–81.

Spindler, Arno, ed. *Der Handelskrieg mit U-Booten.* 4 vols. In the series *Der Krieg zur See, 1914–1918,* edited by E. von Mantey. Berlin: E. S. Mittler & Sohn, 1932. (This is the official German naval history of World War I.)

Steffen, Dick. "The Holtzendorff Memorandum of 22 December 1916 and Germany's Declaration of Unrestricted U-Boat Warfare." *Journal of Military History* 68, no. 1 (January 2004): 215–44.

Stern, Robert C. *The Battle beneath the Waves.* London: Arms and Armour, 1999.

Sterne, Elaine. *Over the Seas for Uncle Sam.* New York: Britton, 1918.

Still, William. *Crisis at Sea: The United States Navy in European Waters in World War I.* Gainesville: University Press of Florida, 2007.

Tarrant, V. E. *The U-Boat Offensive 1914–1945.* Annapolis: Naval Institute Press, 1989.

Taylor, Carl T. *The Commerce War, Unarmed Merchant Ships Against German Submarine in WWI.* Clifton Forge, Va.: Mountain Empire, 1999

Terraine, John. *The U-Boat Wars, 1916–1945.* New York: G. P. Putnam's Sons, 1989.
Thomas, Lowell. *Raiders of the Deep.* Garden City, N.Y.: Garden City Publishing, 1928.
——. *The Sea Devil: The Story of Count Felix von Luckner, the German War Raider.* London: Heinemann, 1928; U.S. edition: *Count Luckner, The Sea Devil.* Garden City, N.Y.: Doubleday, Doran, 1928.
Trask, David F. *Captains and Cabinets: Anglo-American Naval Relations, 1917–1918.* Columbia: University of Missouri Press, 1972.
Tuchman, Barbara. *The Zimmermann Telegram.* New York: Macmillan, 1958.
Tumulty, Joseph. *Woodrow Wilson as I Know Him.* Garden City, N.Y.: Doubleday, Page, 1921.
U.S. Bureau of Customs. *Merchant Vessels of the United States.* Washington, D.C.: Government Printing Office, 1916 and 1917.
U.S. Department of Commerce. *Annual List of Merchant Vessels of the United States.* Washington, D.C.: Government Printing Office, 1914–17.
U.S. Department of State. *Diplomatic Correspondence with Belligerent Governments Relating to Neutral Rights and Duties.* FRUS. Washington, D.C.: Government Printing Office, 1916.
——. *Foreign Relations of the United States.* FRUS. Selected volumes, 1915–17.
——. *Papers Relating to the Foreign Relations of the United States.* FRUS. *The Lansing Papers, 1914–1920, Volume I.* Washington, D.C.: Government Printing Office, 1939.
U.S. Office of Naval Records. *German Submarine Activities on the Atlantic Coast of the United States and Canada.* United States Office of Naval Records and Library. Washington, D.C: U.S. Government Printing Office, 1920.
U.S. Office of Naval Records and Library. *American Ship Casualties of the World War including Naval Vessels, Merchant Ships, Sailing Vessels and Fishing Craft.* Washington, D.C.: Government Printing Office, 1923.
United States Shipping Board Emergency Fleet Corporation. Division of Operations. *Register of Ships Owned by United States Shipping Board.* 5th ed., Washington, D.C.: U.S. Government Printing Office, 1920.
——. *Passenger Ships Owned by the United States Government.* Washington, D.C.: United States Shipping Board Emergency Fleet Corporation, 1923.
United States Shipping Board National Headquarters Recruiting Service. *The Merchant Mariner: Devoted to the Men of the American Merchant Marine.* Boston [weekly: issue 1, July 20, 1918].
von Arnauld de la Perrière, Lothar. *'U-35' auf Jagd.* Gütersloh: C. Bertelsmann, 1938.
von Rintelen, Captain [Franz]. *The Dark Invader: Wartime Reminiscences of a German Naval Intelligence Officer.* London: Penguin, 1936.
Williams, William J. *The Wilson Administration and the Shipbuilding Crisis of 1917: Steel Ships and Wooden Steamers.* Lewiston, N.Y.: E. Mellen Press, 1992.
Winton, John. *Convoy: The Defence of Sea Trade 1890–1990.* London: M. Joseph, 1983.

Index

Aberdeen, Scot., 50
Aderholde, Carl F., 9, 109, 173
Admiralty, British, 18, 23, 91, 113
Adriatic Sea, 59, 83
Alderney, 11, 116–17, 119, 150, 175
Alexandria (ship), 76
Algonquin (American Star Line ship): cargo on, 100, 101, 102, 103; and casus belli/acts of war, xiv, 11, 13, 101, 103, 104, 106, 147; Congress and, 147, 149, 152, 154, 159; construction of, 100, 104; crew of, 100, 102–3, 119, 135; description of, 13, 100, 175; and Lansing memorandum to Wilson, 135, 147, 154, 160, 194n34; ownership of, 100, 119, 175, 194n34; photo of, 101; press and, 102–3, 193n21; registry of, xiv, 100, 101, 102, 103, 104, 109, 119, 135, 147, 154, 194n34, 200n5; scholarship on, xv; significance of, 166; sinking of, 13, 101–4, 119, 175; U.S. reaction to sinking of, 184n38
Algonquin (Clyde Steam Ship Company ship), 193n21
Alicante (ship), 59
Allies, World War I: and blockades, xii, xiii, 5, 29, 33, 59; countries in, xii, 4, 7, 14, 104; and credit, 31, 162, 180n1; and Gore Bill, 28; political systems of, 104–5; and trade, 2, 9, 21, 32, 57, 107–8, 148, 162; Wilson and, 14, 16, 65, 165. *See also* Ocean liners
Allies, World War II, 162, 163
American Clothing Workers, 145
American Federation of Labor, 2, 145
American-Hawaiian Line, 41, 119, 143, 156, 175, 197n31
American-Hawaiian Steamship Company, 54
American Star Line, 100, 175
American Union against Militarism, 179n21
Amsterdam, Netherlands, 167
Ancona (ship), 147, 178n9
Anglo-Californian (ship), 178n9
Angora (ship), 169, 170

Anna Maria (ship), 79
Arabia (ship), 178n9
Arabic (ship): and casus belli/acts of war, 61, 95, 106, 147; Congress and, 21, 147, 152, 162; press and, 26; sinking of, 26, 179n18; U.S. public and, 21, 162; U.S. response to, 61; Wilson and, 21, 95, 147
Arabic Pledge, 26, 29, 179n18
Archangel, Russia, 45, 48, 49, 108
Argentina, 66
Arizona, 91, 92
Arkansas, 159
Armed Ship Bill: Congress and, 93, 95–96, 99, 145–46, 157, 158, 159; press and, 95; Theodore Roosevelt and, 96; Wilson and, 93, 94, 95–96, 191n51, 192n7
Armed Ship Policy, 191n51
Armenian (ship), 21, 106, 151, 178n8, 178n9
Arthur Sewall Company, 36–37
Ashtabula Steamship Company, 107
Associated Press, 95–96, 102, 124
Atlanta, Ga., 102
Atlanta Journal-Constitution, 102
Atlantic Ocean: *Columbian* and, 54; German submarines and, 63, 77, 88, 144; *Housatonic* and, 76; *Lyman M. Law* crew and, 54; and ocean liner crossings, 3, 20; safe lane in, 88; and U.S. foreign policy, xi; *Vigilanica* and, 9
Atlantic Transport Company, 100
Augustine, Saint, 138, 198n26, 198n27
Austria-Hungary: and attacks on merchant ships, 20; and Central powers, 4, 105; and *Chemung* sinking, 59–60; and entry into World War I, 7; and espionage and subversion, 97; and Italy, 59; and mutual defense treaties, 6; and naval summit, 18
Austro-Prussian War, 16
Axis powers, 163
Azores, 108

Aztec (ship): arming of, 141, 142, 143, 146, 159; cargo on, 141; and casus belli/acts of war, xv; Congress and, 141, 146, 152, 154, 159; construction of, 141; crew of, 141; description of, 13, 141, 175; fatalities on, 13, 142–43, 151, 152, 159, 173, 174; and Lansing memoradum to Wilson, 154; ownership of, 141, 175; photo of, 142; scholarship on, xv; significance of, 166; sinking of, 141–43, 146, 175; Wilson and, 141

Bailey, Thomas, 179n13
Baker, Newton, 88
Baker, Ray Stannard, 197n2
Balkan Wars, 16
Balmaha, Scot., 44, 183n32
Baltimore, Md., 192n9
Balto (ship), 55–56
Bangor, Maine, 81
Baralong (ship), 27
Barbrito, Manuel, 114
Barclay, Curle & Company, 75
Barry, Wales, 53
Bath, Maine, 36
Bavaria (ship), 39
Bayonne, N.J., 127
Beesly, Patrick, 92, 191n4
Belfast, Ireland, 48, 49
Belgium, 4, 6, 7, 17, 153, 154
Benas, J. D., 100, 104, 194n34
Benedict-Manson Marine Company, 81
Bergen, Norway, 128, 169
Berlin, Germany: and communication with Washington, D.C., 93; and subversion, 153; and unrestricted submarine warfare, 79, 186n4; U.S. diplomats in, 43, 51, 53, 55, 64, 67, 68, 72; and Zimmerman Telegram, xiii
Bernstorff, Johann von: and *Arabic* Pledge, 26, 179n18; Hans Rose and, 76; memorandum by, 155, 201n35; and severing of U.S.-German diplomatic relations, 67, 68–69, 70; and submarine attacks off Nantucket, 77; and unrestricted German submarine warfare, xiii, 122; and Zimmerman Telegram, 91
Berryman, Clifford, 12, 15, 25
Berwindale (ship), 152
Bethmann-Hollweg, Theobold von, 33, 66, 67
Bevill, H. O., 114

Bilbao, Spain, 54
Bishop Rock Lighthouse, 9, 39
Bishops, 101
Bizerta, Tunisia, 144
Blockades: Allies and, xii, xiii, 5, 29, 33, 59; Arthur Conan Doyle on, 33; attempts to run, 12; Austrian, 60; British, xii, 17, 29, 31–32, 45, 57, 64, 83, 155, 180n2; Central powers and, 5; Denmark and, 29, 31, 32; France and, 60, 63; German, 59, 60, 63, 66, 79, 97, 148; Holland and, 29, 31, 32, 88; impact on U.S. neutrality, 5; impact on U.S. shipping, 88; and international law, 7–8, 18, 32, 97, 177n4; Italy and, 60, 63; press and, 180n2; and safe lanes, 84, 88, 128, 155, 169; during U.S. Civil War, 32, 180n2. See also Mines; Submarine warfare
Blommersdyk, SS (ship), 77
Boer War, 16
Bordeaux, France, 193n27
Borland, William P., 156
Borre, Norway, 54
Borum, Lewis P.: and *City of Memphis* sinking, 113, 114, 115, 118, 175, 180n2; reputation of, 112, 119; and voyage to Germany, 111; and voyage to Turkey, 112
Boston, Mass., 45, 54, 111
Boulogne, Fr., 28
Bowling, Scot., 52
Brandaris Light, 169–70
Brazil, 36, 66
Bremerhaven, Ger., 111
Brest, Fr., 141, 175
Bristol, Eng., 190n27
British National Archives, 171
Brodie, Bernard, 177n1 (chap. 1)
Brooklyn, N.Y., 128
Brown, F., 9, 109, 173
Bryan, William Jennings: and Congress, 32; and diplomatic protests, 19, 32; and *Falaba* incident, 178n11; and loan ban, 162, 180n1; and *Lusitania* sinking, 24; and *Nebraskan* sinking, 43; as pacifist or neutralist, 24, 58; resignation of, 19, 24, 179n15, 180n1; and Robert Rose, 58
Buenz, Karl, 75–76
Bulgaria, 7, 105
Bureau of War Risk Insurance, 170, 203n11
Burleson, Albert, 12, 121

Cabinet: and *Algonquin* sinking, xiv; and Armed Ship Bill, 192n7; and arming of U.S. merchant ships, 93; Newton Baker and, 88; William Jennings Bryan and, 24, 179n15; Albert Burleson and, 121; and casus belli/acts of war, xiv; and *City of Memphis* sinking, xiv, 11, 117, 120, 123, 156; Josephus Daniels and, 90, 121, 132, 179n15; and declaration of war, 12, 107, 117, 120–21, 122, 123, 124, 126, 130, 156, 160, 165; and diplomatic relations with Germany, 67–68, 72; and *Healdton* sinking, 124; and *Housatonic* sinking, xiv, 88; David Houston and, 65, 88, 90, 121, 132; and *Illinois* sinking, xiv, 11, 117, 120, 123, 156; Franklin Lane and, 90, 121; Robert Lansing and, 68, 90, 120–21, 125, 132; and *Lyman M. Law* sinking, xiv, 90; and *Marguerite* sinking, 144; William Gibbs McAdoo and, 67, 90, 132; and merchant mariners, 166; and press, 126, 131–32; and shipping crisis, 588; and unrestricted German submarine warfare, 64, 88; and *Vigilancia* sinking, xiv, 11, 117, 118, 120, 123, 156; and war preparations, 124; and Zimmerman Telegram, 92

Cadiz, Spain, 59
Cagliari, Italy, 82, 83, 84, 85, 86
California, 49, 65
Camarinas, Spain, 55, 56
Camden, N.J., 39, 41
Canada, 44, 46, 107
Canadian Northwest Steamship Company, 100
Canadians, 108
Cape May, N.J., 39
Cape Ortega, Spain, 54
Cape Spartivento, Sardinia, 82, 84
Cape Town, South Africa, 108
Cardiff, Wales, 53, 113, 149
Cardine, George A., 81
Cargo. *See* Trade goods
Carib (ship), 155, 181n8
Caribbean, 111, 112
Cash and Carry legislation, 162–63, 164
Cattaro, Yugoslavia, 83
Central Georgia Railway, 111
Central powers: Americans and, 16; countries making up, 4, 7, 105, 112; defeat of, xii; and outbreak of World War I, xii; political systems of, 104–5; press and, 2; and trade, 5, 28, 32; Wilson and, 65

Chadwin, Mark Lincoln, 202n2 (epilogue)
Chandler, W., 128, 173
Channel Islands, 11, 116
Chapaneta (mariner), 39, 182n16
Charleston, S.C., 75
Chemung (ship): and casus belli/acts of war, 35, 79, 106; Congress and, 147; crew of, 119; and Lansing memorandum to Wilson, 135; ownership of, 57, 58, 185n28, 186n35; as precedent, 74, 87; sinking of, 35, 58, 59–60, 79, 83, 109–10, 119
Chester, Pa., 107, 111
Chicago, Ill., 94, 128
Chicago Tribune, 94
Christian Knudsen, SS, 77
Christian Science Monitor, 102
Christina, Norw., 53
Christopher, Charles: and *Healdton* sinking, 128–29, 167, 169, 170, 171, 172, 175; and press, 198n15
City of Macon (ship), 111
City of Memphis (ship): cabinet and, 11–12, 120, 121, 124, 156; cargo on, 111, 112, 113, 118, 196n18; and casus belli/acts of war, xiv, xv, 15, 106, 117, 118, 120, 130, 135, 136, 138, 139, 157, 162; Congress and, 131, 149, 152, 154, 156, 159; construction of, 111, 118; crew of, 112–13, 118; damage to, during voyage to Turkey, 112; description of, 13, 111, 112, 175; as government transport ship, 111, 143, 195n15; and Lansing memorandum to Wilson, 135, 154; ownership of, 111, 112, 118, 120, 149, 175; photo of, 112; press and, 114–15, 117–18, 120, 196n20; registry of, 106, 111, 118, 149; scholarship on, xv, 139–40; significance of sinking of, 166; sinking of, 11, 13, 106, 112–15, 117, 119, 131, 149, 157, 175, 196n20; stopping of, 180n7; and trade, 111–12; Wilson and, 12, 124, 130, 136
Civil War, U.S., xi, 18, 32, 75
Civitas Dei (City of God) (Saint Augustine), 138
Civita Vecchia, Italy, 86
Clark, Champ, 98
Class, 1, 2–3, 4, 20–21, 94, 165
Clausen, N. P., 114
Clyde Steam Ship Company, 193n21
Coast Guard, U.S., 163
Coast Seamen's Union, 1
Codebreakers, The (Kahn), 92

Coffee, Thomas, 94, 95, 173, 192n9
Columbian (ship): cargo on, 55, 56, 57; and casus belli/acts of war, 35, 106; Congress and, 147; construction of, 54; crew of, 59, 119; and Lansing memorandum to Wilson, 134; ownership of, 54; as precedent, 74; press and, 185n22; sinking of, 35, 54–56, 57, 109–10, 114, 119; size of, 54
Comerford, Frank, 192n11
Commager, Henry Steele, 177n2
Committee of Public Information, 165
Communipaw (ship), 35, 180n7
Congress, U.S.: and *Algonquin* sinking, 147, 149, 152, 154, 159; anti-war sentiment in, 131, 144, 145; and *Arabic* sinking, 21, 147, 152, 162; and Armed Ship Bill/arming of U.S. merchant ships, 90, 93–94, 95–96, 98–99, 145–46, 157, 158, 159; and *Aztec* sinking, 141, 146, 152, 154, 159; and casus belli/acts of war, xv, 6, 134, 165; and *Chemung* sinking, 147; and *City of Memphis* sinking, 11, 120, 131, 149, 152, 154, 156, 159; and *Columbian* sinking, 147; convening of Apr. 2, 1917 session of, xii, xiv, xv, 12, 92, 121, 122, 123, 124, 167; and declaration of war debate, xv, 13–14, 139, 145–57, 158–60; and declaration of war votes, xiv–xv, 12, 14, 140, 143, 144, 150, 157–58; and diplomatic relations with Germany, 11, 68–70; and *Falaba* incident, 21, 147, 151; and foreign policy, 161, 163; and German Americans, 6; and *Gulflight* incident, 147, 151; and *Healdton* sinking, xiv, 130, 150, 152, 154, 157, 159, 167; and *Housatonic* sinking, 152, 154, 157; and *Illinois* sinking, 11, 120, 131, 149, 150, 152, 154, 156, 159; and Irish Americans, 153; and Lansing memorandum to Wilson, 158; and *Leelanaw* incidents, 147, 152; and *Lusitania* sinking, 21, 147, 151; and *Lyman M. Law* sinking, 147, 152, 154, 157, 159; and *Marguerite* sinking, 144; and merchant mariners, 166; and *Missourian* sinking, 143, 154, 156, 159; post-World War I, 161, 164; and press, 126, 143, 198n19; pro-Ally/prowar members of, 69, 70; and Puerto Ricans, 108, 134; and responsibility for declaring war, 107, 127; and shipping crisis, 90; and *Sussex* sinking, 21, 29, 147, 149, 152; and U.S. neutrality, 27; and *Vigilancia* sinking, 13, 120, 131, 149, 150, 152, 156, 157, 159; and Wilson, 73; Wilson's Apr. 2, 1917, address to, 12, 13, 136, 138–39, 140, 141; Wilson's Aug. 19, 1914, address to, 16; Wilson's Feb. 3, 1917, address to, 68–72, 73, 78, 79–80, 93, 120, 135; Wilson's Feb. 26, 1917, address to, 89, 93–94, 95, 147, 157; Wilson's fifth annual message to, 198n26; and Wilson's Fourteen Points, xii; and World War II, 162–63; and Zimmermann Telegram, 131
Congressional Record, 150, 154, 201n27, 201n28
Connecticut, 75
Conrad, Joseph, 3
Contraband: on *Algonquin*, 102; in Berryman cartoon, 15; box shooks as, 82, 84, 87; British and, 32; and Cash and Carry laws, 162; and casus belli/acts of war, 39, 49; on *Chemung*, 59; on *City of Memphis*, 113; on *Columbian*, 56; conditional, 32, 56; cotton as, 76; cotton goods as, 45; direct, 162; flax as, 48, 51; foodstuffs as, 102, 103; on *Gulflight*, 40; on *Housatonic*, 78; indirect, 162; and international law, 18, 32, 52, 177n4; on *Lanao*, 53; on *Leelanaw*, 49, 50, 51; loss of ships carrying, 60; lumber as, 84; on *Lyman M. Law*, 82, 85, 87; metals as, 56; motorcycle parts as, 56; neutralists and, 28; petroleum as, 162; removal of, 50; rice as, 53; on *Vigilancia*, 9, 110; wheat as, 37, 78; on *William P. Frye*, 37. *See also* Cotton and cotton goods; Trade goods
Cooper, Henry Allen, 155
Cornwall, Eng., 21, 39, 78
Cotton and cotton goods: British blockade of, 31, 32, 45, 48, 49, 57, 76, 146; *City of Memphis* and, 111, 113, 146, 196n18; as conditional contraband, 32; Gaston, Williams & Wigmore and, 108; Harriss-Irby-Vose Company and, 45, 48, 49, 57, 58, 186n30; McAdoo and, 186n30; as noncontraband, 31; price of, 57, 58; purchase of, by belligerent nations, 31; Sen. Gore and, 28; U.S. Foreign Trade Office and, 57, 58; *Vigilancia* and, 107
Credit, 31, 32, 162, 180n1
Creel, George, 165
Crimean War, 16
Crist (mariner), 182n16
Crow Sound, 39
Cruiser rules: and *Arabic* Pledge, 179n18; and *City of Memphis* sinking, 115; and *Colum-*

bian sinking, 134; destruction of ships under, 18; and evasive or defensive action, 22, 23–24; and *Falaba* incident, 22; German interpretation of, 27; and *Housatonic* sinking, 79, 135; and *Leelanaw* sinking, 134; and *Lusitania* sinking, 24; and *Lyman M. Law* sinking, 83, 87, 135; and *Marguerite* sinking, 144; ships sunk under before Feb. 1, 1917, 200n5; and submarine warfare, 27, 77; treatment of passengers and crews under, 18, 146, 147; U.S. government and, 18–19. *See also* Declaration of London; International law

Cuba, 107, 108
Cummins, Albert B., 145, 158
Cunard Line, 3, 22, 23, 94
Curtis, Frederick, 55, 56, 57, 114
Cushing (ship), 35, 44, 147, 151
Cussler, Clive, 203n14
Cuxhaven, Ger., 45

Dacia (ship), 76
Dana, Richard Henry, 3
Daniels, Josephus: and arming of merchant ships, 90, 99, 124; and cabinet, 90, 121, 179n15; as pacifist or neutralist, 11, 121; and reluctant support for war, 11, 121, 132
Danzig, Pol., 164
Davis, Captain, 22
Declaration of London: articles of, 177n4; and blockades, 7–8, 18, 32, 97, 177n4; and communication with warships, 56; and failure to ratify, 165; Germany and, 110, 115; Great Britain and, 18, 32; impact of, 8; and neutral ships and crews, 7, 18, 63, 177n4; press and, 54; Senate and, 177n4, 183n36; text of, 180n2; and transfer of ships' registries, 46, 103–4, 177n4, 180n2, 183n36, 194n34; United States and, 38, 51, 52, 61; during World War II, 165–66
De Grey, Nigel, 91
Dekalb (ship), 38
Delaware, 49
Delaware River International Building and Engine Works, 107
Delk, Eugene, 48, 50, 51
Delto (ship), 178n9
Democrats and Democratic Party: and antiwar sentiments, 145, 157; and Congress, 28, 68, 145, 149, 156, 157, 158, 159; and diplomatic relations with Germany, 68; neutralist, 162; and prowar sentiments, 149, 156, 158, 159; Southern, 162; Wilson and, 28, 68
Den Helder, Neth., 172
Denmark: and blockades, 29, 31, 32; mariners from, 109, 116; and neutrality, 7, 29; and unrestricted German submarine warfare, 67
Dennison, E. H., 48, 50
Department of State, U.S. *See* State Department, U.S.
Der Handelskrieg mit U-Booten (Spindler), 168, 178n10, 202n2 (App. A)
Der Krieg in der Nordsee, 169
Deutsche Amerikanische Petroleum Gesellschaft (DAPG), 104
Dmitrios, E., 10, 109
Dochra (ship), 193n27
Doyle, Arthur Conan, 33
Duffy, John L., 59
Duncan, Robert, 44
Dundee, Scot., 48, 51
Dutch National Archives, 172

Eagle Point (ship), 152
Easter Island, 181n14
Eavestone (ship), 106, 173, 174
Edward R. Hunt (ship), 200n5
Elder Line, 22
El Monte (ship), 57
English Channel, xiii, 116
Englishman (ship), 152, 178n9
Ensor, Thomas A., 76, 77, 78, 175, 188n4
Entente. *See* Allies
Eopolucci, John I., 142, 143, 173
Espionage, 14, 97, 136
ESSO, 124, 164, 167. *See also* Standard Oil
Evelyn (ship), 57, 58, 155, 181n8

Falaba (ship): attack on, 179n18; William Jennings Bryan and, 178n11; and casus belli/acts of war, 95, 106; Congress and, 147, 151; fatalities on, 21, 22, 106; press and, 21, 178n11; sinking of, 22, 61, 147, 150; U.S. public and, 21, 22; U.S. response to sinking of, 22, 61, 106; Wilson and, 21
Fastnet, Ire., 41, 43, 113
Fastnet Light, 94
Fayle, C. Earnest, 191n51

Ferris, Scott, 156–57, 159
Findlay, Miller & Company, 52, 54
First World War. *See* World War I
Fisher, John "Jacky," 33
Fiske, Bradley, 77
Flood, Henry de la Warr: and declaration of war debate and vote, 150, 153, 155, 156, 158, 159, 160; and House Foreign Relations Committee report, 150, 153–54, 160, 201n28; and Lansing memorandum to Wilson, 201n26
Foreign Office (Germany), 51, 52, 56, 61, 168
Foreign Relations of the United States, 99, 134, 177n4
Foreign Trade Office, U.S. Department of State, 57
Fort McPherson, Ga., 38
Fourteen Points, xii, 165, 199n26
France: and Allies, 4; *Aztec* sinking near, 141; and Belgium, 6; and blockades, 60; and British propaganda, 17; and Channel Islands, 11; and Declaration of London, 177n4; and entry into World War I, 7; and German blockade, 63; and Italian border, 143; and mutual defense treaties, 6; and naval summit, 18; and ocean liners, 16, 17; and Quasi War, xi; *Sussex* in, xiii; and trade, 9, 31, 32, 40, 52, 53, 54, 55, 59, 101, 108, 112, 113, 141; and transfer of ships' registries, 46, 103, 194n34; and unrestricted German submarine warfare, 119; and World War II, 162
France and Canada Steamship Company, 54, 143
Franco-Prussian War, xii, 16
Franz Ferdinand, Archduke, 16
French Indo-China, 52
French Revolution, xii
Frost, Arthur C., 114, 192n9
Frye, William Pierce, 181n10. For ship *Frye*, see *William P. Frye* (ship).
Furuseth, Andrew, 1, 2

G-13 (ship), 128
Galena (ship), 147
Galitos, A., 10, 109
Gallia (ship), 83
Galt, Edith Boling, 98
Galveston, Texas, 76, 81, 111
Gaston, George, 107, 108
Gaston, Williams & Wigmore: Canadian branch of, 107; U.S. branch of, 9, 107–8, 109, 118, 128, 175, 194n3
G. Cavallero (business), 81
Geer, Edward F., 76
Genoa, Italy, 54, 56, 143, 175, 193n27
George A. Cardine Syndicate, 175
Georgia (ship), 75. *See also Housatonic* (20th-century ship)
Gerard, James: and Johann von Bernstorff, 179n18; and *Cushing* incident, 183n30; and *Gulflight* incident, 40; and international law, 18–19, 177n3; and *Leelanaw* incident, 51; and *Nebraskan* incident, 43; and *Pass of Balmaha* incident, 45–46; and unrestricted German submarine warfare, 64, 66, 67, 72, 186n4; and U.S. diplomatic relations with Germany, 68, 72; and *William P. Frye* incident, 51
German Prize Ordinances, 51, 52, 61
Germany: and Belgium, 6, 7, 17; and Central powers, 4, 105; and compensation for destroyed cargo, 52; and espionage, 14, 97, 133, 136; food shortages in, 64; and France, 7; and *Gulflight* incident, 44; and *Healdton* sinking, xiv, 129, 167; and Italy, 59; and Japan, 92, 191n4; and *Leelanaw* incident, 51; and *Lusitania* sinking, 23, 24, 61; and maritime law, 18–19; and Mexico, xiii–xiv, 13, 14, 91, 92, 93, 136, 191n4; and mutual defense treaties, 6; and *Nebraskan* incident, 43–44; and negotiated peace proposals, 65–66; and Netherlands, 168; and *Pass of Balmaha* incident, 45, 46; and sabotage and subversion, 14, 97, 136; and sinking of civilian ships, 177n3; Spanish legation in, 133; Standard Oil ships in, 163; and *Sussex* Pledge, xiii, 29–30; and trade, 17, 29, 31–32, 36, 45, 57, 58, 76, 88, 107, 111, 146, 168, 185n29, 186n30; and transfer of ships' registries, 45, 46–47, 52, 101, 102, 103, 183n36, 194n34; treatment of U.S. citizens in, 14, 133–34, 136, 153; U.S. diplomatic relations with, xiii, 11, 29, 67–70, 95, 113, 120, 122, 131, 133, 152, 153; and U.S. diplomats, 18, 131, 136; and U.S. neutrality, 60, 93; and U.S.-Prussian treaties, 38, 46, 50, 51, 52; and U.S. public opinion, 16, 17, 136; and U.S. shipping, 60; and *William P. Frye*

incident, 51; Wilson and, 14; and World War II, 161, 162, 163. *See also* Submarine warfare
Germany's High Sea Fleet in the World War, 186n4
Gessner & Marr Company, 81
Gibbons, Floyd, 94–95, 192n11
Gibson & Church Company, 183n32
Glasgow, Scot., 44, 75, 100, 114, 127, 183n32
Globe Steamship Company (aka Globe Line), 107, 108, 109, 118, 119, 195n7
Godinez, Chief Officer, 53
Gold Shell (ship), 193n27
Golena (ship), 134
Gompers, Samuel, 2
Gonzales, R., 10, 109
Gore, Thomas P., 28
Gore Bill, 28, 161, 179n21
Gothenburg, Sweden, 48, 49, 75
Graeff, Ernst, 45
Grand Banks, 82
Graves, John Temple, 102–3
Gray, Edwyn, 79
Great Britain: and Allies, 4, 154; Americans in, 22; and Belgium, 6, 7; cabinet of, 18, 177n4; concerns about submarine warfare in, 33; and entry into World War I, 7; and Germany, 146; *Housatonic* sinking near, 77; and killing of German seamen, 179n19; and *Lusitania,* 23; mariners from, 116; and naval summit, 18; naval technical experts in, 43; and ocean liners, 16; post–World War I, 162, 164; and propaganda, 17, 179n19; and Q-ships, 185n29; reactions to Wilson's statements in, 65; safe lane near, 128; submarine attacks near, 9; submarine warfare zone around, 33; and trade, 21, 31, 36–37, 55, 57, 75, 76, 78, 84, 101, 104, 107, 109, 185n29; and transfer of ships' registries, 46, 103, 194n34; and United States, 158; and unrestricted German submarine warfare, 63, 92; U.S. diplomats in, 65, 67; and U.S. Navy, 124; and U.S. neutrality and neutral rights, 60, 146; and *Vigilancia* sinking, 10, 109; voyages to and from, 76, 100; and War of 1812, xi; Wilson advisors and, 24–25; Wilson and, 14; and Zimmerman Telegram, xiii, 91, 185n29. *See also* Blockades: British; Mines: British
Greece, 10, 63, 88, 108, 109, 163

Green, George W. F., 85
Greenbrier (ship), 181n8
Greene, J. S., 41, 43, 56
Greenock, Scot., 127
Greenock and Grangemouth Dock Yard Company, 127
Grenada, 14
Gresham, William Fuller, 143
Grew, Joseph, 53, 55, 64, 186n4
Grotius, Hugo, 5
Growth of the American Republic, The (Morison, Commager, and Leuchtenberg), 177n2
Guaranty Trust Company, 107, 108, 118
Gulflight (ship): attack on, 34, 35, 39–41, 56, 109, 134, 147; and casus belli/acts of war, 34, 35, 106; Congress and, 147, 151; crew of, 39, 40; description of, 39; fatalities on, 34, 39, 41, 60, 61, 133, 134, 182n16; German offer of compensation for, 40, 42, 44; and Lansing memorandum to Wilson, 133, 134; ownership of, 39; photo of, 41; press and, 39, 40; scholarship on, 182n21
Gulf of Mexico, 111
Gulf of Tonkin, 167
Gulf Refining Company, 39
Gulf War, xi, 14
Gunter, Alfred, 39, 56, 134, 182n16

Hague, The, 38, 172
Halifax, Nova Scotia, 100, 128
Hall, William Reginald "Blinker," 91, 92
Hamburg, Germany, 38, 45, 51, 52, 75, 127
Hamburg-American Line, 39, 75
Hamilton, Norman, 38, 181n14
Hamilton, Ontario, Canada, 100
Hampton Roads, Va., 37
Hannevig, Christian, 54
Hannevig, Hans, 52
Hannevig Brothers, 54
Hansa Line, 75
Hansen, Claus, 42, 43, 48
Harby Steamship Company, 57, 58, 185n28. *See also* Harriss-Irby-Vose Company
Harriman, E. H., 111, 118
Harriman, W. Averell, 118–19
Harriman Line, 163
Harriss, Magill & Company, 58
Harriss, Robert M., 45

Harriss, William, 58
Harriss-Irby-Vose Company: and cotton trade, 57–58; and Harby Steamship Company, 57, 58, 185n28; and *Leelanaw*, 48, 49; and *Pass of Balmaha*, 45, 46, 47; revenues of, 186n30; ships lost by, 57–58, 185n29
Hartman, Richard, 55–56
Hashagen, Ernst, 175
Havana, Cuba, 108, 167
Havre, France, 52, 54, 108, 113, 119, 149
Hawaii, 141, 164
Healdton (ship): cargo on, 128, 168; and casus belli/acts of war, xiv, 130; Congress and, xiv, 150, 152, 154, 157, 159; construction of, 127, 129; crew of, 128; description of, 13, 128, 175; fatalities on, 13, 128, 130, 133, 149, 150, 151, 152, 154, 159, 167, 173, 174; insurance claims on, 203n11; and Lansing memorandum to Wilson, 132, 133, 134, 135, 154, 198n23, 202n6; last voyage and sinking of, xiii, xiv, 13, 123, 128–30, 141, 167–72, 175, 193n21, 193n27, 198n15, 198n17, 201n21, 203n11; ownership of, 100, 124, 127, 129, 130, 149, 175; photo of, 129; press and, xiv, 129, 135, 170, 171, 201n21; registry of, 127–28, 129; scholarship on, xv, 129–30, 135, 168–69, 198n17, 202n6; significance of, 166; Wilson and, xiv, 123, 125, 126, 127, 130
Healey, George, 128, 173
Hearst news organization, 95, 102
Helsingborg, Swed., 75
Hesperian (ship), 152, 178n9
Hillebrand, Leo, 142, 175
Hillman, Sidney, 145
Hindenberg, Paul von, 66
"History of British Minefields, 1914-1918" (Leith), 169, 170
Hitchcock, Gilbert, 145–46
Hitler, Adolph, 164
Hoboken, N.J., 128
Holland. *See* Netherlands
Hood, E. M., 95
Housatonic (20th-century ship): cabinet and, 88; cargo on, 75, 77; and casus belli/acts of war, xiv, 11, 78, 79–81, 84, 87, 89, 93–94, 97, 98, 103, 106, 109; Congress and, 152, 154, 157; construction of, 75; description of, 13, 75, 175; and Lansing memorandum to Wilson, 135, 154; last voyage and sinking of, 13, 75, 76, 77–78, 81, 109, 119, 175, 188n4; and *Lyman M. Law* sinking, 87; ownership of, 119, 175; press and, 78–79, 80, 103, 189n11; registry of, 75; scholarship on, xv, 190n23; significance of, 166; and unrestricted German submarine warfare, 74, 76, 80–81, 106, 119, 147; Wilson and, 79–80, 93–94, 97, 98
Housatonic, USS (19th-century ship), 75
Housatonic River, 75
Housatonic Steamship Company, 75, 76, 175
House, Edward: and declaration of war, 123, 130; and diplomatic relations with Germany, 187n13; and Robert Lansing, 125; memoirs of, 122, 125; photo of, 125; pro-Ally sentiments of, 73; and Texas state militia, 179n16; and Wilson, 24, 63, 67, 73, 122, 123, 125, 130, 167, 179n16, 187n13
House Foreign Relations Committee: chairman of, 150, 156; and *Missourian* sinking, 156; report printed by, 13, 150–55, 157, 159, 160, 201n27, 201n28, 201n30, 202n6
House of Representatives, U.S.: and arming of U.S. merchant ships, 95, 98–99; and declaration of war, xiv–xv, 13, 14, 144, 150–58, 200n12; majority leaders of, 157, 162; McLemore Resolution in, 28; sessions of, 192n17; Speaker of, 98; and World War II, 163
Houston, David F., 25, 65, 88, 90, 121, 132
Hoy, Arthur Harris, 94
Hoy, Elizabeth, 94, 95, 173, 192n9
Hoy, Mary E., 94, 95, 173, 192n9
Hoyer, George, 49
Hudgins, C. F., 128, 173
Huerta, Victoriano, 195n15
Hughes, Charles Evan, 65
Hunley (ship), 203n14
Husting, Paul Oscar, 147–48, 156, 159, 200n12
Hydrographic Office, U.S., 88

Iago (ship), 40
Iberian (ship), 178n9
Ideals and Self Interest in America's Foreign Relations: The Great Transformation of the Twentieth Century (Osgood), 202n2 (epilogue)
IJmuiden, Neth., 172

Illinois (ship): cabinet and, xiv, 11–12, 121, 124, 156; cargo on, 116, 118; and casus belli/acts of war, xiv, xv, 15, 106, 117, 118, 130, 135, 136, 138, 139, 157, 162; Congress and, 131, 149, 150, 152, 154, 156, 159; construction of, 116, 118; crew of, 116, 118, 196n26; description of, 13, 116, 175; final voyage and sinking of, 11, 13, 106, 116–17, 119, 120, 150, 175, 194n1, 196n30, 201n21; and Lansing memorandum to Wilson, 135, 154; ownership of, 115, 116, 119, 120, 149, 175; photo of, 117; press and, 11, 117–18, 120, 201n21; registry of, 106, 116, 118, 150; scholarship on, xv, 139–40; significance of, 166; Wilson and, 12, 124
Illinois (state), 65, 186n4
Illinois Central Railway, 111, 118–19
Immigrants. See under Mariners
Imperial Navy, 33, 46, 66
Independence Party, 102
Independent (publication), 79, 87
International law: and *Algonquin* sinking, 102; and *Arabic* Pledge, 179n18; concept of, 6; and continuous voyage doctrine, 29, 32; and declaration of war, 136, 137; and just war, 138; and land travel, 177n3; and mutual defense treaties, 6–7; on naval warfare, 17–18; press and, 102; and sea travel, 177n3; and transfer of ships' registries, 104, 154. See also Cruiser rules; Declaration of London
International Longshoremen's Union, 2
International Mercantile Marine Company, 89, 100
International Seamen's Union, 2
Iowa, 158
Iraq War, 14
Ireland, 3, 33, 41, 114, 175
Irish Americans, 2, 145, 153
Irish coast, 22
Irish Sea, 11
Isles of Scilly, 39–40, 76, 109, 113, 119
Italy: and Allies, 154; and blockades, 60; and entry into World War I, 7; and German blockades, 63; and Germany, 59; and *Lyman M. Law* sinking, 84; and naval summit, 18; and ocean liners, 16; and trade, 54, 57, 58, 59, 81, 101, 112, 143; U.S. diplomats in, 86
Iverson, H. H., 116, 117, 119, 175, 194n1

Jackson, David, 114
Jacobsen (mariner), 59, 60
Jagow, Gottlieb von, 40
Jamaica, 84
James, Henry J., 189n9
Japan, 7, 18, 92, 105, 154, 191n4
Java (ship), 128
Jeffery automobiles, 107
Johnson, Walter C., 128, 173
Joor, Johan, 172
J. P. Morgan (company), 107, 118, 128

Kahn, Herman, 92, 93, 95, 191n4, 192n5
Kaiser, The, 24, 26, 64, 67
Kansan (ship), 147
Kenyon, William S., 158
Kew, Eng., 171
Kiene, Herman H., 37, 181n12
Kiene, Mrs. Herman H., 181n12
Kirby, William F., 159
Kirkwall, Scot., 48, 49
Kitchin, Claude, 145, 157–58
Korean War, xi
Kurson, Robert, 203n14

Labaree, Benjamin W., 177n1 (chap. 1), 198n17
Labor, 2, 14, 144, 145, 164. See also Merchant marine
Laconia (ship): and casus belli/acts of war, 95, 98, 106, 178n9, 192n11; construction of, 94; crew of, 94; description of, 94; fatalities on, 21, 94, 110, 151, 173, 174, 190n23, 192n9; scholarship on, 190n23, 192n11; sinking of, 94, 141; Wilson and, 98
La Coruña, Spain, 55
Lady of the Lake (Scott), 44
LaFollette, Robert: anti-war sentiments of, 144, 145, 146; and Armed Ship Bill, 96, 144, 146; and *Aztec* sinking, 146; and declaration of war, 155, 158, 159; and Seamen's Act, 1, 3, 144
LaFollette, William, 155
Lamm (mariner), 45, 47
Lanao (ship): cargo on, 52, 53, 184n15; and casus belli/acts of war, 35; construction of, 52; and Lansing memorandum to Wilson, 134; owernship of, 52–53; registry of, 53, 54, 56, 109, 200n5; sinking of, 35, 52–54, 147; size of, 52

222 / Index

Lane, Franklin K., 90, 121
Lansdowne, Lord, 18, 177n4
Lansing, Robert: and *Algonquin* sinking, 101, 104, 140, 154, 160; appointment of, as secretary of state, 19, 24; and Armed Ship Bill/arming of U.S. merchant ships, 90, 98, 192n7; and attacks on passenger ships, 20; and cabinet meetings, 90, 120–21, 132, 192n7; and casus belli/acts of war, 19, 73, 101, 120–21, 130; and *City of Memphis* sinking, 120, 154; and Congress, xv; and credit, 162; and declaration of war, xv, 120, 122–23, 125, 130, 132, 137, 201n19; and diplomatic relations with Germany, 29, 67, 68, 72, 73, 122, 187n13; and *Falaba* incident, 178n11; and *Healdton* sinking, 124, 127, 128, 130; and *Housatonic* sinking, 89, 154; and Edward House, 125; and *Illinois* sinking, 120, 154; and *Lanao* incident, 53; and *Leelanaw* sinking, 50, 51; and loan ban, 162, 180n1; and *Lyman M. Law* sinking, 89, 154; and Mar. 30, 1917, memorandum to Wilson, 127, 132–35, 136, 147, 152, 153–54, 158, 181n9, 194n34, 198n23, 201n26, 202n6; and members of Congress, xv, 149, 150, 153–54, 201n19, 201n26; memoirs of, 120; and Frank Polk, 120; and press, 68, 95, 96, 124, 127, 132, 137; pro-Ally sentiments of, 19, 24, 58, 73; and relationship with Wilson, 19, 24, 67, 68, 73, 90, 93, 97, 120, 122–23, 160, 179n16, 187n13; on sinking of U.S. ships, xv; and Edward N. Smith, 191n53; and standard for going to war, 81; as State Department legal counsel, 19; and *Sussex* incident, 29; and unrestricted German submarine warfare, 63, 67, 68, 72, 186n4; and *Vigilancia* sinking, 120, 154; and White Sulphur Springs, W. Va., 90, 91, 93; and *William P. Frye* sinking, 51; and Zimmerman Telegram, 93, 95, 96
Lathrop, Lorin A., 53
Latin Americans, 21
Leelanaw (ship): cargo on, 48, 49, 51; and casus belli/acts of war, 35, 49, 52, 79, 106; Congress and, 147, 152; crew of, 48–49; and Lansing memorandum to Wilson, 134; photo of, 49; as precedent, 74, 87; seizure and sinking of, 35, 48, 49–52, 58, 79, 109–10
Le Havre, France, 9, 141

Leith, Lockhart, 169, 170
Leo (ship), 152
Lerwick, Scot., 45
Leuchtenberg, William E., 177n2
Leveaux, E., 128, 173
Liberia, 164
Link, Arthur, 123, 124, 132, 177n1 (chap. 1), 197n2, 197n4
"List of Neutral Ships Sunk by the Germans, A," 200n5
Liverpool, Eng.: U.S. consul at, 43; voyages to and from, 3, 21, 22, 26, 41, 42, 193n27
Livio, Joseph, 10, 109, 195n12
Lloyd's War Losses: The First World War Casualties to Shipping through Enemy Causes, 1914-1918, 170
Loans, 31, 32, 162, 180n1
Loch Lomond, 44
Locomobile automobiles, 107
Lodge, Henry Cabot, 73, 87, 90
Loeria, Joseph, 9, 109, 173, 195n12
London, England: businesses in, 54, 94, 108; naval summit in, 17–18; and trade, 77, 108, 116; U.S. diplomats and diplomatic offices in, 43, 50, 52, 73, 91, 97; voyages to and from, 101, 116, 150, 193n27
London, Meyer, 144
London Daily Chronicle, 53
Londonian (ship), 193n27
Longshoremen, 2, 145
Lopez, Estphan, 9, 109, 173
Lopez, Manuel, 114
Lord Duffer (ship), 107
Louisiana, 159
Lowe, William, 81
Lowery, Michael, 168–69, 172
Luckner, Felix von, 46
Ludendorff, Erich Friedrich Wilhelm, 66
Ludvigsen, S., 114
Lusitania (ship): cargo on, 19, 23, 24; and casus belli/acts of war, 61, 95, 106, 118; Congress and, 21, 147, 151; fatalities on, 23, 41, 71, 80, 106, 110, 118, 156, 190n23; press and, 24, 194n2; Theodore Roosevelt on, 80; scholarship on, 23, 34, 179n13, 190n23; sinking of, 22–24, 33, 179n18; State Department and, 61; survivors of, 114; U.S. public and, 21, 24, 34, 40; Wilson and, 21, 24, 71, 95

Lusitania Disaster, The (Bailey and Ryan), 179n13
Lyman M. Law (ship): cargo on, 81, 82, 83, 84, 85, 87; and casus belli/acts of war, xiv, xv, 11, 84, 87, 89, 93–94, 97, 98, 103, 106; Congress and, 147, 152, 154, 157, 159; construction of, 81; crew of, 81–82, 84–85, 190n26; description of, 13, 81, 175; and Lansing memorandum to Wilson, 135; Robert Lansing and, 154; ownership of, 81, 119, 175; photo of, 82; press and, 84–87, 103; significance of, 166; sinking of, 13, 82–84, 88, 89, 109–10, 119, 143, 147, 175; supplies on, 85, 86, 87; Wilson and, 89, 93, 97, 98
Lyonesse (ship), 40
Lyons, William, 143, 175

Maddox, USS (ship), 167
Maine, 48, 181n10
Maine, USS (ship), 167
Mainland, Henry, 52, 53, 54, 56–57
Malta, 84
Manchester Engineer (ship), 152
Manila, Phil., 52
Marguerite (ship), xv, 13, 143–44, 154, 166, 175
Marina (ship), 61, 106
Mariners: African Americans as, 1, 21, 94; bonuses and wages paid to, 1, 2, 100, 193n20; carpenters, 9, 109, 173; chief officers, 53; and class, 1, 2–3, 4, 20–21, 165; coal-passers, 113; cooks, 2, 84; coxswain's mates, 45, 47; deckhands, 2; engineers, 2, 9, 53, 102, 109, 116, 128, 173, 178n11, 182n16; and ethnicity, 20–21, 85; firemen, 94, 113, 192n9; historical records on, 166; immigrants as, 1, 2, 3, 4, 9, 10, 21, 84, 108, 109, 113, 116, 128, 141, 143, 178n6; mates, 2, 81, 109, 113, 128, 173; mess boys, 9, 109, 173; muleteers, 21, 106, 178n8; oilers, 10, 109, 128, 173; petty officers, 45; pilots, 31, 36; public and, 2–3, 8; quartermasters, 9, 173; seamen, 34, 39, 112–13, 128, 173; ships' surgeons, 114; stewards, 2, 128, 173; stokers, 173; third officers, 9; wireless operators, 39
Maritime Transportation Company, 81, 85
Maryland Steel Company, 143
Massachusetts, 157, 159
Mauretania (ship), 3
McAdoo, William Gibbs: and 1916 presidential election, 65, 186n4; and arming of merchant ships, 90; and cabinet, 67, 90; and cotton exports, 186n30; prowar sentiments of, 67, 123, 132, 186n4; and Wilson, 90, 123
McBride, L. B., 43
McCafferty, H. W., 37–38
McDonough, Stephen W., 81, 83, 85–86, 88, 175
McDonough, Walter, 81
McKay, A. B., 100
McLemore, Jeff, 27–28
McLemore Resolution, 27–28, 161, 179n21
Mediterranean Sea: *Chemung* sinking in, 59; *Communipaw* incident in, 180n7; German submarines in, 59, 63, 83, 144; *Lyman M. Law* crew and, 82; mariners on, 82; safety zone in, 84, 88
Melville, Herman, 3
Merchant marine, 1–2, 3, 8. *See also* Mariners
Mexican-American War, xi, 91
Mexico: and Germany, xiii–xiv, 13, 14, 91, 92, 93, 136, 191n4; and Japan, 92; and United States, xiv, 91, 111, 143, 158, 195n15
Mexico City, Mexico, 91
Michigan, 128
Middleton, Frank A., 9, 108, 109, 175
Millis, Walter, 177n1 (chap. 1), 202n1 (epilogue)
Mines: British, xiii, 36, 58, 123, 124, 129, 130, 141, 146, 155, 169, 170, 171, 172, 174, 175, 198n17, 202n7; German, xii, 33, 36, 58, 155; Harriss-Irby-Vose Company ships and, 57; maps of, 169, 202n7; Russian, 36, 58; scholarship on, 169, 170; ships sunk by, 35, 60, 181n8, 200n5. *See also* Blockades
Mississippi, 149, 159
Missouri, 28, 69, 148, 154, 156
Missourian (ship): and casus belli/acts of war, xv; Congress and, 143, 154, 156, 159; construction of, 143; crew of, 143, 156; description of, 13, 143, 175; as government transport ship, 143; and Lansing memorandum to Wilson, 154; ownership of, 175; significance of, 166; sinking of, 13, 175
Mixed Claims Commission, 170–71, 203n11
Mogilev, Russia, 104
Mongolia (ship), 100, 193n27
Montenegro, 154
Montera, Julio, 10, 109
Montreal, Canada, 75

Morgan, J. P., 31, 155
Morison, Samuel Eliot, 177n2
Mueller, Edward, 196n20
Muskogee (ship), 35
Mutual defense treaties, 6–7, 13, 16
My Four Years in Germany (Gerard), 179n18, 186n4

Nantucket, Mass., 189n9
Nantucket Lightship, 77
Napier, Shanks & Bell, Limited, 100
Navy, U.S., 77, 99–100, 124–25, 141, 142, 149, 166
Nebraska (state), 145, 148
Nebraskan (ship): attack on, 25, 34, 35, 41–44, 48, 56, 109, 147; cargo on, 41; and casus belli/acts of war, 34, 35, 44, 106; construction of, 41; House Foreign Relations Committee and, 151; and Lansing memorandum to Wilson, 134; ownership of, 41; photo of, 42; significance of, 44
Nesz, Jaun, 10, 109, 195n12
Netherlands: and blockades, 29, 31, 32, 63, 88; British submarines off of, 171; and *Healdton,* xiii, xiv, 128, 167, 168, 175; and naval summit, 18; and neutrality, 7, 29, 32, 168, 171; and trade, 168, 171; and unrestricted German submarine warfare, 66, 67; Web sites in, 172
Neutrality Acts, 161–63
Newcastle, England, 141
New England, 85
New Jersey, 49
New Mexico, 91, 92
Newport, R.I., 76, 77
Newport News, Va., 21, 76, 82, 116
Newspapers. *See New York Times;* Press
New York, N.Y.: *Algonquin* and, 100, 101; *Alicante* and, 59; *Arabic* and, 26; *Aztec* and, 141; *City of Memphis* and, 113; *Columbian* and, 54, 55; *Husatonic* and, 75; Irish Americans in, 145; *Laconia* and, 94; *Leelanaw* and, 48; longshoremen in, 145; *Missourian* and, 143; newspapers in, 23; *Pass of Balmaha* and, 45; press in, 34, 71; pro-Ally sentiment in, 34; shipping firms and agents in, 54, 58, 81, 85, 100, 107; and trade, 111; and transatlantic crossings, 3; *Vigilancia* and, 9, 107, 108, 119, 149; vulnerability of, 77

New York Maritime Register, 179n14
New York State, 48–49, 57, 144
New York Times: and *Algonquin* sinking, 102; and *Chemung* sinking, 59, 185n28; and crew information, 49; and declaration of war, 126–27, 131, 144; and *Falaba* incident, 178n11; and fatalities from ship sinkings, 194n2; and *Golena* incident, 134; Harriss, Magill & Co., 186n35; and *Healdton* sinking, 124, 130, 131, 167; and *Housatonic* sinking, 78, 84; and *Laconia* sinking, 192n9; and *Lanao* incident, 53; and *Leelanaw* incident, 48–49, 50; and *Lusitania* sinking, 194n2; and *Lyman M. Law* sinking, 84, 85; and *Nebraskan* incident, 42, 43; pro-Ally/pro-war sentiments of, 126, 144; and *St. Helen's* incident, 134; and unrestricted German submarine warfare, 78, 186n4; use of phrase "overt act" by, 188n24; and *Vigilancia* sinking, 109; and *William P. Frye* incident, 53, 84
New York Times Current History, 89
Nicholas II, csar of Russia, 104
Nicosian (ship), 27, 152
Norberg, A., 175
Nordberg, A., 100
Norfolk, Va., 38, 128
Norfolk Public Library, 181n14
Norlina (ship), 35
Norma Pratt (ship), 110
Norris, George W., 148–49
North, Neils P., 9, 109, 173
North American Society of Oceanic History, 172
North Sea, 31, 44, 128
Norway and Norwegians, 7, 32, 66, 116, 178n6
Nova Scotia Steel and Coal Company, 100
Nyanza (ship), 35
Nye, Gerald, 161

O'Brien, Walter, 142, 175
Occupations, marine. *See* Mariners
Ocean liners: armed, 27; attacks on, 16, 17, 19, 21–22, 26; British Admiralty and, 23; and class, 3, 20, 21, 165; as cultural icons, 3, 4; and ethnicity, 21; German policies toward, 24, 26, 27, 29; and international law, 18; Lansing and, 19, 20; press and, 3, 4, 20, 21; scholarship on, 178n6; speed of, 3; U.S. pas-

sengers on, 5, 17, 19, 20, 27–28; U.S.-registered, 33–34; Wilson and, 17, 18, 19, 20, 21; women and children on, 17, 21, 165. *See also Arabic* (ship); *Falaba* (ship); *Laconia* (ship); *Lusitania* (ship)
Ocean Steamship Company, 111, 175, 197n31. *See also* Savannah Line
O'Connor, T.V., 2
Odessa, Ukraine, 75
Okasan (ship), 107
Oklahoma (ship), 39
Oklahoma (state), 28, 57, 156, 159
Orders in Council, British, 45, 57
Orduna (ship), 152, 188n4
Oriental Navigation Company, 141, 175
Orkney Islands, 48, 51
Orleans (ship), 141
Osenber, W., 116
Osgood, Robert E., 202n2 (epilogue)
Oswego [sic] (ship). *See Owego* (ship)
Ottoman Empire, 7, 105
Outlook, 80, 190n23
Owego (ship), 35, 56, 134, 147
Oyster Bay, N.Y., 73

Pacific Ocean, 76, 84
Packard automobiles, 107
Page, Nelson, 86
Page, Walter Hines: and British attacks on German seamen, 179n19; and *Falaba* incident, 178n11; and *Housatonic* sinking, 188n4; and *Leelanaw* incident, 50; and *Nebraskan* incident, 43; pro-British/pro-Ally sentiments of, 65, 73, 179n19; and unrestricted German submarine warfare, 67; and Wilson, 25, 65, 97, 179n16; and Zimmerman Telegram, 91, 192n5
Palermo, Italy, 81
Panama, 14, 163, 164, 202n4 (epilogue)
Paris, France, 59, 108
Pass of Balmaha (ship): cargo on, 186n30; and casus belli/acts of war, 35, 106; construction of, 44; descriptions of, 44, 46; and Lansing memorandum to Wilson, 134–35; ownership of, 183n32; as precedent, 52, 103, 104, 184n38; press and, 183n32; registry of, 44–45, 103, 104, 109; scholarship on, 183n34; seizure of, 35, 44–47, 48, 58

Patria (ship), 152
Pearl Harbor, Hawaii, 163
Penobscot Bay, 81
Persia (ship), 178n9
Peru, 10, 108, 109
Petrolite (ship), 35, 147
Philadelphia, Pa., 24, 100, 112, 128
Philippines, 52
Pickhuben (ship), 75. *See also Housatonic* (20th-century ship)
Pierce automobiles, 107
Pierre Loti (ship), 37
Pittman, Key, 125
Pittsburgh, Pa., 128
Pless Castle, 66
Plymouth, Eng., 10, 40, 101
Poland, 17, 161, 162, 163
Polk, Frank, 90, 91, 93, 120
Port Arthur, Texas, 116, 119, 150, 182n16
Port Colborne and St. Lawrence Navigation Company, 100
Porto Maurizio, Italy, 143
Portsmouth, England, 169
Portugal, 52, 108
Press: 21st-century, 14; and *Algonquin* sinking, 102–3; and *Arabic* sinking, 26; and Armed Ship Bill/arming of U.S. merchant ships, 95, 99; and *Aztec* sinking, 142; and blockades, 180n2; British, 95, 192n9; and *Carib* sinking, 155; and casus belli/acts of war, 74, 120; and Central powers, 2; and *City of Memphis* sinking, 11, 106, 114–15, 117–18, 120, 180n7, 196n20; and class, 21, 94, 165; and *Columbian* incident, 56, 57, 185n22; and *Communipaw* incident, 180n7; and crew lists, 84–85; and Declaration of London, 54; and declaration of war, 122, 131, 143, 144, 198n19; and ethnicity, 21; and *Evelyn* sinking, 155; and *Falaba* incident, 178n11; and gender, 21, 165; German, 63, 64; and *Gulflight* incident, 39, 40; and *Healdton* sinking, 124, 128, 129, 131, 135, 167, 170, 171, 201n21; and *Housatonic* sinking, 79, 103, 189n11; and *Illinois* sinking, 11, 106, 117–18, 120, 201n21; Italian, 86; and labor, 2; and *Laconia* sinking, 94–95; and Robert Lansing, 124; and *Leelanaw* incident, 50; and *Lusitania* sinking, 40; and *Lyman M. Law* sinking, 82, 84, 85, 86–87,

226 / Index

Press—*continued*
103, 147; and *Marguerite* sinking, 143; and merchant mariners, 166; and *Missourian* sinking, 156; and *Nebraskan* incident, 42, 43, 44; neutralist, 79; and ocean liners, 3, 4, 21; and passenger lists, 20; and *Pass of Balmaha* incident, 45, 183n32; pro-Ally, 34, 79; Rep. William LaFollette and, 155; and Hans Rose, 76, 77, 189n11; and Sen. Norris of Nebraska, 148; and ship casualties and survivors, 4, 178n8; and ships lost at sea, 87, 114, 158, 165; and submarine attacks, 26; and submarine policy, 77; and submarines off Nantucket, 189n9; and *Sussex* incident, 29; and unrestricted German submarine warfare, 63, 64, 65–66, 68, 72, 79, 117–18, 186n4; and U.S. diplomatic relations with Germany, 68, 69; and *Vigilancia* sinking, 10, 11, 106, 108, 109, 111, 114, 117–18, 120; and *William P. Frye* incident, 37, 39, 50, 54, 165; and Wilson, 122, 126–27, 131, 179n14; and Wilson's Feb. 3, 1917, address to Congress, 71; and Zimmerman Telegram, 95–96, 134. *See also New York Times*
Prince Charles (ship), 45
Princess Margaret (ship), 169
Princeton University, 123, 132
Prinz Eitel Friedrich (ship), 37, 38, 84, 181n14
Prize court, 38, 45, 50, 51, 52, 56
Progressives, 145, 148
Prohibition, 163, 164
Prussia, 38, 46, 50, 51
Prutting, Fred, 114
Puerto Rico and Puerto Ricans, 21, 108, 164
Pure Light (ship), 127, 129. *See also Healdton* (ship)
Pure Light Oil Company, 127
Pustkuchen, Herbert, 29, 113, 114–15, 175

Q-ships, 26–27, 45, 179n19, 185n29
Quasi War, xi
Quebec, Canada, 75
Queenstown, Ire., 36–37, 42, 79, 114

Rankin, Jeannette, 145, 157
Rayburn, Sam, 162
Rebecca Palmer (ship), 35, 134, 147
Reed, James A., 148

Republicans, 73, 145, 155, 158
Rio Pirahn or *Rio Piranha* (ship), 184n15
Roach, John, 111
Road to War: America, 1914-1917 (Millis), 177n1 (chap. 1), 202n1 (epilogue)
Rochester (ship), 193n27
Rockingham (ship), 193n27
Rodriquez, Alexander, 10, 109, 134, 173
Rogers, John P., 157, 159
Rome, Italy, 82, 86, 108, 190n27
Rona, Scot., 45
Rondon, T., 10, 109
Room 40 (Beesly), 92
Roosevelt, Franklin, 149, 163
Roosevelt, Theodore: and Armed Ship Bill, 96; and Henry Cabot Lodge, 87, 90; pro-war sentiments of, 80, 81; on sinking of U.S. ships, xiii, 80, 81; and unrestricted German submarine warfare, 96; and Wilson, 73, 80, 87, 96, 97
Rose, Hans: and activities off Nantucket, 189n9; and cruiser rules, 79, 81, 119, 144, 146; description of, 76; and *Housatonic*, 76, 78–79, 81, 119, 175; in Newport, R.I., 76–77; and press, 76, 79, 189n11; scholarship on, 79; ships sunk off of Nantucket by, 77; war record of, 83
Rose, Robert F., 58
Rosenberg, Erich, 40
Rotterdam, Neth., 100, 112, 128, 168, 203n11
Rouen, France, 39
Roumania, 154
Royal Navy (U.K.), 26, 79
Royal Netherlands Navy, 171, 172
Russia: and Allies, 4, 104; civil war in, 105; and entry into World War I, 7; mariners from, 119; and mutual defense treaties, 6; and naval summit, 18; and ocean liners, 16; and Serbia, 6; and trade, 108; trade with, 45, 48, 49; tsar's abdication in, 104, 105; and U.S. neutrality, 60; withdrawal of, from World War I, 105
Russian (ship), 178n9
Russian Revolution, 131
Ryan, Paul B., 179n13

Sabin, Charles, 107, 108
Sabotage, 14

Sacramento (ship), 35, 76, 134, 147
Saigon, French Indo-China, 52, 54
Sailor's Union of the Pacific, 1
Saltzwedel, Reinhold, 116, 117, 119, 175
Salvator (ship), 78
Salvatore Giner (ship), 59
Sandford, Edward, 75
San Francisco, Calif., 41, 54, 128
Sarajevo, Bosnia, 16
Sardinia, 82, 84, 143, 175
Savannah, Ga., 111, 119
Savannah Line: and Central Georgia Railway, 111; Harriman family and, 111; history of, 196n20; mariners hired by, 112; number of ships owned by, 197n31; ownership of, 111, 118–19; routes operated by, 111; routes run by, 111–12, 119, 128; ships owned by, 111, 112, 197n31. *See also City of Memphis* (ship)
Scalanova, Turkey, 112
Scandinavians, 2, 3, 108
Scheer, Reinhard, 47, 179n18, 186n4
Schneider, Rudolf, 26
Schull, Ireland, 114
Schultz, Charles, 102, 193n28
Schultze, Otto, 53
Schwieger, Walther, 22, 23
Scilly, Isles of, 39–40, 76, 109, 113, 119, 175
Scotland: *City of Memphis* survivors in, 11, 114–15; *Leelanaw* incident near, 47, 48, 50–51; and name of *Pass of Balmaha*, 183n32; *Pass of Balmaha* incidents near, 45, 47; ships built in, 44, 52, 75, 100, 127, 129; U.S. consuls in, 48, 50, 51
Scott, Walter, 9, 10, 44, 109, 183n32
Seaconnet (ship), 134, 147, 181n8
Sea Hunters II, The (Cussler), 203n14
Seaman's Act, 1–2, 144
Sea Power in the Machine Age (Brodie), 177n1 (chap. 1)
Searsport, Maine, 190n25
Seattle, Wash., 36
Sebek (ship), 178n9
Second World War. *See* World War II
Seeadler (ship), 46, 47, 184n37
Selene (ship), 53
Senate, U.S.: and Armed Ship Bill, 96, 99, 145–46; and cloture rules, 96, 99, 123, 144, 146, 192n12; and Declaration of London, 177n4, 183n36; and declaration of war, xiv, 13, 14, 144, 145–50, 200n12; Foreign Relations Committee of, 18, 28, 32, 69, 95–96; Gore Bill in, 28; and Lansing, 24; rules of, 148; and Wilson, 123, 192n12; and World War II, 163; and Zimmerman Telegram, 96
Serbia/Servia, 6, 7, 105, 154
Seward (ship), 200n5
Shackleford, Dorsey W., 144, 154–55, 201n30
Shadow Divers (Kurson), 203n14
Shea, Robert, 114
Shetland Islands, 45
Short (mariner), 39, 182n16
Siberia, Joseph, 9, 109, 173
Sierra Leone, 22
Silesia, 66
Silius (ship), 152
Sino-Japanese War, 16
Smalls Light, 22
Smith, Edward N., 137, 191n53
Smith, R. W., 128, 173
Socialists, 144
Sour Lake, Texas, 115
South America, 10, 181n14
Sovereignty for Sale (Carlisle), 164, 202n4 (epilogue)
Spain: *Chemung* sinking off coast of, 59; *Columbian* incident near, 54; and Germany, 66; mariners from, 10, 21, 108, 109, 116; and neutrality, 7; representation of U.S. in Germany by, 133; and trade, 108; U.S. consuls in, 54
Spanish-American War, xi
Spanish Civil War, 163
Sparrow, G. S., 10, 109, 195n12
Sparrows Point, Md., 143
Spindler, Arno, 168, 202n2 (App. A)
Spindle Top, Texas, 115
Standard Oil: and *Communipaw*, 180n7; and *Cushing*, 44; and *Healdton*, 100, 126, 127, 128, 129, 131, 149, 171, 175, 193n21, 197n31, 203n11; ships owned by, 164, 194n34, 197n31; and ships' registries, 104, 127–28, 163–64; subsidiaries of, 104; and unrestricted German submarine warfare, 89, 128

228 / Index

State Department, U.S.: and *Algonquin* sinking, 101, 103; and *Armenian* sinking, 21; and attacks on U.S. merchant ships, 34; von Bernstorff and, 26; and casus belli/acts of war, xiv, 134, 139, 147; and *Chemung* sinking, 59; and *City of Memphis* sinking, 114; and *Columbian* incident, 54, 55, 56; and *Congress*, 158; and crises following Wilson's Feb. 3, 1917, address to Congress, 73; and Declaration of London, 180n2; *Foreign Relations of the United States* published by, 99; Foreign Trade Office in, 57, 58; on German crew members breaking parole, 38; and *Gulflight* incident, 40; and Harriss-Irby-Vose Company, 57, 58; and *Healdton* sinking, xiv, 124, 167, 203n11; and *Housatonic* sinking, 78, 135; and *Lanao* incident, 52–53; and *Leelanaw* incident, 50–51; and *Lusitania* sinking, 61; and *Lyman M. Law* sinking, 82, 84, 85, 135; and Mar. 30, 1917, Lansing memorandum to Wilson, 153; and *Marina* sinking, 61; and minor submarine-merchant ship encounters, 180n7; and *Nebraskan* incident, 43, 44; and *Pass of Balmaha* incident, 45; protests by, 20, 52; and ships destroyed by mines, 36; and shipwreck survivors, 4; and sinking of civilian ships, 18–19, 81; and sinking of *Healdton*, xiv; and *Sussex* incident, 29; and tally of ship losses, 147; and transfer of ships' registries, 103, 183n36, 194n34; and *Vigilancia* sinking, 10; and *William P. Frye* incident, 50, 53; and Zimmerman Telegram, xiii, 91
Steamshipmen's Protective Union, 1
Steiner, John, 128, 173
Stephanidis, John, 100, 102, 104, 194n34
Stephano, SS (ship), 77
Stephens, Joseph G., 10, 101
Stettin, (formerly Ger.), 75
St. Helen's (ship), 134, 147
St. Lawrence and Chicago Steam Navigation Company, Limited, 100
St. Nazaire, France, 54
Stockton Springs, Maine, 81, 190n25
Stone, William J., 28, 69
Stovall, Pleasant Alexander, 188n20
St. Paul (ship), 51

Straits of Otranto, 83
Strand Magazine, 33
Strathdene, SS (ship), 77
St. Vincent, Port., 53
Submarines: Austrian, 35; bases for, 83; British and, 26–27, 61, 80, 171, 172; defensive measures by, 59; Dutch, 171–72; *E-43*, 171; first German uses of, 33; hulls of, 27; *Hunley*, 75; invention of, 5; and *Lyman M. Law* sinking, 82–83; *O-2*, 171, 172; official records on, 178n10; scholarship on, 79, 168–69, 202n2 (App. A); *U-20*, 22; *U-24*, 26; *U-28*, 22; *U-30*, 40; *U-35*, 86, 143, 175; *U-36*, 45, 58, 183n34; *U-38*, 21, 58, 59, 83; *U-41*, 42, 43, 48; *U-46*, 142, 175; *U-49*, 55, 58; *U-52*, 143, 175; *U-53*, 76, 77, 78, 175; *U-62*, 101, 175; *U-63*, 53, 184n15; *U-70*, 10, 11, 109, 175; *UB-29*, 28, 29, 113; UB class of, 180n22; *UC-21*, 116, 117, 175; *UC-66*, 113, 175; and U.S.-registered passenger liners, 33–34
"Submarines" (Fisher), 33
Submarine warfare: advocates of, 33, 66, 186n4; and *Arabic* Pledge, 26, 29; Congress and, 157; and Declaration of London, 110, 115; defenses against, 26–27, 33, 45, 87, 88; Dutch and, 168; factors leading to, 64–65, 162; and firing single torpedo, 168; German adoption of unrestricted, 33, 66–67; German announcement of unrestricted, xiii, 10, 62, 63, 65–66, 72, 76, 79, 81, 82, 88, 92, 93, 100, 101, 122, 128, 130, 137, 144, 151, 152, 156; German debates over, 27; and Lansing memorandum to Wilson, 133; and *Lusitania* sinking, 179n18; and merchant ships, 30, 33; and neutral ships, 33, 43, 60; and nighttime attacks, 168, 202n3 (App. A); and ocean liners, 179n18; press and, 65–66, 78–79, 117–18, 186n4; purposes of, xii, xiii, 5; and reporting of attacks, 168; scholarship on, 177n2; and *Sussex* Pledge, xiii, 29–30, 66; U.S. casualties from, xv, 151, 159; U.S. ships sunk by, xiii, xiv, 13, 159. *See also* Cruiser rules
Suez Canal, 52, 54
Sussex (ship): attack on, 28–29, 113; and casus belli/acts of war, 61, 106; Congress and, 21, 147, 149, 152; Lansing and, 29; ownership of, 28; reaction to, xiii, 21, 34, 61; U.S. pas-

sengers on, xiii, 29; Wilson and, 21, 29, 68, 70, 71, 72
Sussex Pledge, xiii, xviii, 29–30, 66, 69, 71, 95
Swan, Hunter & Wigham Richardson, 94
Swanson, Claude, 13, 149–50, 159, 201n19, 201n21, 201n26
Sway of the Grand Saloon, The (Brinnin), 178n6
Sweden and Swedish, 7, 49, 116, 178n6
Swienmunde, Germany, 153
Switzerland and Swiss, 7, 67, 188n20

Taft, WIlliam, 1
Tampico crisis, 111, 195n15
Temple, Henry, 201n35
Terschellingbank Lightship, 170
Terschelling Island, 169, 170, 172
Terschelling Light, 128, 167, 168, 169, 203n11
Texaco, 115–16, 119, 128, 175, 197n31
Texas, 27, 49, 57, 91, 92, 115
Thierichens, Max, 37, 38, 181n14
Thrasher, Leon, 22, 178n11
Tirpitz, Alfred von, 33, 64
Titanic (ship), 4, 203n14
T. J. Stewart Company, 81
Toronto, Canada, 100
Torsdal (ship), 184n15
Towers, John, 43
Trade goods: acids, 101; ammunition, 8, 32; arms, 8, 32; automobile parts, 108; blasting caps, 59, 60; box shooks, 81, 82, 84, 87; bunker coal, 113; coal, 76; copper, 56, 57, 101; flax, 48, 49, 51; flour, 75; food, 5, 8, 31, 35, 57; foodstuffs, 100, 101, 102, 103, 141; formaldehyde, 101; fruit, 149; general cargo, 142, 143; grain, 75, 77, 100, 101; horses, 21, 55, 112; licorice, 112; locomotives, 108; lumber, 84; machinery, 101, 108; motorcycle parts, 56, 57; mules, 21; munitions, 2, 5, 17, 31, 162; and Neutrality Acts, 162; noncontraband, 31; oil, 31, 35, 39, 49, 116, 168; petroleum, 128, 162, 164; provisions, 108; railway equipment and supplies, 108; rice, 52, 53, 184n15; rum, 163; shoes, 108; soap, 77–78; steel, 56, 57; steel rails, 108; straw, 149; sugar, 41; tin, 101; transport equipment, 8, 31, 32; troops, 17; trucks, 107; typewriters, 108; weapons, 32; wheat, 36,

37, 78, 84; and World War II, 162–63. *See also* Contraband; Cotton and cotton goods
Tredwell, Roger Culver, 82, 84, 85, 190n27
Tripoli, 84
Tromp (ship), 53
Tsingtao, China, 37
Tubantia (ship), 152
Tuchman, Barbara, 92, 95, 191n3, 191n4, 192n5
Tumulty, Joseph: and Lansing, 120; memoirs of, 122, 186n1; and press, 68; and Wilson, 24, 63, 98, 122, 179n16
Tunisia, 144
Turin, Italy, 190n27
Turkey, 112
Turner, W. J., 23
Turner Joy, USS (ship), 167

U-boat.net, 168–69
U-boats. *See* Submarines
Union League Club, 96
United States: and Great Britain, 158; and isolationism, 139, 161, 165; isolationist areas of, 137, 159; and maritime rights, xi, xv, 16, 17; and Mexico, xiv, 91, 111, 143, 158, 195n15; and mutual defense treaties, 7, 13, 16; and naval summit, 18; and neutrality, 5, 32; and Quasi War, xi; and ships' registries, 163–65; sovereignty of, 14; and trade, 31, 36; and transfer of ships' registries, 46, 104, 194n34; and treaties with Prussia, 38, 46, 50, 51, 52; and unrestricted German submarine warfare, 63; and War of 1812, xi. *See also* Civil War, U.S.
United States Line, 163
United States Shipping Board, 193n20
Ushant Light, 141

Valencia, Spain, 59
Valentiner, Max, 59–60, 83
Vanderbilt, Alfred, 23
Varing (ship), 55, 56, 185n22
Vasquez, M., 10, 109
Veaux, Henry Lee, 128, 173
Venezuela, 10, 108, 109
Veracruz, Mex., 111, 195n15
Versailles Treaty, 163, 164, 165
Victorian (ship), 45, 58

230 / Index

Vienna, Austria, 59
Vietnam War, 14
Vigilancia (ship): cabinet and, 121, 156; cargo on, 107, 108, 110, 149, 195n7; and casus belli/acts of war, xiv, xv, 11, 13, 14, 15, 106, 110, 117, 118, 130, 135, 136, 138, 139, 157, 162; Congress and, 13, 131, 149, 150, 152, 156, 157, 159; construction of, 107, 109, 118; crew of, 108, 109, 118, 195n7, 195n8; description of, 9, 10, 108, 175; fatalities on, 9–10, 11, 12, 13, 14, 109, 110, 115, 120, 138, 149, 150, 151, 152, 157, 159, 173, 174, 195n12; final voyage and sinking of, 9–10, 11, 12, 13, 106, 108–9, 113, 116, 119, 120, 124, 131, 133, 149, 175, 193n27; flag and registry of, 10, 106, 108, 109, 110, 149; Lansing and, 120; and Lansing memorandum to Wilson, 133, 134, 135; ownership of, 9, 11, 107, 109, 118, 120, 149, 175, 194n3; photo of, 10; press and, 10, 11, 108, 109, 111, 114, 117–18, 120; registry of, 11, 106, 107, 109, 118; scholarship on, xv, 139–40; significance of, 166; U.S. public and, 131; Wilson and, 124
Vincent (ship), 58, 181n8
Virginia, 149, 150, 159
Vladivostok, Russia, 108
von Arnauld de la Perière, Lothar, 82–83, 85–86, 143, 144, 146, 175
von Eckhardt, Heinrich, 191n4
von Forstner, Siegfried, 22
von Holtzendorff, Henning, 27, 33, 65, 66, 73, 186n4
von Muller, Georg, 67

Wahine (ship), 169
Wald, Lillian, 179n21
Walker, Charles, 114
Wallace, Richard, 173
Walther, Hans, 143, 175
Ward and Armstrong, 194n3
Ward Line, 107, 194n3
Warhawks: American Interventionists before Pearl Harbor, The (Chadwin), 202n2 (epilogue)
War of 1812, xi
War Risk Bureau, 170, 203n11
Wars of the French Revolution and Empire, xii
"War with Germany" (Roosevelt), 80
Washington, D.C.: and communication with Berlin, 93; German ambassador in, xiii, 26, 76; German notes in, 26, 40, 53, 86; press in, 42, 86, 102, 126, 131; Edward House in, 125; and report on *Lyman M. Law* sinking, 86; and report on *Missourian* sinking, 143; and report on *Nebraskan* incident, 43; State Department in, 4, 58; U.S. Hydrographic Office in, 88
Washington, George, 7, 16, 154
Washington State, 155
Watertown, N.Y., 137
Watkins, John Thomas, 147–48, 159, 200n12
Way of the Neutral Is Hard (cartoon), 15
Weser River, 111
West Africa, 22
Western Union, 93
West Haven, Conn., 81
Westpoint, SS (ship), 77
Westwego (ship), 35
White Sulphur Springs, W. Va., 90, 93
Wilber, David F., 143
William Chase, 175
William P. Frye (ship): attack on, 30, 35, 36–38, 49, 51, 106, 109; cargo on, 84; and casus belli/acts of war, 30, 35, 38, 106; and Lansing memorandum to Wilson, 134–35; as namesake for Sen. William Pierce Frye, 181n10; as precedent, 39, 40, 51, 52, 53, 54, 59, 60, 74, 84, 87; press and, 165; reparations for, 38–39
Williams, John Sharp, 149, 159
Williard, Charles W., 175
Wilmington, Del., 9, 108
Wilson, Woodrow: and 1916 presidential election, 65; advisors to, xiii, 6, 14, 24–25, 97, 123, 126, 187n13; and *Algonquin* sinking, xiv, 11, 101, 147, 160; and announcement of unrestricted German submarine warfare, 10–11, 63, 64, 65–66, 67, 70, 122, 152; and Apr. 2, 1917, address to Congress, 13, 14, 136, 138–39, 140–41, 144, 153, 154, 165, 198n26; and *Arabic* incident, 21, 95; and Armed Ship Bill/arming U.S. merchant ships, 89, 90, 93, 95–96, 97–98, 157, 192n7; and attacks on passenger ships, 17, 18, 19–20, 21; and attempts to negotiate peace, 65; and Aug. 19, 1914, address to Congress, 16–17; and beginning of World War I, xii, 5, 16; and William Jennings Bryan, 24; and cabi-

net, 12, 67–68, 72, 88, 90, 93, 107, 120–22, 124, 126, 130, 131, 192n7; cartoon depiction of, 12; and casus belli/acts of war, xiii, xiv, xv, 6, 11, 49, 80, 81, 89, 92–94, 95, 97, 101, 130, 133, 135, 147, 160, 188n24, 191n4, 192n5; and *City of Memphis* sinking, xiv, 107, 117, 122, 124, 130, 135, 136, 139; and class, 21, 165; and convening of Congress to declare war, xiv, xv, 12, 92, 121, 123, 124, 128, 130; critics of, 73, 80, 87, 96, 97, 139–40; and decision making, 25, 68, 73, 120, 122, 123, 160; and declaration of war, 107, 122–27, 130, 131, 132, 136–37, 151, 157, 159, 160, 167, 172, 197n2, 197n4, 198n26, 198n27, 200n5; and diplomatic relations with Germany, xiii, 10–11, 67–72, 113, 122, 152, 187n13; and ethnicity, 21; and expansion of U.S. Navy, 124–25; and *Falaba* incident, 21, 95; and Feb. 3, 1917, address to Congress, 69–72, 73, 78, 79–80; and Feb. 26, 1917, address to Congress, 89, 93–94, 95, 135, 157; and fifth annual message to Congress, 198n26; and foreign policy, 28, 96, 161; Fourteen Points of, xii, 165, 198n26; and freedom of the seas, xi–xii; German foreign minister on, 72; and Gore Bill, 28, 161; and *Healdton* sinking, 123, 125, 127, 128, 130, 167, 172; health of, 97, 124, 197n4; and *Housatonic* sinking, xiv, 11, 80–81, 93, 135, 147; and Edward House, 24, 63, 73, 122, 123, 125, 179n16, 187n13; and David Houston, 25, 132; idealism of, 14, 96, 127, 136, 139, 140, 165, 198n20, 198n26; and *Illinois* sinking, xiv, 107, 117, 122, 124, 130, 135, 136, 139; and international law, 138; Jan. 22, 1917, address by, 65, 66; and just war, 138–39, 198n26; and *Laconia* sinking, 95; and Lansing, 24, 29, 63, 67, 68, 72, 73, 93, 97, 120, 122, 123, 127, 132, 160, 179n16, 187n13; and Lansing memorandum, 136, 147, 152, 153, 158, 181n9, 198n23, 201n26, 202n6; and League of Nations, 198n26; and *Leelanaw* sinking, 49; and loss of merchant mariners, 165; and *Lusitania* sinking, 19, 21, 23, 24, 95; and *Lyman M. Law* sinking, xiv, 11, 93, 135, 147; and William Gibbs McAdoo, 132; and McLemore Resolution, 28, 161; and Mexico, 195n15; and morality, 198n27; and Walter Hines Page, 25, 65, 73, 97, 179n16; photo of, 97; and press, 71, 95, 122, 126–27, 179n14; press and, 87, 131; and relationship with Lansing, 19; scholarship on, 14, 123–24, 132, 139–40, 161, 165, 177n1 (chap. 1), 197n2, 197n4, 198n20, 198n26; and Seaman's Act, 1; second inauguration of, 97–98, 124, 192n15; and Senate cloture rules, 192n12; and shipping crisis, 88; and *Sussex* Pledge, 95; and *Sussex* sinking, 21, 29, 68, 72, 113; and Joseph Tumulty, 24, 63, 122, 179n16; and U-boat visit to Newport harbor, 77; and U.S. Constitution, 138; and U.S. neutrality, xii, 5, 10–11, 16, 20, 27, 31, 65, 96–97, 161; and U.S. passengers on belligerent ships, 17; *Vigilancia* (ship), 136; and *Vigilancia* sinking, xiv, 107, 117, 122, 124, 130, 135, 139; and Zimmerman Telegram, xiv, 91–93, 95–96, 192n5

Wilson Papers, The (ed. Link), 123–24, 132
Wilson the Diplomatist: A Look at His Major Foreign Policies (Link), 177n1 (chap. 1)
Winterport, Maine, 81
Wisconsin, 1, 155, 159
Women: and 1916 presidential election, 65; and attacks on ships, 148; as casualties, 23, 118, 148, 150, 165; and class, 21; and declaration of war, 157; German treatment of, 38; on ocean liners, 165; as passengers, 8, 17, 21, 196n20; public perceptions of, 21
Woolsey, Lester, 68
World War I: duration of, xii; end of, 161; escalation of, 7; first U.S. serviceman killed in, 142, 143; impact of maritime transportation on, xii; impact of U.S. participation on, xii; merchant marine and, 1; outbreak of, xii, 4, 7, 16; scholarship on, xii, xv, 14, 80, 161, 165, 166, 169, 177n1 (chap. 1), 202n1 (epilogue), 202n2 (epilogue); U.S. casualties in, 14; U.S. entry into, xi–xii, xiv–xv, 5–6, 16, 38–39, 92, 164; and U.S. neutrality, xii–xiii; Wilson's depiction of, 14
World War II, xi, xii, 161, 162, 165–66
Wotherspoon, William, 100, 104, 194n34
Wünsche, Otto, 10, 11, 109, 110, 175
www.wrecksite.eu, 172

Yarrowdale (ship), 153
Yoker yards, 100

Zimmerman, Arthur, 53–54, 56, 72, 91, 96, 191n4

Zimmerman Telegram: British and, xiii, 90–91, 185n29; and casus belli/acts of war, 92, 93, 94, 97, 98, 134, 136, 191n3; contents of, xiii–xiv, 13, 14; delivery of, to U.S. government, xiii; House Foreign Relations Committee and, 153; impact of, 192n5; interception of, xiii, 91; and Lansing memorandum to Wilson, 133, 134; noted in Mar. 30, 1917, Lansing memorandum to Wilson, 153; press and, 95–96, 134; public and, 92, 95–96, 131; scholarship on, 92, 95, 191n3, 191n4, 192n5; significance of, 105; text of, 92, 191n2; transmission of, 93; and U.S. neutrality, 92, 93; Walter Hines Page and, 192n5; Wilson and, 92–94, 97, 98, 192n5

Zimmerman Telegram, The (Tuchman), 92

Zurich, Switzerland, 153

New Perspectives on Maritime History and Nautical Archaeology
Edited by James C. Bradford and Gene Allen Smith

Maritime Heritage of the Cayman Islands, by Roger C. Smith (1999; first paperback edition, 2000)
The Three German Navies: Dissolution, Transition, and New Beginnings, 1945–1960, by Douglas C. Peifer (2002)
The Rescue of the Gale Runner: *Death, Heroism, and the U.S. Coast Guard*, by Dennis L. Noble (2002; first paperback edition, 2008)
Brown Water Warfare: The U.S. Navy in Riverine Warfare and the Emergence of a Tactical Doctrine, 1775–1970, by R. Blake Dunnavent (2003)
Sea Power in the Medieval Mediterranean: The Catalan-Aragonese Fleet in the War of the Sicilian Vespers, by Lawrence V. Mott (2003)
An Admiral for America: Sir Peter Warren, Vice-Admiral of the Red, 1703–1752, by Julian Gwyn (2004)
Maritime History as World History, edited by Daniel Finamore (2004)
Counterpoint to Trafalgar: The Anglo-Russian Invasion of Naples, 1805–1806, by William Henry Flayhart III (paperback edition, 2004)
Life and Death on the Greenland Patrol, 1942, by Thaddeus D. Novak, edited by P. J. Capelotti (2005)
X Marks the Spot: The Archaeology of Piracy, edited by Russell K. Skowronek and Charles R. Ewen (2006; first paperback edition 2007)
Industrializing American Shipbuilding: The Transformation of Ship Design and Construction, 1820–1920, by William H. Thiesen (2006)
Admiral Lord Keith and the Naval War Against Napoleon, by Kevin D. McCranie (2006)
Commodore John Rodgers: Paragon of the Early American Navy, by John H. Schroeder (2006)
Borderland Smuggling: Patriots, Loyalists, and Illicit Trade in the Northeast, 1783–1820, by Joshua M. Smith (2006)
Brutality on Trial: "Hellfire" Pedersen, "Fighting" Hansen, and the Seamen's Act of 1915, by E. Kay Gibson (2006)
Uriah Levy: Reformer of the Antebellum Navy, by Ira Dye (2006)
Crisis at Sea: The United States Navy in European Waters in World War I, by William N. Still Jr. (2006)
Chinese Junks on the Pacific: Views from a Different Deck, by Hans K. Van Tilburg (2007)
Eight Thousand Years of Maltese Maritime History: Trade, Piracy, and Naval Warfare in the Central Mediterranean, by Ayse Devrim Atauz (2007)
Merchant Mariners at War: An Oral History of World War II, by George J. Billy and Christine M. Billy (2008)
The Steamboat Montana *and the Opening of the West: History, Excavation, and Architecture*, by Annalies Corbin and Bradley A. Rodgers (2008)
Attack Transport: USS Charles Carroll *in World War II*, by Kenneth H. Goldman (2008)
Diplomats in Blue: U.S. Naval Officers in China, 1922–1933, by William Reynolds Braisted (2009)
Sir Samuel Hood and the Battle of the Chesapeake, by Colin Pengelly (2009)
Voyages, The Age of Sail: Documents in Maritime History, Volume I, 1492–1865, edited by Joshua M. Smith and the National Maritime Historical Society (2009)
Voyages, The Age of Engines: Documents in Maritime History, Volume II, 1865–Present, edited by Joshua M. Smith and the National Maritime Historical Society (2009)
H.M.S. Fowey Lost . . . and Found!, by Russell K. Skowronek and George R. Fischer (2009)

American Coastal Rescue Craft: A Design History of Coastal Rescue Craft Used by the United States Life-Saving Service and the United States Coast Guard, by William D. Wilkinson and Commander Timothy R. Dring, USNR (Retired) (2009)

The Spanish Convoy of 1750: Heaven's Hammer and International Diplomacy, by James A. Lewis (2009)

The Development of Mobile Logistic Support in Anglo-American Naval Policy, 1900–1953, by Peter V. Nash (2009)

Captain "Hell Roaring" Mike Healy: From American Slave to Arctic Hero, by Dennis L. Noble and Truman R. Strobridge (2009)

Sovereignty at Sea: U.S. Merchant Ships and American Entry into World War I, by Rodney Carlisle (2009; first paperback edition, 2011)

Commodore Abraham Whipple of the Continental Navy: Privateer, Patriot, Pioneer, by Sheldon S. Cohen (2010)

Lucky 73: USS Pampanito's *Unlikely Rescue of Allied POWs in WW II,* by Aldona Sendzikas (2010)

Cruise of the Dashing Wave: *Rounding Cape Horn in 1860,* by Philip Hichborn, edited by William H. Thiesen (2010)

Seated by the Sea: The Maritime History of Portland, Maine, and Its Irish Longshoremen, by Michael C. Connolly (2010)

The Whaling Expedition of the Ulysses, *1937–1938,* by LT (j.g.) Quentin R. Walsh, U.S. Coast Guard, edited and with an Introduction by P.J. Capelotti (2010)

Stalking the U-Boat: U. S. Naval Aviation in Europe During World War I, by Geoffrey L. Rossano

In Katrina's Wake: The U.S. Coast Guard and the Gulf Coast Hurricanes of 2005, by Donald L. Canney (2010)

A Civil War Gunboat in Pacific Waters: Life On Board USS Saginaw, by Hans K. Van Tilburg (2010)

The U.S. Coast Guard's War on Human Smuggling, by Dennis L. Noble (2011)

The Sea Their Graves: Archaeology of Death and Remembrance in Maritime Culture, by David J. Stewart (2011)

www.ingramcontent.com/pod-product-compliance
Lightning Source LLC
Chambersburg PA
CBHW022111150426
43195CB00008B/360